GERMAN MINORITIES IN EUROPE

GERMAN MINORITIES
IN EUROPE

Ethnic Identity and Cultural Belonging

Edited by Stefan Wolff

Berghahn Books
New York • Oxford

First published in 2000 by **Berghahn Books**

www.berghahnbooks.com

© 2000 Stefan Wolff

Library of Congress Cataloging-in-Publication Data

German minorities in Europe : ethnic identity and cultural belonging /
edited by Stefan Wolff.
    p. cm.
    ISBN 1-57181-738-7 (alk. paper) – ISBN 1–57181–504–X (alk. paper)
    1. Germans – Europe – History. 2. Minorities – Europe – History.
3. Return migration – Germany. 4. German – Europe, Eastern. 5.
Europe – Ethnic relations. I. Wolff, Stefan, 1969–

D1056.2.G45 G47 2001

                                                            2001018454

British Library Cataloguing in Publication Data
A catalogue record for this book is available from the British
Library.

Printed in the United States on acid-free paper
ISBN 1-57181-738-7 hardback
1-57181-504-X paperback

Table of Contents

List of Maps

List of Tables

List of Contributors

Wolfgang Bergem, Dr. phil., University of Wuppertal, Germany

Anny Schweigkofler, M.A., South Tyrol, Italy

Bruce Donaldson, Ph.D., University of Melbourne, Australia

Gerd Stricker, Dr. phil., Glaube in der 2.Welt, Zollikon, Switzerland

Hans-Joachim Heintze, Dr. jur. habil., University of Bochum, Germany

Karen Margrethe Pedersen, M.A., Danish Institute of Border Region Studies

Judith Broadbridge, Ph.D., University of Staffordshire, England

Karl Cordell, Ph.D., University of Plymouth, England

Lucy P. Marcus, M.Phil., Consultant, England

Patrick Stevenson, Ph.D., University of Southampton, England

Peter H. Nelde, Ph.D., Professor, Catholic University of Brussels, Belgium

Richard Wagner, Writer, Berlin, Germany

Stefan Wolff, Ph.D., University of Bath, England

Zeljko Sevic, Ph.D., University of Greenwich, England

Preface

The study of ethnic minorities and their role in the domestic politics of their host-states has long attracted scholars from a wide range of disciplines in the Social Sciences and Humanities.

National minorities, or diaspora groups, have until recently been somewhat under-represented in the literature on ethnic minorities. With the collapse of communism in Central and Eastern Europe and the subsequent upsurge of ethnic conflicts in many countries of the region, interest in this particular subject has increased. Studies on Russian minorities in the Baltic republics and in member states of the Commonwealth of Independent States (CIS) as well as on Hungarian communities in the neighbouring countries of the Republic of Hungary, have been carried out since 1990. The violent escalation of the conflict in Kosovo in 1998/99 has raised awareness about Albanian external minorities. A fourth important diaspora community, still numbering millions and spread over twenty countries in both Western and Central and Eastern Europe, has attracted only little attention. Ethnic German minorities in Europe have been widely neglected in academic literature over the past few decades. Once crucial players in Nazi Germany's attempted revision of European boundaries, they suffered expulsion and deportation in Central and Eastern Europe after 1945 and there, as well as in some of their host-countries in the West, assimilation seemed to be their inevitable fate.

Nevertheless, German ethnicity is still claimed by a significant number of people outside the Federal Republic of Germany. To examine their ethnic identity and national belonging is one of the tasks this book seeks to accomplish. In order to do so, case studies of all the major individual minority groups are provided. Recognised scholars provide different perspectives on the social and political circumstances under which German minorities live today. Set against the background of their own unique conditions, assessments are made of the character of each German community as a distinct ethno-cultural group, now and in the future. While the vitality of German language and culture is essential for the group's survival, many other factors ranging from the minority's origin and role in European history to the state of bilateral relations between Germany and the host-country, and minority rights policies of the latter, are of no less importance and are examined as well.

In this way, a comprehensive picture of Germans and German culture in Europe emerges that provides both historical and contemporary perspectives on a diaspora community with an uncertain future lying between assimilation, segregation, and emigration.

INTRODUCTION

Culture, Identity, and Distinction: Ethnic Minorities between Scylla and Charybdis

Wolfgang Bergem

Ethnic minorities are constantly challenged by two equally threatening perspectives – maintaining their ethnicity and insisting on their cultural distinctiveness bears the danger of marginalisation in their host-state, while attempts aimed at integration imply the no less troublesome possibility of being absorbed into the majority culture and the consequential loss of their particular identity. Taken to extremes, efforts by ethnic minorities to mobilise their group members on the basis of a collective identity and to distinguish the cultural specificity upon which this identity rests, can result not only in dissimilation but also in segregation.

At the beginning of the twenty-first century, a renaissance of ethnic identity seems to be the most common response to the end of the east-west conflict, to various migration movements, to the erosion of the concept of the nation-state, and to the globalisation process, which is more often than not perceived as ever-increasing homogenisation. At the same time, there is also a renaissance of the concept of culture in the interpretation of social developments, in the justification of politics, and above all in the quest for the fundamentals of individual and collective identity.

In this context, it is in particular the construction of collective identity that requires a framework in which the conceptualisation of the self and the distinction from the other become possible. The European nation-states and their emphasis on a 'national' identity, which dominated and homogenised cultural identities especially in the nineteenth century (Lepsius

1997: 948), are increasingly challenged and complemented by sub-national loyalties to a particular territory or ethnicity. In competing for economic resources, social opportunities, and democratic participation, ethnicity has come to be an ever more important reference point around which actors in the public sphere can be rallied. Yet, ethnicity as a concept itself is still an object of debate between primordialists and functionalists/constructivists. Heckmann (1997: 52), mediating between these two schools, describes ethnicity in a genealogical definition as 'constituted by the belief in common origin, to which are added real or imagined socio-cultural similarities, common historical and current experiences and social relationships, a collective identity based on in-group and out-group definition, . . . and a certain feeling of solidarity (among group members)'.

The contemporary renaissance of ethnicity and its increasing political importance at the level of the state have been analysed by Leggewie (1994: 47f.) as the result of three simultaneous, even though not necessarily coinciding, tendencies. There is, first, the 'ethnic restoration', that is, the ethnic redefinition of statehood, as, for example, in the case of the successor states of the former Soviet Union or Yugoslavia. A second tendency is 'ethnic revitalisation', describing the process of reviving ethnic identities as a basis for regionalist, and occasionally separatist, movements in Western Europe. The third tendency, 'ethnic reconstruction', refers to ethnic minorities as a result of transnational migration. Inasmuch as these minorities, in their demands for opportunities to realise their cultural distinctiveness, including appropriate political and territorial structures, challenge a majority perception of homogeneity, they simultaneously provoke an ethnically orientated redefinition of the titular national group. The recent experiences of German-speaking minorities in Europe, however, fit, if any, then the third of these tendencies. Yet even this, for two reasons, is only a partial match. First, because Leggewie uses the term in the context of minorities that came into existence as a result of transnational migration, which neither applies to German minorities in Western Europe (i.e., Alsace, South Tyrol, Belgium and Denmark), nor to those in Poland or the Czech and Slovak Republics. And second, because the foremost aim of all German minorities today – the preservation of their distinct ethnic identities – hardly conflicts with the principle of the nation-state any more. As the concept of ethnic identity is fundamentally linked to that of culture, this introductory chapter will focus on three problematic issues in this context – the need for culture vs. the dangers of an exaggerated 'culturalism', the potential transformation of cultural distinctiveness into a friend–enemy dichotomy and its political implications, and the twofold challenges of assimilation and segregation to the ethno-cultural identity of diaspora minorities.

Culturalism as Danger?

In contrast to terms like power, rule, or conflict, political science is so far still lacking a stringent concept of culture. In order to be able to use the term, the political scientist is required to look across the boundaries of his or her own discipline, to fields such as cultural anthropology, ethnology, or philosophy. Even though there are an enormous number and variety of definitions of culture, there seems to be a certain core consensus in cultural studies about culture as a semiotic or symbolic system as defined by Cassirer and Geertz. Focussing on the meaningful character of social action, this concept of culture emphasises the social need for meaning and meaningful interpretation, without which neither orientation nor identification would be possible. This desire for meaning is particularly relevant in periods of social turmoil, mental insecurity, and the loss of normative systems, and especially important for diaspora minorities, who, constantly challenged by a culturally different environment, require a minimum of permanence for their survival as a distinct group. For ethnic minorities, the preservation, or (permanent) reconstruction, of their own ethno-cultural environment implies the possibility to maintain their collective identity despite a dominant majority culture, and to generate – in processes of reflexive classification – group cohesion and internal stability. The desire for meaning, which cannot be satisfied without a secure and accepted position in a familiar cultural environment, is an elementary human need. Hannerz (1992: 3) contends that humans as 'creatures who "make" sense' could not live in a world without meaning.

From a semiotic point of view, then, culture is a communicatively generated, socially passed on, yet over time changing and changeable, collectively memorised ensemble of symbols that allows human actions to be interpreted, and thus enables human beings to create meaning.[1] But this is a complex and multi-facetted process, and even though the integrative effects of a common culture cannot be denied, there is no direct causal relationship between cultural socialisation and the behaviour of political actors. Geertz (1983: 21) emphasises the complexity of the relationship between culture on the one side, and society and politics on the other, when he insists that culture is the framework in which social processes, behaviour, or institutions can be described, but not causally linked to it. The causal connections between culture and identity on the one hand, and political and social phenomena on the other, form an entangled web, in which the quest for dependent and independent variables just rarely can succeed.

Such a semiotic understanding of culture, however, does not clarify the empirical meaning of the term. For the past forty years, culture has acquired an ever broader meaning. Williams (1958: xvi) describes it as 'a whole way of life, material, intellectual, and spiritual'. In its intention to overcome the differentiation between high culture and low culture, the influential definition of culture by the Centre for Contemporary Cultural Studies in Birmingham was similarly all-encompassing (Clarke et al. 1979: 40–42; Agger 1992: 78f.). Since the 1960s and 1970s, definitions have further expanded the term culture as one of the determining forces in history (on an equal level with social structures, politics, and economic developments), and eventually to Agger's (1992: 6) programmatic phrase 'Culture is us'.

However, the broader the empirical meaning of culture became, the more such culturalist approaches were also criticised. As early as the 1970s, Johnson introduced the term 'culturalism' as a polemic criticism of the understanding of history represented by Williams and Thompson, and claimed that a cultural-anthropological approach to history would unfairly deny the importance of social and economic processes as

---

1. I use ensemble, rather than structure or system of symbols, because culture is better understood as a plural and dynamic phenomenon than as static system or causally organised structure of a coherent whole.

political institutions (Kaschuba 1995: 14). From a different point of view, Kaschuba (Kaschuba 1995: 14–16) has drawn attention to the dangers implicit in a culturalisation of social theory. According to him, references to 'culture' become empty gestures pointing to higher morality while neglecting 'society' as the only context that can be influenced by human action.

This danger and its political implications are very real in the context of ethnic minorities. Once culture has become a substitute for society, differences between an ethnic minority and the majority population of its host-state in areas such as education, income, employment, and social mobility are no longer seen in a political context, but become inevitable consequences of cultural differences. In turn, this can also lead to an instrumentalisation of culture for political purposes by manipulating a perception of threat to the majority's own culture. Here, four different strategies are possible – cultural racism, religious or ideological fundamentalism, ethnicisation of power struggles or resource competition, and the neo-nationalist legitimation of the state in relation to culture and/or ethnicity (Kaschuba 1995: 22–28). Thus, the difficult task for ethnic minorities of mediating between the two extremes of cultural marginalisation and assimilation can be further complicated by a 'cultural policy' of their host-state that instrumentalises existing differences between majority and minority cultures to exclude, oppress, monitor, and manipulate ethnic minorities (Hannerz 1995: 75). At the same time, however, the very nature of culture and identity, which implies the distinction between in-group and out-group, also poses a challenge for the state to pursue minority policies that try to avoid these potentially destabilising consequences. The core of the danger of culturalism in public and academic discourses can thus be discerned in the delimiting and potentially excluding character of culture and identity.

Culture and Identity as Categories of Distinction

A relatively recent school of cultural studies focuses on culture from the perspective of identity politics and in the context of ethnic minorities (J. Assmann 1992, A. Assmann 1994, Hall 1994 and 1996, Said 1994, and Bhabha 1996), rather than using traditional concepts like class, alternative, or subcultures. By emphasising the authenticity and originality of a collective identity, these studies give prominence to the delimiting form of the culture on which it is based. Culture and identity are used as categories of distinction and demarcation. Their differentiating character is the basis upon which an identity-generating culture can be built. In turn, culture, as a communicatively generated phenomenon, creates collective identity through processes of inclusion and exclusion; i.e., collective identity is the result of defining relationships of similarity and difference vis-à-vis identities – real or imagined – of other groups.

However, this construction of collective identity as a perception of difference, which implies the duality of internal affiliation and external differentiation, is dangerously close to potentially aggressive friend-enemy dichotomies. The transition from the cultural differentiation of one's own/one's group's identity to the exclusion of another identity is a dynamic process. The borderline beyond which the image of the other turns into the image of the enemy, i.e., the point at which the construction of an identity is transformed into the creation of an enemy, cannot be determined precisely and, above all, not reliably.

At the same time, the question of cultural roots has become all the more pressing since the end of the Cold War and the collapse of the no longer valid good–evil, us–them dichotomy with its system-stabilising functions in East and West. The creation of images of the self and the other is an expression of the search of individuals and groups for security. The symbolical and metaphorical drawing of these images is a characteristic of the human being as 'animal symbolicum' (Cassirer 1990: 51) and thus a universal and trans-historic phenomenon. The subsequent differentiation from the other is – although to varying degrees – vital for the survival of nations and ethnic groups as collective actors. As a result of exaggeration and fusion of negative stereotypes, enemy images serve a variety of purposes for individuals, societies, and ruling elites.

In giving simple explanations for complex processes, they offer individuals security and orientation. By projecting responsibility for unpleasant experiences onto the out-group, they excuse the individual or his/her group from an examination of their share of responsibility, suggest superiority, and thus stabilise individuals psychologically. Thus, a desire for subjective certainty is one of the primary causes for policies of exclusion and hatred of everyone and everything 'deviating' from the norms of the in-group and disturbing the simplicity of one's own world view.

Qua individual stabilisation, collective identity serves the purpose of integration in, and homogenisation of, nations and ethnic groups alike. The channelling of aggressions towards declared enemies increases the coherence and unity of the in-group, because the imagination of a common and threatening 'other' increases the desire to stress internal similarities and to close ranks. The level of stability of a society, regardless of the essence of its cultural identity, and its need for a friend–enemy dichotomy, are negatively correlated – the less a cultural self-concept is developed, the more are (negative) differences emphasised and enemy images created, in relation to which the respective group can define itself as the (positive) opposite of its enemy.

The integrative effects of enemy images also contribute to the consolidation of rule. Culturally relatively homogeneous societies are perceived to be more easily to control than culturally fragmented ones. The perception of the other as enemy induces a preparedness to follow a determined leadership. Thus, enemy images stabilise and legitimate a system of rule the more the political class in charge is trusted to avert the perceived threat posed by the enemy. The decisionist approach of Carl Schmitt defines politics on the basis of the differentiation between enemy and friend and the joint struggle against the enemy, who becomes a threat simply because of its difference from the (collective) self (Bergem 1993). Schmitt's conception of the political power of democracy as elimination of everything that threatens homogeneity (Schmitt 1969: 13f.) has no room for the existence of something culturally distinct, such as an ethnic minority. Rule that finds its justification only in the annihilation of an imagined external threat lacks democratic legitimacy. This, in turn, means that a lack of democratic legitimacy requires the intense projection of enemy images so that an existing system of rule can consolidate itself and become stable. In the context of ethnic minorities, the obvious implication is that democracy (or successful democratisation) ensures that the differentiating character of culture-based identity constructions becomes less salient. In other words, the deconstruction of friend–enemy dichotomies reduces the potential for (ethnic) conflict.

Cultural Identity between Assimilation and Segregation

The complexity of culture as a plural and processual ensemble of symbols makes it very difficult, if not outright impossible, to develop unambiguous and non-contradictory, or at least not mutually overlapping, identities. With culture no longer a static phenomenon, collective identities become dynamic constructions with a more or less strongly developed capability and willingness to preserve collective memory.

The increasing importance and attractiveness of ethnic and regional identities in most European democracies is not only a particularist response to universalism, but also a reaction to the (perceived) inability of liberal nation-states to generate meaning, allow orientation, and offer affective ties. Liberal democracies preserve their stability because of their ability to negotiate and achieve, often less than attractive, compromise in a complicated and painstaking political and social process, rather than through recourse to holistic utopias. While the nation-state has thus become a 'cold project' (Dahrendorf in: Probst 1994: 1289), which, as a consequence of globalisation and the growing importance of supranational political structures is increasingly losing its role as an essential reference point for collective identities, humans seek to satisfy their desire for meaning at other levels that still provide a sense of homogeneity and cohesion; one of these levels is ethnicity.

In this context, the French *nouvelle droite* has developed the concept of ethno-pluralism, which is closely related to Schmitt's friend–enemy dichotomy and other ideas of the 'conservative revolution' during the Weimar Republic. The essence of ethno-pluralism is the argument of the self-sufficient uniqueness of the ethnically determined culture of any given people, which can be used against universalist ideas, transnational human rights, and liberal pluralism, while supporting the concept of 'organic' democracy rooted in the ethno-cultural homogeneity of a people (Herzinger 1993: 1390f.). In this discourse, the differentiating character of culture and identity is being instrumentalised to justify a policy segregation of one's own collective self from ethnically different other collective selfs. In close analogy to friend-enemy dichotomies, the danger of radicalising difference, therefore, lies in its potential to be used as a weapon against pluralism and as a rationale for an aggressive policy towards the other (A. Assmann 1994: 29), as the praise for cultural difference turns into the verdict of cultural incompatibility (Kaschuba 1995: 23). Emphasis on cultural distinctiveness then results in social and political processes of inclusion and exclusion, and (collective) identification is inevitably followed by segregation. Thus, for ethnic minorities, it may be only a small step from preserving their ethno-cultural identities to the political and social disassociation from majority culture and society, with the consequence of growing conflict potentials.

In recognising these implications, there have recently been a number of attempts to overcome the radical concept of cultural difference, which was also a topic in the post-modern discourse, and its implicit ban on assimilation and integration. For example, Welsch (1995: 42–44) describes 'transculturality' as a phenomenon that symbolises that the categories of self and other in their definite sense of strict distinction without overlap do not exist anymore. Rather, he argues, cultures are characterised internally by a plurality of possible identities, while externally they share common spaces with other cultures. The relationship between cultures, then, is no longer one of distinction and separation, but increasingly one of interrelation, mixture, and similarity. Politically, this means understanding and interaction instead of isolation and conflict. The understanding of such overlapping cultures is also the basis of terms like 'multiple identity' (Grossberg 1996: 89) or 'patchwork-identity' (Keupp 1997: 11) in the diagnosis of modern society. While any such transcultural society would give ethnic minorities the opportunity to participate in the wider social and political process and become an integrative part of their host-state, it simultaneously bears the danger of the opposite extreme of segregation – that of assimilation by and into a dominant majority culture and the subsequent loss of what previously constituted the cultural basis of a distinct ethnic identity. Yet, this Western European perception of ethno-cultural and ethno-national identities being replaced by other, less boundary-related ways of collective identification is limited in its universal applicability. The transition period in Eastern Europe and Islamic movements in the Arabian world have, in particular, demonstrated that the 'need for distinction and identity has never before been so urgent' (A. Assmann 1994: 32).

Clearly, the age of globalisation has brought cultures closer together and has made them, to some extent, more similar. While the other is no longer as clearly identifiable as before, there is a corresponding tendency to create the image of this other particularly sharply in order to preserve (cultural) distinction as the basis of one's own (collective) identity. The renaissance of ethnicity as an important category of a distinctive identity cannot therefore, at least in a non-western context, be explained by recourse to theories of cultural hybridity as developed by Hall (1994). While ethnic diasporas in Western Europe, because of their familiarity with at least two distinct national cultures, have demonstrated their ability to bridge cultural gaps and to avoid both assimilation and segregation, the situation for diaspora minorities and ethnic groups in Eastern Europe is much more difficult, because there the response to the loss of ethno-cultural distinctiveness has been its reconstruction. This has particularly affected minority groups who, in order to resist assimilation pressure, had to preserve, and insist on, their particularity vis-à-vis a less and less distinct majority culture, while at the same time avoiding the trap of (re-)constructing their identity on the basis of a radical friend-enemy distinction, which, in a political context, has the potential to be transformed into territorial separatism, or at least to be perceived as such by the majority.

The balance in identity construction and preservation between segregation and assimilation is difficult to maintain for diaspora communities; it is the navigating between Scylla and Charybdis. While bilingualism and biculturalism, on the one hand, open a window of opportunity to construct a plural identity that manages to overcome traditional ethnic boundaries, on the other hand the necessarily growing contact and exchange with a majority culture increase the dangers of an initially gradual, yet eventually inevitable, complete assimilation.[2]

The responsibility to maintain a sensible balance between segregation and assimilation, however, does not only rest with diaspora minorities. In order to master this constant challenge successfully, they depend on the willingness of their host-state

---

2. Barker (1998) has exemplified the complexity of this process in relation to the literature of the Sorbian minority in Eastern Germany.

to provide conditions in which both majority and minority can maintain their ethno-cultural distinctiveness and in which the minority can be an integral part of the social and political process of the country they live in.

References

Agger, B., *Cultural Studies as Critical Theory*, London and Bristol, 1992.

Assmann, A., 'Zum Problem der Identität aus kulturwissenschaftlicher Sicht', in *Die Wiederkehr des Regionalen. Über neue Formen kultureller Identität*, ed. Rolf Lindner Frankfurt a. M. and New York, 1994, pp. 13–35.

Assmann, J., *Das kulturelle Gedächtnis. Schrift, Erinnerung und politische Identität in frühen Hochkulturen*, München, 1992.

Barker, P., '"Die Schmerzen der endenden Art" oder das "Neuwasser" der bikulturellen Poetik: Sorbian Literature since the *Wende*', lecture at the 24th New Hampshire Symposium *Difference(s) in the East. East Germany between New Beginnings and Marginalization*', Conway, New Hampshire, 24 June – 1 July 1998.

Bergem, W., *Tradition und Transformation. Eine vergleichende Untersuchung zur politischen Kultur in Deutschland*, Opladen, 1993.

Bhabha, H.K., 'Culture's In-Between', in *Questions of Cultural Identity*, eds. Stuart Hall and Paul du Gay, London, 1996, pp. 53–60.

Cassirer, E., *Versuch über den Menschen. Einführung in eine Philosophie der Kultur*, Frankfurt a. M., 1990.

Clarke, J., Hall, S., Jefferson, T., and Roberts, B., 'Subkulturen, Kulturen und Klasse', in *Jugendkultur als Widerstand. Milieus, Rituale, Provokationen*, eds. Axel Honneth, Rolf Lindner, and Rainer Paris, Frankfurt a. M., 1979, pp. 39–131.

Geertz, C., *Dichte Beschreibung. Beiträge zum Verstehen kultureller Systeme*, Frankfurt a. M., 1983.

Grossberg, L., 'Identity and Cultural Studies: Is That All There Is?', in *Questions of Cultural Identity*, eds. Stuart Hall and Paul du Gay, London, 1996, pp. 87–107.

Hall, S., *Rassismus und kulturelle Identität. Ausgewählte Schriften 2*, Hamburg, 1994.

——, 'Who Needs "Identity"?', in *Questions of Cultural Identity*, eds. Stuart Hall and Paul du Gay, London, 1996, pp. 1–17.

Hannerz, U., *Cultural Complexity. Studies in the Social Organization of Meaning*, New York, 1992.

——, '"Kultur" in einer vernetzten Welt. Zur Revision eines ethnologischen Begriffs', in *Kulturen – Identitäten – Diskurse. Perspektiven Europäischer Ethnologie*, ed. Wolfgang Kaschuba, Berlin, 1995, pp. 64–84.

Heckmann, F., 'Ethnos – eine imaginierte oder reale Gruppe? Über Ethnizität als soziologische Kategorie', in *Kollektive Identität in Krisen. Ethnizität in Region, Nation, Europa*, eds. Friedrich Hettlage, Petra Deger, and Susanne Wagner, Opladen, 1997, pp. 46–55.

Herzinger, R., 'Revolutionärer Aufbruch in die Stammesgemeinschaft? Die Ideologie(n) der Neuen Rechten und ihre Zeitschriften', in *Deutschland Archiv* no. 12, 1993, pp. 1389–1403.

Kaschuba, W., 'Kulturalismus: Vom Verschwinden des Sozialen im gesellschaftlichen Diskurs', in *Kulturen - Identitäten - Diskurse. Perspektiven Europäischer Ethnologie*, ed. Wolfgang Kaschuba, Berlin, 1995, pp. 11–30.

Keupp, H., 'Diskursarena Identität: Lernprozesse in der Identitätsforschung', in *Identitätsarbeit heute. Klassische und aktuelle Perspektiven der Identitätsforschung*, eds. Heiner Keupp and Renate Höfer, Frankfurt a. M., 1997, pp. 11–39.

Leggewie, C., 'Ethnizität, Nationalismus und multikulturelle Gesellschaft', in *Nationales Bewußtsein und kollektive Identität. Studien zur Entwicklung des kollektiven Bewußtseins in der Neuzeit 2*, ed. Helmut Berding, Frankfurt a. M., 1994, pp. 46–65.

Lepsius, M. R., 'Bildet sich eine kulturelle Identität in der Europäischen Union?', in: *Blätter für deutsche und internationale Politik*, no. 8, 1997, pp. 948–55.

Probst, L., 'Das Dilemma der Intellektuellen mit der Nation. Ein Plädoyer gegen die Kontinuitätslogik', in *Deutschland Archiv* no. 12, 1994, pp. 1287–91.

Said, E. W., *Kultur und Imperialismus. Einbildungskraft und Politik im Zeitalter der Macht*, Frankfurt a. M., 1994.

Schmitt, C., *Die geistesgeschichtliche Lage des heutigen Parlamentarismus*, Berlin, 1969.

Welsch, W., 'Transkulturalität. Zur veränderten Verfaßtheit heutiger Kulturen', in *Zeitschrift für Kulturaustausch*, no. 1, 1996, pp. 39–44.

Williams, R., *Culture and Society 1780-1950*, London, 1967.

PART ONE

German Minorities in Western Europe

CHAPTER 1

A National Minority with a Transethnic Identity – the German Minority in Denmark

Karen Margrethe Pedersen

L iving in the German-Danish border region of Sønderjyl-land/Nordschleswig, the bilingual German minority came into existence after a 1920 referendum that determined the present-day border between the two countries. The members of the minority have a German national identity linking them to the monocultural and monolingual norms upon which Germany has been established as a nation-state.

In terms of ethnic identity, which might be seen as a subcategory of national identity, the case is less clear cut. The minority is characterised by an ethnic identity that is composed of German and Danish elements alike, thus indicating the duality of a transethnic identity. Such a transethnic identity is due to the members' relations to, and interaction with, the majority group in the private as well as the social sphere, a situation resulting in bilingualism and in specific ways of thinking, feeling, and acting. These traits enable members of the minority to perceive differences between themselves and the majority population and to make a choice between German and Danish national identity. Thus, membership in the minority is a conscious act of self-ascription, and individuals can choose to leave the minority if they wish, as no external or physical conditions prevent them from doing so, because neither cultural attributes, such as dress, food or residence, nor physical characteristics or religious affiliations distinguish the minority from the majority. What does divide them is the difference in national identity, the difference between a (minority) transethnic identity and a (majority) ethnic identity, and the difference in self-ascription that makes members of the minority feel that they belong there, whereas members of the majority do not.

The reason for the majority's feeling is that it has a Danish national identity and an analogous ethnic identity merging into one as the very homogeneous majority population is deeply rooted in a Danish monolingualism and a Danish monoculture. This has led to the widely accepted view among members of the majority that it only has a national identity, while ethnic identities are reserved for those minority groups that have always lived in Denmark and other European nation-states or have recently migrated there.

The German minority in Denmark does not see itself as an ethnic group either, but rather as a national group that is part of the titular nation of the neighbouring state. So the members share the view of the majority regarding national and ethnic identity. Nevertheless, it is at the same time a widespread belief among members of the German minority that their national identity is neither German nor Danish, but rather German as well as Danish, a combination that is called *Zweiströmigkeit* (duality/parallelism) (Cornett 1986, Weitling 1991, 1994, 1997). This *Zweiströmigkeit* is not, however, within the national identity, it is within the ethnic identity, and therefore the minority might be said to have a German national identity and a transethnic German and Danish identity.

Byram (1986) describes the German minority as an ethnic group, because its members consider themselves to be a distinct group in their own right. Yet he considers this identity to be based only on cognitive ethnicity: 'The minority is an ethnically distinct group in the sense that the members of the minority consider themselves to be so. For them, the cognitive category of "*deutscher Nordschleswiger*" contains a set of attitudes, opinions and beliefs which are attributed to them by themselves and outsiders' (Byram 1986: 139).

German and Danish Populations in the History of the Border Region

The Duchy of Schleswig belonged to the Danish Crown until 1864, when it was annexed to Prussia as a result of the

Prussian–Danish War and remained under Prussian control for more than half a century. A policy of Germanisation was not very successful during this period, resulting in nothing but a consolidation of the Danish identity of the local majority population, who expressed their national identity in the 1920 referendum carried out under the regulations of the Versailles Peace Treaty. On the other hand, however, Germanisation resulted in a consolidation of the group that had gradually developed a German identity over the centuries, under the strong cultural and economic influence from neighbouring Holstein. Denmark acknowledged that it had also acquired a national minority and accorded its members a number of rights as early as summer 1920 to meet their special needs in the fields of education, religion, law, administration, and election to the Danish parliament, the Folketing.

After the end of the Second World War in 1945, the German minority was deprived of some of its former rights within education, and property officially belonging to the educational system of the minority was confiscated as indemnity. The reason for this was its active cooperation with the German occupation forces. The very same year the German minority began to follow a new political approach and founded the *Bund deutscher Nordschleswiger* (BDN) as its official organisation. Its members clearly stated that they acknowledged the border and, while they would remain loyal to their German cultural identity, they also pledged to be loyal Danish citizens. The *Deutscher Schul- und Spachverein für Nordschleswig*, an association dealing with education and language, was established in 1945 and managed to reopen several German kindergartens and schools in the following ten years. In 1946, the BDN started publishing a weekly paper in German. From 1951, it became a daily paper that still exists today under the name *Der Nordschleswiger.*

The 1955 Copenhagen–Bonn Declarations regulated the status of the German minority in Denmark and that of the analogous Danish minority in the Federal Republic on the basis of reciprocity between two sovereign states. They stated that the profession of Danish and German nationality and culture is a civil right, which must neither be disputed nor controlled by the authorities. Minority members must not be prevented from using the language they prefer – neither verbally nor in writing. No discrimination must be made in the allocation of financial support and other public means. Public

announcements should also be published in the newspapers of
the minorities, and due regard should be paid to the broad-
casting possibility of the minorities. When municipal councils
are appointed, the representatives of the minorities participate
in the activities of the committees according to their number.
Finally the Copenhagen–Bonn Declarations promise the
minorities the right to establish religious, cultural and professional links with the respective mother countries (Becker-
Christensen 1992).

The Present Situation

The German minority numbers about 10–15,000 people, i.e.
4–6 percent of the population in the administrative region
Sønderjylland/Nordschleswig. However, these figures are
only estimates as the Copenhagen–Bonn Declarations do not
allow official inquiries into an individual's membership in the
minority. They are based upon the number of members of the
BDN, upon the votes for the German minority's political party
Schleswigsche Partei (SP), and upon the number of pupils in the
private German minority schools run by the *Deutscher Schul-
und Sprachverein.*

The minority is primarily organised within these cultural and
political organisations. In addition, there is a youth and sports
association, the *Deutscher Jugendverband für Nordschleswig,* the
Association of German Libraries, *Verband deutscher Büchereien,*
and the *Nordschleswigsche Gemeinde der Nordelbischen Kirche,* the
acknowledged Lutheran Free Church of the German minority
in Denmark.

Because of its relatively small size, the minority does
not have an all-encompassing economic network. Socially,
the German minority is in neither an inferior nor a supe-
rior position. In order to deal with social aspects of community life, such as nursing, care for the elderly, and
counselling, it has established the *Sozialdienst Nordschleswig*
(Pedersen 1996).

Minority Organisations and Organisation of the Minority

The BDN was restructured in 1995 (Grenzland '96'). It has now
an assembly of delegates acting as an umbrella organisation.

These delegates represent the different cultural associations, the political party SP, and the governing body, the BDN executive board. Part of this horizontal structure comprises two secretariats, a local one in Aabenraa, the *Deutsches Generalsekretariat,* and one in Copenhagen, the *Sekretariat der deutschen Volksgruppe in Kopenhagen.* The minority also has a committee liasing with the Danish government and parliament in Copenhagen and dealing with the minority's interests in relation to domestic policy issues (the *Kontaktausschuss für die deutsche Volksgruppe bei Regierung und Parlament in Kopenhagen*), and a committee at the state legislature in Kiel in the state of Schleswig–Holstein that plays a consultative role on questions regarding the minority from a German point of view (the *Gremium für Fragen der deutschen Minderheit beim Schleswig– Holsteinischen Landtag in Kiel*).

Demography

Members of the German minority live scattered throughout Sønderjylland/Nordschleswig, and the only apparent settlement pattern is their increasing concentration closer to the border. Members of the minority are drawn primarily from three sources. First, there are those families who have their roots in the region and have been attracted to and identified with German culture and language for generations. Second, there are artisans, businessmen, and administrators that immigrated from Holstein and other German principalities during the eighteenth and nineteenth centuries. Today, the largest group of migrants from the Federal Republic are teachers in the minority education system and their families. These teachers, who make up 60 percent of the staff at minority schools, are civil servants from Schleswig–Holstein granted leave for service in Nordschleswig. Third, there is a small group of people who originally belonged to the Danish majority but have come to identify more and more with German culture, eventually choosing to be a member of the minority even if they were born in Copenhagen. In an interview, the director of the minority school system said the following about parents from the majority sending their children to minority schools: 'And today we have more instances where parents have grown into German culture' (Nordslesvigerne er mere pragmatiske, *Flensborg Avis,* 30 May 1995).

The Linguistic Situation

Although the Copenhagen–Bonn Declarations protect the right to use German as a minority language, most minority members do not speak it as their first language. Their first language is the Danish dialect Sønderjysk (Southern Jutland dialect). However, they learn German as a minority language in kindergarten and school, and become bilingual. Standard Danish is also mastered by some of them, having acquired it either in school or Danish society, but a regional variety of Danish is more common as the third language.

Sønderjysk is neutral in relation to national identity for the minority as well as the majority, but standard Danish is only regarded as neutral by the majority. The minority regards standard Danish as a national majority language that is not compatible with their national identity, which requires German as a national language.

Although standard Danish is not a part of their identity, many members of the minority have had to realise that competence in it is necessary in order to be accepted in some jobs and political contexts. However, this is a linguistic context in which they are not alone, as they share these conditions with dialect speakers of the majority.

Byram (1986) regards a minority language as an element of cognitive ethnicity, but within the German minority he considers it to be only a symbol of ethnicity. The symbolic function arises because the minority is presumed to be German-speaking, even though most minority members only speak German at a very limited number of cultural events. German becomes a symbol of belonging to the minority, rather than a significant feature in everyday communication among its members. As the terms 'ethnic minority' and 'linguistic minority', according to Byram (1986) and others, are synonymous, this symbolic function of the language leads him to conclude that the minority has a particular ethnic identity, which I describe as transethnic.

The Cultural Situation

In Nordschleswig/Sønderjylland, neither origin nor first language are definite indicators of whether somebody belongs to minority or majority. Observable indicators revealing minority affiliation, nevertheless, do exist. They include education in the minority school system, membership of one of the minority organisations, attendance at church services with German Lutheran ministers in the local church, and a personal subscription to the daily minority paper *Der Nordschleswiger*, which has a circulation of 3,000. The use of the minority language, i.e., German, at formal, institutional occasions and at cultural events organised by the minority, may also be seen to indicate that somebody belongs to the minority.

Apart from the minority language, it is difficult to see any specific minority culture expressed in the activities of the minority organisations. The sports which are played are the same within minority and majority, even though the daily activities are conducted in minority associations and sometimes also at minority sports grounds. Matches, however, take place both inside and outside a minority context, in the wider region, or in Schleswig–Holstein. The minority youth clubs and cultural, political, or professional meetings are housed in buildings owned by the minority, very often the minority school. These activities have a specific minority character, but this manifests itself in form rather than in content. What is specifically German in the German minority tends to be imported directly from the Federal Republic, for example theatre groups, orchestras, lecturers and art exhibitions. (Federal) German radio and television programmes are also received, as the minority does not have electronic media of its own in Denmark.

Identity

Die deutsche Volksgruppe is the official name of the German minority used by the BND and reflecting on the national identity of the minority. When members define themselves not only as Germans, but also as *deutsche Nordschleswiger* or simply as *Nordschleswiger* (in Danish *nordslesviger*), this self-concept might be said to have its origin in their transethnic identity. Apart from their relations with Germany, members of the minority stress their local relations within the minority and the majority, and the region Sønderjylland/Nordschleswig is seen as an important component of their identity. Although regional affiliation plays a similar role for members of the majority, the difference in national identity accounts for a terminological distinction. The Danish majority refers to the area as Sønderjylland, and its members identifying with the region speak of themselves as *sønderjyder* (Southjutlanders).

A recent trend among younger minority members is that they describe themselves as *tyske sønderjyder* (German Southjutlanders), a very obvious expression of their transethnic German–Danish identity. Some members of the minority belonging to the post-war generation are worried about this new identity, seeing it as the last step towards total assimilation. (Danish) Southjutlanders from the same generation who have a strong Danish national identity regard it as self-contradictory. According to them, one can either be a Southjutlander or a German *Nordschleswiger*, a polarity indicating that they only take national identity into consideration. Generally open towards other ethnic identities, the young generation of German *Nordschleswiger*, on the other hand, says that they have developed an independent minority identity integrated, but not assimilated, in Danish society.

The majority often characterises members of the minority as *hjemmetyskere* (Home Germans, i.e., Germans who feel at home wherever they live), a term earlier on bearing negative associations based on the former conflict between minority and majority. Today, *hjemmetyskere* is used as a neutral expression in Danish contexts by the minority as well. Among them, Günter Weitling used the expression several times during a lecture about identity in the borderland: 'Both from a general and individual viewpoint, the concept *Zweiströmigkeit* is the most positive constituting concept of a Home German identity' (My translation. Weitling 1994: 30).

Developing Minority Identity

In the self-perception of the German minority, the development of its identity is dependent on the education process where children are influenced by German culture and language. For children living in minority homes, it is part of the minority's lifestyle and includes linguistic competence in German. For children coming from a Danish background, it is a supplement to the Danish way of living.

Although the minority lives scattered over a rather large

area it is possible for all members to send their children to German kindergartens and schools. There are several small kindergartens and schools throughout the region, and a free bus service is offered to those living far away. Such a decentralised system is expensive, but the Danish state pays about 80 percent of the costs, a percentage equal to the subsidies given to private Danish institutions, and the neighbouring country covers the rest. Thus, parents do not have to pay for their children to attend minority schools, and the fees for kindergartens are at the same level as those paid by majority parents.

In 1998, there were twenty-four minority kindergartens attended by 584 children. The aim of the German kindergarten is to prepare the children for German school by introducing them gradually to German language and culture. Two-thirds of the kindergarten children continue at a minority school, while one-third goes on to Danish schools. Their parents might have wanted to profit from two languages and two cultures as a basis for their children's future development. Probably one or both of such parents will not belong to the minority. If only one of the parents belongs to the minority, the change from minority to majority education system could be the result of a compromise in the family.

In the minority school, German is the medium of instruction in all subjects, apart from Danish, and the final exam is fully recognised in both Denmark and the Federal Republic. In the academic year 1997/98, the minority had 1277 pupils in grades 1–10 at fifteen schools. These were approximately 2.8 percent of the total number of pupils in the region. There is also an upper secondary school that had 106 pupils divided between three grades and a *Nachschule* (a boarding school for grades 9 and 10) with 71 pupils.

According to its educational goals, the minority school system prepares its pupils for a life in both Denmark and Germany, and it wants to contribute actively to the cultural and socio-political development in the border region. In relation to culture, the school first of all aims at establishing awareness and knowledge of German culture. This includes German customs and traditions, ways of living, as well as literature, history, and music. The perspective is mostly that of the Federal Republic and especially that of Schleswig–Holstein, where most of the teachers grew up and were educated. Hardly ever is German culture elsewhere focussed on. Danish culture is dealt with in the subject Danish, but very often it is restricted to the literary tradition and the study of modern fiction and non-fiction productions in various Danish media. Many young teachers of Danish are educated in Denmark in a Danish educational and cultural tradition, but they have far fewer lessons available to familiarise pupils with their culture than all the other subjects, which are taught in German and with a German perspective. Innovative steps have been taken to introduce coordinated German-Danish teaching (Pedersen 1990, 1991) according to which the two cultures and languages would have equal status, yet so far this is restricted to the lower grades and a few schools only.

If contemporary social issues are regarded as elements of culture, they are, however, equally taught in relation to Denmark and the Federal Republic. However, there can be no doubt that the German minority school is German and not bilingual or bicultural German–Danish, at least not in the sense of an equal status of German and Danish in the curriculum. The Danish elements are first of all brought to school by the pupils.

Language Use and Bilingualism

The pupils' use of the Danish dialect Sønderjysk is one of these elements. The language of conversation among friends inside and outside class is primarily Sønderjysk, except among those few who have German as their first language. Even though pupils also speak German to their teachers, this does not imply that they speak a lot of German. One student has realised that: 'I thought that I would speak much more German here in the school, but it was not much at all; Danish, standard Danish, we only speak that in the Danish lessons, well not even then so much, but otherwise a lot of Sønderjysk and then a little German with the friends' (Byram 1986: 70).

As this statement indicates, pupils speak both standard Danish and Sønderjysk in the subject Danish, but it is the only place where they speak standard Danish. Having acquired German as a minority second language, and standard Danish as a school language primarily at minority institutions, the pupils have only been in contact with a limited part of the two languages. Compared to monolinguals at majority schools in

Table 1: Language Use in North Schleswig

Language use in the family	German	Sønderjysk	Danish
with the parents	23.7 percent	72.4 percent	3.9 percent
with the children	27.8 percent	70.7 percent	1.5 percent

(Translated from Figure 7, Toft, 1982, p. 44, Table 19.b, 'Das Sprachverhalten innerhalb der Familie')

Denmark and the Federal Republic their linguistic and communicative competence is therefore different (Wieczerkowsky 1978, Søndergaard 1981, Byram 1986, Pedersen 1993).

Nevertheless, minority pupils become bilinguals. A study (Pedersen 1986) of the communicative competence of two groups of children (4–5 years and 12–13 years) and the language use of their parents showed that no young children and only a few of the pupils were regarded as speakers of standard Danish. It also turned out that none of the young children were bilinguals at that age, some of them still being monolingual German or Sønderjysk speakers. But the pupils regarded themselves as bilingual Sønderjysk–German-speakers and a few of them felt that they had a command of Sønderjysk, German and standard Danish. In comparison to the children, more parents regarded themselves as monolingual Sønderjysk speakers.

There are no official statistics regarding language use, and within existing research there are only a few surveys covering this aspect. The results of Sievers (1974), Toft (1982) and Pedersen (1986) confirm, however, the general assumption that the Danish dialect Sønderjysk is used in everyday communication. Toft (1982) has shown the distribution of languages mostly used inside the family, and the respective figures of 72.4 percent and 70.7 percent make it evident that Sønderjysk is the most commonly used means of communication within the family.

Functional Regional Bilingualism

The linguistic variation within the languages used by the German minority has first of all been studied within the context of the minority children's use of Danish in Pedersen (1986, 1987, and 1993). A number of characteristic regional features of German, caused by the influence of the regional variety of German spoken in Schleswig–Holstein and by the contact with

Sønderjysk and standard Danish, were established in these studies as well. With regard to vocabulary, these features include 'false friends', a type of interference where German words similar to Danish words are chosen instead of standard German expressions. The most characteristic feature, however, is a prosody different from that of standard German. It is influenced by the intonation and stress patterns in Danish, which has also been observed by Byram (1986: 149): 'There is official recognition that North Schleswig German is different from West German standard and a tendency to nurture the regional dialect.' This, in part, has been caused by the linguistic example set by teachers in the minority education system, which can be described as 'formal *Hochdeutsch* spoken with a regional accent, sometimes with a North Schleswig intonation breaking through' (Byram, 1986: 67).

The teachers' attitude towards the pupils' development of a North Schleswig German variant is one of acceptance. Corrections towards standard German do not take place very often. If it happens, then it is in lessons where the attention is on formal aspects of the language. Only then, deviations in syntax, morphology, and semantics might be corrected. Prosody, on the other hand, nobody cares about.

Those minority members who speak two varieties of Danish – the dialect Sønderjysk and a regional variety of standard Danish – and a variety of German, namely North Schleswig German, have no command of a standard language. Their language competence is, however, nevertheless a kind of bilingualism that can be characterised as a functional regional bilingualism. It is functional because it satisfies the communicative demands within the minority and is today accepted widely within the border region by most majority members (Pedersen, 1993). Their positive attitude towards a bidialectism consisting of the dialect Sønderjysk and a regional variety of standard Danish has been growing concurrently with the increasing economic strength of the region, no longer being dependent on Copenhagen as the economic, cultural and linguistic centre.

Maintaining Minority Language and Identity

As the members of the German minority speak Sønderjysk or a Danish regional language in communication with the members of the majority, they are seldom liable to linguistic prejudice in the border region, they might even be envied for their proficiency in German. It is not in its function as a minority language, but rather as an important foreign language for the majority in cross-border cooperation and trade that competence in German is regarded as an asset. As a minority language, German is of no importance in public administration, the judicial system, politics, media, or local trade. The only exceptions in this context are the minority party's election campaigns, which are in German and Danish, and the minority paper which is published in German. There are also a few public signs in German in Aabenraa, where the minority has its headquarters. Bilingual signs, however, are never used, and outside Aabenraa the minority is fairly invisible in everyday life.

Strong national feelings on the part of some of the majority members have emerged recently in Sønderjylland/Nordschleswig against the background of formalised Danish–German cross-border cooperation. They were, however, not directed against the German minority, which is fully recognised as having the same economic framework for its activities as the majority. Furthermore, it is subsidised from the Federal Republic. The minority's legal rights seem to be fulfilled, and the minority does not deviate from the majority in relation to demands of an economic nature.

The decreasing importance of national concepts, the invisibility of the German minority, and the lack of specific minority-defined demands might be the reasons why the majority's attitude towards the German population in the region is one of indifference. 'If they think they are German, let them do so, but I don't understand why,' was an answer to the question about the importance of the minority in spring 1998. In its simple terms, it represents an attitude of surprised disinterest that seems to be widespread. This is not so much an expression of ignorance about the origins of the minority, but rather a disbelief that one part of the population can keep insisting on its distinct national identity at a time when national feelings no longer seem to be of the same importance as they were a few decades ago.

On the whole, the conditions the minority finds for maintaining its national and transethnic identity are considered ideal. According to Byram (1986), it is, however, less clear whether the minority would continue to exist without financial subsidies from the neighbouring country: 'Without financial subsidy, the minority could not exist as it does. Indeed without financial subsidy, the minority might not exist at all. Yet the members of the minority would not cease to exist; they would have to reinterpret their identity in different economic circumstances.' (Byram, 1986: 113).

References

Becker-Christensen, H., *The Danish–German Minority Arrangement – a Model for Others?* Aabenraa, 1992.

Byram, M., *Minority Education and Ethnic Survival. Case Study of a German School in Denmark.* Clevedon, 1986.

Cornett, A., 'Integration eller assimilation. Nationale mindretal i nutidens samfund', in *Økonomi og Politik* 59.3, 1986, pp. 225–33.

Nordslesvigerne er mere pragmatiske, *Flensborg Avis*, 30 May 1995.

Pedersen, K.M., *Mødet mellem sprogene i den dansk-tyske grænseregion. En-, to- og flersprogede børn i Sønderjylland.* Institut for grænseregionsforskning, Aabenraa, 1986.

——, 'German Minority Children in the Danish Border Region: Code-switching and Interference', in *Journal of Multilingual and Multicultural Development*, vol. 8, nos. 1 and 2, 1987, pp. 111–20.

——, ed., *Sprache und Unterricht in der deutschen, dänischen und friesischen Minderheit*, Aabenraa, 1990.

——, 'Intentions and Innovations in Minority Language Education', in *European Lesser Used Languages in Primary Education*, eds. J. Sikma and D. Gorter, Ljouvert, 1991, pp. 179–89.

——, 'Functional Regional Bilingualism', in *Journal of Multilingual and Multicultural Development*, vol. 14, no. 6, 1993, pp. 463–81.

——, 'Die deutsche Minderheit in Dänemark und die dänische Minderheit in Deutschland', in *Handbuch der mitteleuropäischen Sprachminderheiten*, eds. R. Hinderling and L.M. Eichinger, Tübingen, 1996, pp. 31–61.

Sievers, K.D., *Beiträge zur Frage der ethnischen Identifikation des Bundes Deutscher Nordschleswiger*, Flensburg, 1996.

Søndergaard, B., 'Tosprogethed med diglossi – højtysk, rigsdansk, sønderjysk i Nordslesvig. (Mit deutscher Zusammenfassung: Zweisprachigkeit mit Diglossie. Hochdeutsch, Reichsdänisch und Süderjütisch in Nordschleswig)', in *Danske Studier* 1981, pp. 73–90.

Toft, G., *Die bäuerliche Struktur der deutschen Volksgruppe in Nordschleswig.* Flensburg, 1981.

Weitling, G. 'Tysk mindretalsliv i Nordslesvig i et fremtidigt perspektiv', in *Pluk*, no. 1, 1991, pp. 17–21.

——, 'Tysk identitet i Nordslesvig', in *National identitet*, ed. H. Becker-Christensen, Aabenraa, 1996, pp. 25–36.

——, *Sønderjyder set med tyske briller*, *Flensburg Avis*, 22 November 1997.

Wieczerkowsky, W., *Zum sprachlichen Können zweisprachiger Schüler in deutschen Schulen Nordschleswigs*, Hamburg, 1978 (unpublished).

CHAPTER 2

The German-speaking Minority of Belgium

Bruce Donaldson

Compared with other such small linguistic minorities in Europe, Belgium's German-speaking population has fared well as far as its linguistic rights are concerned. But this particular minority has the good fortune to reside in a country where one's whole existence revolves around one's membership of one or other language community. Of course the usual obsession of Belgian politics is Dutch versus French, where Dutch-speakers constitute the majority, but it would have been difficult for the Flemings and Walloons to press for linguistic equality while riding rough-shod over similar rights for the country's third linguistic group, the German-speakers of the east of the country.[1]

According to the most recent national census (1 March 1991),[2] of the almost ten million population of the Kingdom of

1. Nevertheless, the editors of *Deutsch als Muttersprache in Belgien – Forschungsberichte zur Gegenwartslage*, writing back in 1979, felt compelled in their preface (p. 5) to comment (my translation): 'In a country whose very marrow is affected by the problem of the linguistic–cultural contact and conflict of the two 'large' Belgian population groups – the French and the Dutch speakers – it is not by any means automatic that numberswise less important minorities like the German-speakers are free to develop linguistically and culturally.'
2. The population figures quoted here are as given in Alen and Ergec (1994: 9, footnote 12). It should also be noted that somewhere between 10,000 and 12,000 of the German-speakers in the Eupen area are German nationals, residing in Belgium because of the favourable living conditions. In Raeren, for example, 45 percent of the population of 9,500 individuals falls into this category, and in Kelmis (population 10,000) it is approximately 35 percent.

Belgium, less than one per cent belong to the German-speaking community. The largest group are the 5,768,925 Dutch-speakers (i.e. Flemings), followed by the 3,188,093 French speakers (i.e. Walloons), and 954,045 Bruxellois, who

1. Old Belgium Welkenraedt
2. New Belgium Eupen
3. New Belgium St Vith
4. Old Belgium Bocholz
5. New Belgium Malmédy
6. Old Belgium Arel
7. Vurgebiet

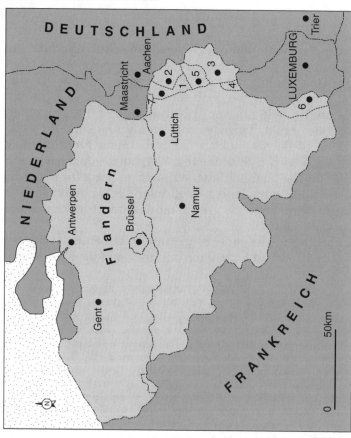

German-speaking Areas in Belgium

may be Dutch- or French-speaking or bilingual, although the majority would consider themselves francophone.

Location of the German-speaking Area

The German-speaking area is neither a single entity historically nor are its constituent parts all geographically contiguous. The present-day state of Belgium was created in 1831 out of the United Kingdom of the Netherlands which had consisted of what we now call the Netherlands, Belgium and Luxemburg. Some of the German-speaking areas were part of Belgium from long before that time (Old Belgium), but others were only incorporated into the Belgian state after the First World War (New Belgium). Due to the geographic distribution of these areas along the German border between the south-eastern corner of Holland and the north of Luxemburg, as well as the location of another area in the south adjacent to the western border of the Grand Duchy of Luxemburg, there is not even dialectal homogeneity between them. The Germanic dialects represented here range from north to south through Low Franconian, Ripuarian[3] and Moselle Franconian,[4] whereby the Low Franconian area in the north (area 1 on the map, centred on the town of Welkenraedt) is contiguous with a small Dutch-speaking area in the north of Liège (the Fourons, Voerstreek or Vurgebiet, area 7 on the map), Dutch itself being a Low Franconian dialect of West Germanic. To the east of Old Belgium in the north lies an area of New Belgium (area 2 on the map) which colloquially goes under the name of the main town situated there, Eupen, which is also the largest town in German-speaking Belgium and therefore the region's administrative centre and the home of its only daily newspaper (*Grenz-Echo*, founded 1927) and radio station. South of this region, bordering on both the north of Luxemburg and Germany, lies a second even larger, but economically less significant part of New Belgium which also goes under the name of the main town situated

3. The northern third of areas 1 and 2 on the map is separated from the southern two-thirds by the Benrather Line, which separates the Low Franconian from the Ripuarian dialect.
4. To this dialect, and thus in terms of 'dialect geography' historically part of Luxemburg, belongs the German spoken in Arel, St Vith, parts of Bocholz and the German-speaking communities in Malmédy.

there, St Vith (area 3 on the map). Separating these two parts of New Belgium as well as stretching southwards along the western boundary of St Vith, is a third area of New Belgium (area 5 on the map), also named after its main town, Malmédy, but this differs from the other two parts of New Belgium in that it is regarded as constituting part of the French-speaking community, although it contains a German-speaking minority. To the south-west of the St Vith area, bordering on Luxemburg and lying just inside the Belgian province of Luxemburg, is a small German-speaking area, Bocholz (French Beho), which is part of Old Belgium (area 4 on the map). Finally there is the German-speaking area of the French-speaking Belgian province of Luxemburg (area 6 on the map), which is part of Old Belgium and which forms a continuum with the Letzebuergisch-speaking Grand Duchy, but is not contiguous with the other areas in Belgium where German is spoken, which all lie to the north of the Grand Duchy. *Das Areler Land*, as it is known, takes its name from the capital city of the province of Luxemburg, Arel (French Arlon).[5] What the Arel area has in common with the Malmédy area is that it merely houses a German minority, but German has no official status; there are not even 'linguistic facilities' for Germans as there are in Malmédy. What is more, the Germans of both the Arel and the Bocholz areas really only use the local dialect,[6] French being used for all the higher social functions – retention of German in these highly Frenchified areas was hastened by the stigma attached to German as a result of German invasion in two world wars; similar sentiments towards standard German exist in the Grand Duchy. But all areas of German-speaking Belgium, whether belonging to Old or New Belgium, have varying degrees of diglossia in common.

5. Historically, the overwhelmingly French-speaking province of Belgium called Luxemburg and the present-day independent state of Luxemburg, i.e. the Grand Duchy, were one. The basis of the current border between the two is language, i.e. French to the west and German to the east, a division which occurred in 1831 when Belgium gained independence from Holland. However, some Germans were left behind in the west and because of the last two world wars, French has managed to assert itself alongside German (as well as Letzebuergisch) in the Grand Duchy, thus blurring the historical reason for the original division.

6. In the four northern municipalities of the German-speaking area (i.e. the Eupen area) dialect is seldom heard, and then only among the older inhabitants, but in the five southern municipalities (i.e. the St Vith area) dialect is regularly used by the people when communicating with other locals.

The Size of the German-speaking Population

The three areas of New Belgium (2, 3 and 5 on the map) comprise what is referred to in Belgian politics as the *Ostkantone*. Eupen and St Vith constitute the area where German has official status, as it is the language of the majority, the result of their having become part of the kingdom only in 1919; in the area around Malmédy, while historically part of New Belgium, French has official status as German-speakers do not constitute the majority of the population. The number of German-speakers in Belgium varies according to whether one includes the areas where German is spoken but does not have official status. The website of the Minister-President of the Government of the German-speaking Community in Belgium, for example, quotes the number as being 68,000[7] (and thus 0.68 percent of the total population), where clearly only New Belgium (i.e. areas 2 and 3) is being considered. Various other estimations of the total German population (Hinderdael and Nelde 1996: 481), i.e. including Old Belgium, put the figure at around 100,000, and thus at 1 percent of the total population of the kingdom, but this includes German-speakers who fall outside the jurisdiction of the government of the German-speaking Community; as German-speakers in Old Belgium do not enjoy protection as a recognised linguistic minority, it is difficult to obtain reliable figures as to their number, but it is put variously at between 30,000 and 50,000. As for the number in the Arel region, it seems to be anyone's guess. The municipalities of Old Belgium all show varying degrees of Frenchification, with administration, church and school acting as important contributors to the process. This means that German is relegated in these areas to more intimate spheres, but Hinderdael and Nelde (1996: 482) comment that language consciousness is not highly developed in Old Belgium, added to which French has the advantage of enjoying higher status.

---

7. It is believed that roughly 5 percent of this population figure for the German-speaking area consists of French speakers who have moved into the area (see Hinderdael and Nelde 1996: 482).

The German-speaking Area as a Transitionary Zone

From the above it is clear that Belgium's German-speaking region forms a transitionary zone both between Dutch and German and between French and German. Linguistically and culturally it looks eastwards, whereas politically and administratively it looks westwards to the larger cities of Belgium, while economically it looks in both directions with Eupen having an economic link to the area around Aachen in particular, but it is also well situated to look towards Maastricht in Holland for its economic well-being. The linguistic border between Dutch and French that runs from west to east through Belgium and continues from north to south along the eastern fringe of the country – but here it separates not only Dutch but also German from French – is a living reminder of the collision between Germania and Romania that occurred two thousand years ago with the language border taking another thousand years (until the tenth century) to emerge along it is present course. As elsewhere in Europe, the linguistic and cultural distinctions resulting from this collision do not by any means coincide with the neatly drawn national borders that are of much later origin. There is a certain irony in the fact that this area of the Eastern Cantons should have been at the centre of the Carolingian empire but now finds itself relegated to the periphery of the political entity in which it is now located.

The Historical Origins of the German-speaking Area

The linguistic and cultural differences between the constituent areas of German-speaking Belgium are a direct result of earlier political and ecclesiastical divisions, as well as of topography in an age when such things were a greater impediment to communication than they are today. The dialectal differences are worth noting, as the German dialects of the north, for example, are not mutually intelligible with those of the Arel region. The northern areas belonged historically to the Duchy of Limburg, and Arel of course to the Duchy of Luxemburg, and both were regarded as peripheral to their respective duchies. By the middle of the fifteenth century both duchies found themselves under the House of Burgundy, which led eventually to their passing to the House of Habsburg under Charles V. When the emperor abdicated in 1555, his son, Philip II, inherited from him both Spain and the whole of the Burgundian Netherlands, while the rest of the Holy Roman Empire was bequeathed to Charles's brother, Ferdinand. This all important event in the history of what previously constituted the Netherlands, accounts for the fact that those territories ceased to form part of the German Empire and explains, albeit with numerous minor changes later, the present-day border between Holland, Belgium and Luxemburg on the one hand, and Germany on the other. From 1555 the Netherlands, now in Spanish hands, were governed from Brussels by a stadtholder.

During the eighty-year period from 1568 to 1648 the Netherlanders fought a war of independence. This resistance to Spanish rule was eventually stronger in the Protestant north than in the Catholic south, which explains why Holland ultimately obtained independence, while the southern provinces (present-day Belgium and Luxemburg) stayed loyal to Spain under whose rule they were to remain until the War of the Spanish Succession (1701–14) at the conclusion of which they passed to the Austrian branch of the Habsburg family. Austrian rule lasted until the arrival of French revolutionary troops in 1794, which led to the incorporation of the region into the French Republic. After the defeat of Napoleon it was decided at the Congress of Vienna in 1815 to reinstate the united Netherlands as it had been in the first half of the sixteenth century, i.e. a union of Holland, Belgium and Luxemburg, united under the newly constituted Dutch monarchy. But this union lasted only a few years as the revolutions of 1830 affected the southern Netherlands and led to the creation of the separate Kingdom of Belgium in 1831, while Luxemburg remained under Holland until 1890; the ascension of Queen Wilhelmina to the Dutch throne in that year necessitated the independence of the Grand Duchy of Luxemburg under another branch of the Nassau dynasty, as its medieval constitution did not permit a female ruler at that time. It was the Congress of Vienna that was responsible for drawing the border between the German-speaking areas of present-day Belgium: Holland was given areas 1 (Welkenraedt) and 4 (Bocholz) while areas 2 (Eupen), 3 (St Vith) and 5 (Malmédy) were given to Prussia, thus creating the current border between Old and New Belgium.

During the long period of changing allegiances, the importance of French and Dutch as administrative languages in Belgium waxed and waned according to the political circumstances of the day. Nevertheless, the Burgundian, Spanish, Austrian, Napoleonic and even the final independent period all favoured French, which had always been the language of the aristocracy of the region.

On the foundation of the Belgian state in 1831, possibly more than 250,000 German-speakers found themselves living within the newly founded kingdom. German was recognised and a German version of the first constitution appeared, but subsequent Frenchification at the local level did much to damage the freedom of language that had been granted. In 1839 the German community in the province of Luxemburg was separated from the rest of German-speaking Belgium, and German declined rapidly in that area. Even in the German-speaking territory of Old Belgium further to the north, German declined throughout the nineteenth century and possibly only survived at all due to the existence of bilingual primary schools and the use of standard German in church (Hinderdael and Nelde 1996: 483). The rekindling of linguistic consciousness among Belgium's Germans that occurred at the end of the nineteenth century, no doubt influenced by developments in the Dutch-speaking part of the country, was followed by the German invasion during the First World War. This was an event which obviously aided the spread of the German language. And when in 1920 the Treaty of Versailles assigned the Prussian territories of Eupen, St Vith and Malmédy to Belgium as reparations for its dreadful suffering during the war, the scene was set for the developments we see today. There was a slight setback in 1940 when Germany took back the recently ceded areas, plus some of the older German-speaking territory in areas 1 (Welkenraedt) and 4 (Bocholz) on the map, all of which, however, were returned to Belgium after the war.

The Dominance of French and the Rise of Dutch

The historical events above gave rise, as we have seen, to a domination of French over the other two languages spoken in the country, i.e. Dutch and German, but the majority of the population have always been Flemings. The short period of reunification with Holland after Napoleon, during which time 75 percent of the population of the nation as a whole was Dutch-speaking, saw Dutch briefly make significant inroads into government, the law, the economy, and higher education, and planted the seeds of the Flemish Movement. After the breakup, the Belgian establishment returned to using French for all the higher functions of government and society, but it had been demonstrated that Dutch was just as capable as French in fulfilling these functions. Consequently, from the middle of the nineteenth century to the post-1945 period, Flemings have been campaigning for linguistic equality. It was eventually decided that the least contentious means of attaining this equality while preserving the political unity of the country, was by means of creating a federal state with legally defined geographic areas where Dutch and French were to have sole or dual official status. As Belgian federalism was to be based on linguistic differences, due recognition of the existence of a third, if relatively small linguistic community, also became an issue. Cultural and other autonomy for the country's three linguistic communities was to be granted, and only the most necessary of functions were to be left in the hands of the national government.

What it Means to Be a German-speaking Belgian

Membership of the German-speaking community of Belgium means more than possessing the ability to speak German; it includes not only the ability, but also the desire to speak German at every level of life and to possess the constitutional right to do so, which obviously necessitates the cooperation of government in making living in one's language possible. Membership also presupposes an awareness of the difficult circumstances surrounding the origins of New Belgium and a desire to preserve the specific identity of the region within the recent constitutional reforms of the Belgian state. The German-speaking people of New Belgium may have belonged to the Kingdom of Belgium for only seventy-odd years, but they nevertheless feel themselves to be Belgian. It should be pointed out, however, that in the minds of many there is only one true Belgian, namely the king, all other citizens being Flemish, Walloon or German. 'Belgian' is increasingly perceived as a federal term referring merely to one's nationality, not one's cultural identity.

Although the national obsession is inevitably the peaceful coexistence of the Flemish and Walloon communities, a peace which still flares from time to time, Belgian Germans might well count themselves as lucky that they live in a country where two such large linguistic communities have been striving to find an acceptable *modus vivendi*. Had they found themselves living in an otherwise monolingual state, their linguistic and cultural aspirations may well not have been respected to the degree that they have been. Rather than suffering peripheral damage from the central struggle, they have been the beneficiaries of it. Karl-Heinz Lambertz (1980) commented in an interview: 'There is, however, a negative aspect. We have our own community aspirations and aims. The others understand this because they are more or less in the same situation. But every proposal we put forward for the purpose of solving our own problems is promptly seized upon by the French and Dutch communities and made into a *casus belli* in their own unending battle. This is vastly prejudicial to us German-speakers, because it sometimes forces us to take sides in an argument which has nothing to do with us at all.' Belgian federalism, however, has made great advances since then.

The Creation of the Federal State

The language border between Dutch and French was fixed by language laws in 1962–63[8] as a forerunner to constitutional reform; 'the 1962–1963 laws on languages laid the foundations of the *territoriality principle,* which stipulates that in monolingual linguistic regions the use of a given language – that of the monolingual linguistic region – is compulsory for all public administrative acts, regardless of the tier of government from which they emanate' (Alen and Ergec 1994: 7).

8. As a result of these laws and the constitutional reform of 1970, the Eupen–StVith region was declared an officially German-speaking area, but the Malmédy area (itself also part of New not Old Belgium) was not included, as the majority of its inhabitants spoke French.

There have since been four constitutional reforms, in 1970, 1980, 1988–89 and 1993, which have transformed the country from a unitarian into a federal state. As a result of these reforms, various levels of authority, which all complement one another, are recognised: the Federal Government, the Communities,[9] the Regions, the Provinces and the Municipalities. German-speakers, while possessing their own Municipalities within the province of Liège, constitute the German-speaking Community. 'Communitisation', with inherent linguistic autonomy, was granted on the insistence of the Flemings. The Walloons, on the other hand, insisted on economic autonomy, which led to 'regionalisation', i.e. the creation of three regions, namely the Flemish Region, the Brussels–Capital Region (officially bilingual) and the Walloon Region. The economy of the German-speaking Community is inexorably bound up with that of the French-speaking Community, and thus constitutes part of the Walloon Region. There have been partly legitimate demands in recent times for the recognition of the German-speaking area as a fourth official Region in order to grant the Germans more economic autonomy, but this would require a change of the constitution. The first article of the Belgian Constitution, following the Fourth State Reform of 1993, states, 'Belgium is a federal state made up of Communities and Regions.' One of the main points of the Fourth Reform was the protection of linguistic minorities. The 'principle of subsidiarity' prevails, by which is meant that anything that can be dealt with at a lower level must not be passed on to a higher political level and that this lower level must be the closest possible to the community of which the people feel themselves a part. Reconciling regional and cultural identity on the one hand and a federal structure on the other is obviously not without its problems, but it does bring the decision-making process closer to the people.

'The laws on the use of languages in administrative matters provide "linguistic facilities" for the inhabitants of the 27 communes contiguous to a different linguistic region' (Alen and Ergec 1994: 8). Included in these 27 municipalities are the 9 in the German-speaking area which all have 'linguistic facilities' for French speakers and 2 (Malmédy and Weismes [Fr.

9. Capitalisation of such terms in this paragraph is in accordance with that employed in the publications of the Belgian government consulted in the writing of this chapter.

Waimes]) in the Malmédy area (area 5 on the map), which
have facilities for German-speakers, as Germans constitute
about 25 percent of the population in this area. Although
other municipalities, lying outside the region where German
has official status (i.e. those in area 1 on the map), have the
right to apply for 'linguistic facilities' for German-speakers,
none has yet done so.

The three language communities enjoy autonomy in culture, education, radio and television, health care, welfare, science and technology, use of languages and international
relations in all these areas, as well as cooperating between the
communities in cultural, educational and individual-related
matters. In the German-speaking region the federal government retains authority in matters relating to the use of language in legal proceedings and the armed forces.

The federal parliament of Belgium consists of the Chamber
of Representatives and the Senate and the functions and
responsibilities of these two bodies do not differ greatly from
those in other western countries that employ the bi-cameral
system. Twenty-one of the seventy-one members of the Senate
possess the status of 'community senator', consisting of ten from
the Flemish Community, ten from the French Community and
one from the German Community, all of whom are appointed
by the legislative assemblies of the three communities. The Senate is thus the main venue for inter-community dialogue.

The communities and regions each have their own parliament, called a council, and their own government. On the
non-Flemish side of the complicated political spectrum there is
a Government and a Council of the Walloon Region,[10] which
also includes the German-speaking part of the country for
regional matters, as well as a Government and a Council of the
French Community, which excludes the German-speaking
community. The German-speaking community has a Government and a Council for its own community matters. The
Government consists of 3 members whereas the Council of
the German-speaking Community, its legislative assembly,
consists of 25 directly elected members who are elected every
5 years. These bodies have their own legislative powers and
their own financial resources, in every way comparable to

10. The Flemings on the other hand have merged the institutions of the Flemish
Region and the Flemish Community to form a single Flemish Government.

those of the two larger communities. The 10 provinces are not only subordinate to the federal state but also to the communities, and above all to the regions. This means that there are constitutional safeguards for the German-speaking community residing as it does within the Walloon Region. The lowest level of government, and thus the one closest to the people, is the Municipality (also called Commune in some publications). Since the merger of nearly 3,000 municipalities in 1975, there are now 589, of which 9 are German-speaking (Eupen, Kelmis, Lontzen, Raeren [all in the Eupen area] and St Vith, Bütgenbach, Büllingen, Amel, Burg–Reuland [all in the St Vith area]). Municipalities have a local district council whose size (between 7 and 55 members) depends on the number of inhabitants within its boundaries.

No one in Belgium denies that all these tiers of government are complicated, but they are the price that had to be paid to retain the unity of the Belgian state. *Living in Belgium*, a recent promotional electronic publication of the German-speaking Community, proudly proclaims that this rather complicated federal system:

> reflects honour on this country that its statesmen have wisely decided to endow the 69,000 citizens living in the German-speaking territory with the same institutions and the same autonomy in many important aspects of public and daily life as have been given to the 5.9 million Flemings and the 4 million French-speaking Belgians. It is almost unique in Europe that a state should grant such valuable instruments of self-government to a minority of only 0.7 percent of its population, thereby raising it, in a constitutional sense, beyond the status of a minority.

Interestingly enough, *Living in Belgium* goes on to state the following which may be of relevance to other communities discussed in this book:

> It is no wonder, therefore, that the emergent democracies of Central and Eastern Europe as well as their minority organisations are knocking at the door, asking for more information about this ingenious Belgian solution, with a view to isolating those aspects of the system which are transferable into their own Constitution or basic laws. What was given to the German-speaking Community is much more than the fundamental rights of minority-protection. In fact it represents a constitutionally guaranteed place in the new federal State, on an equal footing with the two other Communities, a position that enjoys a high degree of autonomy and self-determination.

I have chosen in this paragraph to quote at length from this promotional publication as it contains statements that have emanated from within the German-speaking community itself and which reflect the satisfaction of the German-speakers with the results of Belgian federalism. It certainly was not always so. Inter- and particularly post-war attempts to Frenchify government and education in the German-speaking area are now a thing of the past, but attempts '[to impose] the French language without actually prohibiting the use of German was at one time considered as a legal means to facilitate integration into the Belgian State. There were many fields in which the German language wasn't commonly used' (*Living in Belgium*). Dissatisfaction with this situation among the German-speaking minority was growing when the language laws of the early 1960s began to be enacted, the result of Flemish activism, and from then on the German-speaking community was more or less able to ride on the back of legislation being enacted to keep the peace between the country's other two language groups.

Languages in the Schools

In the areas of Eupen and St Vith where German enjoys official status, it is the language of instruction in schools; understandably enough, French is offered as first foreign language. But even in the Eupen area, contrary to the intention of the 1962-63 language laws, there are French schools for the French-speaking minority[11] that attract a certain number of German-speaking children to them.[12] In all other areas where

11. This is a good example of the unevenhanded way in which the provision of 'linguistic facilities' for minority groups in the 1962–63 language laws has been applied: there are greater facilities for the tiny French-speaking minority in the officially German-speaking area than there are for the much larger German-speaking minority in the officially French-speaking area (3 percent of the population in the town of Eupen, for example, versus 25 percent of the population speaking German outside of Eupen–StVith). A few German schools still have so-called French departments where all instruction is given in French but this is soon to change as the classes for the Abiturdiplom will only be conducted in German.

12. One must not lose sight of the fact that, with the exception of the few German-speakers who choose to pursue a university education in Germany (usually in Aachen or occasionally in Cologne), German-speaking Belgians usually proceed to a French-speaking university as there is no facility for tertiary study in German in the kingdom.

German is also spoken but French is the official language, instruction is of course conducted in French. In Malmédy, German is the first foreign language taught in schools and is compulsory. In other areas of Old Belgium, German is usually only offered as an optional foreign language, the competition coming from both Dutch and English; German competes with Dutch as first foreign language in the Welkenraedt area in particular. In secondary education, the situation for German is even less rosy. Hinderdael and Nelde (1996: 489) ascertained that up to two-thirds of instruction even in the official German-speaking area is conducted in French. Outside the Eupen–St Vith areas, where secondary education is of course conducted in French, German has trouble holding its own against Dutch and English, as English is overwhelmingly preferred; but even Dutch usually proves to be more popular than German. One must not of course lose sight of the fact that the majority of Belgians have Dutch as their mother tongue and that whereas Wallonia was the economic powerhouse of nineteenth-century Belgium, Flanders is where the most exciting things are happening now. Having a knowledge of Dutch to function fully in Belgian life has never been more necessary in this country's long troubled history, than it is now. As we seem to be heading into an age where the younger generation of Flemings and Walloons is more comfortable expressing itself in English than in the other national language, there is no reason to expect German-speaking Belgians to be any different.

German and the Electronic Media

Belgium has transmitted radio programmes in German since 1945. To begin with, a French station broadcast several hours a day in German. Eupen acquired its own station in 1960, and in 1977 the German Community was granted an independent *Belgisches Rundfunk- und Fernsehzentrum* which broadcasts in German 24 hours a day. There is no German language television service in Belgium, but it is of course possible for German-speakers to receive German television, as well as Dutch and Luxemburgian transmissions, so the community is in fact very well served in this respect.

German and the Legal System

The right to a trial in German has existed since 1925, but equality with Dutch and French has only existed since 1982. If a crime is committed in the German-speaking area, a trial in German can be requested, but if the accused speaks French, the trial may be conducted in French. In addition, any resident of the German-speaking Eastern Cantons who is a Belgian national, can request a trial in German. Where appeals end up in courts located outside the area in which German enjoys official status (thus even in the city of Liège), the accused retains the right to a trial in German (Hinderdael and Nelde 1996: 493).

Economic Perspectives of the German-speaking Area

Because the rate of unemployment in the German-speaking area is below the national average, and because of the ability to develop cross-border contacts, as well as the favourably central position of the area with first-class transportation infrastructure close at hand, the economic climate of the region is generally positive, although the Eupen area is better situated with regard to infrastructure than the area around St Vith. Increase in light industry has gradually been replacing job losses in the agricultural sector. Nevertheless, both the timber and dairying industries are considered vital to the area, but there is a growing acknowledgement of the fact that the services sector needs to be developed if labour migration, particularly of the young, is to be stemmed. The German-French bilingualism of the population does, however, put the local people in a good position for finding employment outside the German-speaking area of Belgium – in fact 12 percent of the working population have found employment in Germany and Luxemburg, with 3,500 residents commuting on a daily basis to jobs in Germany (Hinderdael and Nelde 1996: 485). Since 1992 the German-speaking community has been a member of the 'Meuse–Rhine Euregio', a body which unites the contiguous economic zones in eastern Belgium, Holland and Germany with the aim of dismantling the frontiers and promoting cross-border cooperation between companies and institutions within the participating areas. There is also a realisation that the natural beauty of the area can be exploited for tourism, which is one field in which the German Community has legislative autonomy.

Conclusion

In conclusion I will quote at length from the work of Hinderdael and Nelde (1996: 486), the latter of whom heads the *Brussels Research Centre on Multilingualism*. The very existence of such an institution in the Belgian capital is a reflection of the all-pervasive presence of an awareness of life with more than one language in the Kingdom of Belgium:

> All investigations into the language habits of German-speaking Belgians which have been conducted by the Brussels Research Centre on Multilingualism by means of field surveys, have confirmed the quite heterogeneous nature of the German-speaking area of Belgium which is not just geographically fragmented. The degree of Frenchification, the transition to language change, the diglossic language combinations, the attitude and the language consciousness of the people are, as a result of their isolation, as varied as the historical structures described hitherto.

The two researchers go on to conclude that there are great pressures on Belgium's German-speakers, particularly on those in Old Belgium, to make the transition to French. The end result of this process is the transformation of the border between Old and New Belgium, the former national border between Prussia and Belgium, into a language border, whereas the two areas formerly shared the same German dialect. They remark that a language border which has scarcely moved eastwards in centuries, may now require only one or two generations to shift considerably further to the east. This is not unconnected with the stigmatisation of German in Old Belgium, and this in turn is not unconnected with the contempt Germany has shown for Belgian sovereignty in the last two world wars. Such factors explain why, despite the favourable legal situation that prevails vis-à-vis German in contemporary Belgium, the German-speaking minority is nevertheless not immune from linguistic assimilation by the French-speaking majority in that part of the country. There seems to be no correlation in Belgium between the two, as indeed was borne out generally by the research project on linguistic minorities, entitled Euromosaic (Luxemburg 1996). Old Belgium seems more than happy to Frenchify, and even New Belgium seems quite willing to make many concessions to French (e.g. some education in French, bilingual signs, French language plays and literature promoted by the Alliance Française), despite the existence of legislation to the contrary and despite its strong economic links with Germany, and thus its economic prosperity.

References

My thanks to the Office of the Minister-Präsident der Deutschsprachigen Gemein-schaft in Belgien, Mr. J. Maraite, for their conscientious replies to my many e-mail enquiries.

'In East-Belgium the German-speakers feel at home' in *Living in Belgium,* an electronic promotional publication distributed by the office of the Minister-President of the government of the German-speaking Community.

Alen, A. and Ergec, R., *Federal Belgium after the Fourth State Reform of 1993,* Brussels, 1994.

Auburger, L., Kloss, H., and Rupp, H., *Deutsch als Muttersprache in Belgien,* Wiesbaden, 1979.

Belgian Federal Government on Line: http: //belgium.fgov.be.

Donaldson, B., *Dutch: a Linguistic History of Holland and Belgium,* The Hague, 1983.

Hinderdael, M. and Nelde, P.H., 'Deutschbelgien', in *Handbuch der mitteleuropäischen Sprachminderheiten,* eds. R. Hinderling and L. Eichinger, Tübingen, 1996, pp. 479–95.

Lambertz, K.-H., *The German-speaking Belgians,* Interview with Karl-Heinz Lambertz, Member of the Party Committee for the Harmonious Coexistence of the Communities, recorded by J.M. Depluvrez, 1980.

Acknowledgement for the Map

'German-speaking Areas in Belgium': Hinderdael, M. and Nelde, P.H., 'Deutschbelgien', in *Handbuch der mitteleuropäischen Sprachminderheiten,* eds. R. Hinderling and L. Eichinger, Tübingen, 1996, p. 479.

CHAPTER 3

The Ethnolinguistic Vitality of Alsatian-speakers in Southern Alsace

Judith Broadbridge

The easternmost region of France, Alsace, is situated between the Vosges mountain range to the west, and the River Rhine to the east. The northern limit follows the River Lauter, while to the south it extends as far as the Territoire de Belfort. It lies along the French–German and, in part, French–Swiss borders. In linguistic terms, Alsace is to be found to the east of the border between Romance and Germanic populations, a frontier not reflected in present-day political mapping of territory. Since Alsace now lies on French soil, French is the official language, used by law in all public domains. The only formal situations in which German or Alsatian occur, but then just on a small scale, are religious services, the media, in court and in specially organised school classes (in addition, of course, to those for German as a foreign language).

While most local varieties of German are to be found in juxtaposition with *Hochdeutsch* or Standard German, this is obviously not the case as far as Alsatian is concerned. Instances in which German is used are rare.

The term Alsatian is misleading, as it suggests homogeneity. In reality, forms of Alsatian differ from one village to another. In broad terms, the different manifestations of Alsatian can be categorised as Alemannic or Franconian. The greater proportion of Alsace is the territory of Low Alemannic as are Baden and Swabia on German soil. However, the northernmost tip of the region forms a stronghold of Rhenish Franconian, while to the far south, in the Sundgau, High Alemannic holds sway, as it does, too, in neighbouring Switzerland. Although Strasbourg lies in the area categorised as Low Alemannic, its variety is Franconian in nature.

Alsace appears to fit neatly into Meic Stephens's (1978, xii) definition of a linguistic minority, described as a community where a language is spoken which is not the language of the majority of the state's citizens. Indeed, Stephens offers Alsace as an example. Leaving aside the political correctness or not of the word *minority*, the notion of language in the above definition also gives rise to debate. For some, Alsatian is merely one variety, among others, of the German language, and therefore Alsatian-speakers essentially form a German-speaking minority. However, others feel the local idiom is a language in its own right, and deny any kinship between the regional variety and *Hochdeutsch*, and thus the Alsatian-speaking population can be considered an Alsatian-speaking minority but not a German-speaking one. There is no doubt that a link does exist between German and Alsatian, explaining the relative ease with which Alsatian-speakers are able to learn German. But unlike most other Germanic idioms, Alsatian includes a considerable number of French lexical items. The extent to which Alsatian-speakers can be considered a German-speaking minority or not, has less to do with linguistic similarities than with the beliefs and perceptions of the Alsatian-speakers themselves.

The discussion which follows is based on the results of a telephone questionnaire interview survey, outlined below, which was carried out in Southern Alsace between 1994 and 1995. The target population was that of Zillisheim, an urban commune seven kilometres from Mulhouse in the *Haut-Rhin*.[1]

---

1. Zillisheim was chosen because it presents several factors pertinent to the study carried out here. Firstly, it is situated in an area in which the form of Alsatian used is classed as High Alemannic. Secondly, its proximity to Mulhouse ensures that it cannot but have stronger economic and cultural links to this town rather than Strasbourg. Thirdly, the researcher wished to examine an urban population, but one which did not demonstrate the high levels of Frenchification evident in long-established conurbations. Zillisheim was only rated as an urban commune in 1990, and thus, whilst it reflects the characteristics of such communities, Alsatian is still very much in evidence in terms of language use. Finally, the urban population needed to be as far away from the Swiss and/or German frontiers (to the extent that this was possible) for cross-border linguistic interference to be at a minimum.

The main objective is to consider the ethnolinguistic vitality of Alsace as defined by Giles et al in 1977 and presented by Appel and Muysken (1987: 33–8) and Giles and Coupland (1991: 136–39). The notion of status is the prime focus of attention here.

Sampling Procedure and Questionnaire

Given that this project took the form of an interview survey requiring detailed comment, it was felt appropriate to limit investigation to those aged fifteen and over, as younger respondents may be less inclined, or able, to provide in-depth discussion.

A quota sample was drawn up according to age and sex, using material from the 1990 INSEE census (see Table 2). The telephone directory was used as a source of information in making the necessary calls. Interviews were carried out with 161 people, representing 10 percent of the population under scrutiny. The sample includes 46 percent men and 54 percent women, 39.8 percent of the respondents are aged between 15 and 39, 34.2 percent between 40 and 59 and 26.1 percent 60 and over. All socio-professional categories are represented as

Table 2: Comparison: Interviews Conducted in Zillisheim and Quotas Sought

	Quota		Interviewed	
By Sex				
Men	80		74	
Women	81		87	
By Age				
15–19	13		13	
20–39	51		51	
40–59	55		55	
60+	42		42	
By Age and Sex	Men	Women	Men	Women
15–19	7	6	5	8
20–39	27	24	26	25
40–59	27	28	24	31
60+	19	23	19	23

are all educational levels. 64 percent of those questioned claimed to speak Alsatian 'easily' or 'moderately well'.

In order to obtain comparable data, a structured interview questionnaire was devised and rigorously pre-tested.[2]

Ethnolinguistic Vitality

Language maintenance is the term used to describe a situation 'where members of a community try to keep the language(s) they have always used, i.e. to retain the same patterns of language choice' (Hoffman 1991, 185). Language shift, on the other hand, indicates that a community does not maintain its language, but gradually gives up its use in favour of another one. In Southern Alsace, all researchers are agreed that the use of Alsatian is on the decline. The latest published study relating to the *Haut-Rhin*, that of Liliane Vassberg, confirms this belief:

> Projected demographic changes in the composition of families (Alsatian, mixed, French and foreign), and the patterns of language use in each of them, make the outlook for the dialect very grim (Vassberg 1993, 181).

2. On the basis of the 1990 INSEE census it was calculated that those aged fifteen and above totalled 1,609 in Zillisheim. Although quota sampling is said to be representative only in terms of number, it has been shown to compare well with probability samples in matters of opinion and attitude, and 'much of the variability in human behaviour is accounted for if the sample is made properly representative in respect of the 'quota' variable' (Hedges 1985: 87).

    In general, the size of the sample is of greater importance than the proportion it represents. This only ceases to be true if the percentage of the sampling universe is ten or higher (Moser and Kalton 1979: 147; Hedges 1985: 56). In the case under discussion, it was considered feasible to successfully question 161 people from the 1,609 possibilities in Zillisheim and thus attain the ten percent figure considered significant.

    Pre-testing took the following forms. In a first phase, comments were sought from a group of specialists: a sociolinguist, two geolinguists, an employee of *Culture et Bilinguisme* – an organisation for the promotion of Alsatian located in Strasbourg, a psychologist, an employee of INED and a market researcher.

    A second phase comprised a series of face-to-face interviews of a participating type. In other words, the respondents were aware that they were taking part in a pre-test. Interviewees had the opportunity, not only of answering the questions but also of commenting on them. In a final phase, pilot interviews were conducted over the telephone in an neighbouring area to that to be examined during the project proper. For this last series of questioning, interlocutors were not informed that this was a preliminary enquiry.

Results of the present author's study of Zillisheim only serve to underline the rejection of Alsatian in favour of French. The reasons for such linguistic movement are many and varied, and cannot be easily defined. However, it is clear that they occur as a result of a series of collective decisions, whether conscious or unconscious, in relation to language choice. The notion of linguistic vitality developed by Giles et al, is an attempt to categorise the factors which operate in such linguistic change. According to them: 'the more vitality a linguistic group has, the more likely it will survive and thrive as a collective entity in an intergroup context' (Appel and Muysken 1987: 33). Three major components are highlighted by Giles et al: status, demography and institutional support. In terms of the last two, Alsatian's vitality would appear to be somewhat low. A decrease in the use of Alsatian, as well as in the numbers of those capable of using it, is evident. The support which Alsatian receives on a national level is minimal. The Deixonne Law of 1951 recognised the right of regional idioms to exist, but omitted Alsatian from the list as it was considered to be merely a dialect of a foreign language, German, and was not indigenous to France. Only in 1961 were provisions extended to include Alsatian. The Savary Circular of 1982 further emphasised the value of regional varieties. The mid-eighties saw the creation of a European Bureau for Lesser-Used Languages which has had an Alsatian office in Strasbourg since 1993. A national initiative of 1984/85 introduced a language and regional culture option to secondary schools and made it available as a component of the baccalaureate. However, the hours devoted to such a component do not allow for the teaching of Alsatian itself but simply an examination of Alsatian as a phenomenon. In education in general, Alsatian has to resist substitution by another majority language, German. Some favour French/Alsatian bilingual education whilst others believe French/German classes to be of greater value. A bilingual edition of *L'Alsace*, the most popular daily newspaper in the *Haut-Rhin*, does exist, but is published in French and German, not French and Alsatian. The only Alsatian which appears is in comic articles. Radio and television (the regional channel FR3) are sources of programmes in Alsatian, but they are often at times when many people are unavailable or of a type which appeals only to a minority. Thus a bleak picture is revealed in terms of demography and institutional support.

Status

The status factor is defined by Giles et al as being made up of four components, namely socio-historical, economic, social and language. It is proposed to examine these individually in the light of responses made to a series of attitude statements posed in the research project detailed above. The comments made by interlocutors are provided here in English, although they were obviously given in French originally.

Socio-Historical Status

As the term implies, socio-historical status is derived from the shared history of the community. Historical instances in which a group suffered linguistic oppression may serve to strengthen its internal loyalties and incite it to the defence of its linguistic heritage. This cannot but be the case for Alsace, whether North or South. Alsace has a unique history, dictated in part by its geographic location at the crossroads of Europe. It is a history that is shared neither by its cross-border neighbours nor by the rest of France, and its significance in linguistic terms cannot be overestimated. In the fifth century AD, invasion by the Alemans resulted in Alsace becoming part of a Germanic linguistic area which subsists to this day. More recent history can be examined in five parts.

Alsace as Part of France, 1648–1870

The Treaty of Westphalia of 1648 marked the end of the Thirty Years War and resulted in the annexation of Alsace by France. Already in 1539 the Ordinance of Villers–Côteret in France had declared French to be the only official language of the realm, to be used in courts and administration and thus implicitly condemning Latin and regional varieties. 'So, to some degree, the French linguistic domination began as soon as Alsace–Lorraine passed to France' (Strauss 1981: 190). Nevertheless, until the Revolution the German language held its own. A common language policy was introduced for the whole of the Republic, as a single language was seen as the natural extension of the political aim of equality. Although the intention was to eradicate all regional varieties, the Alemannic and Franconian spoken in Alsace were considered particularly suspect as they were the idioms of the enemy and, as such, monarchist and counter-revolutionary as well as, according to Abbé Grégoire, 'degenerate idioms' (Schwengler 1989: 25).

As a result of linguistic policies, French became the language of officialdom and of education. Nevertheless, it was principally the preserve of the well-to-do and the intelligentsia. This process of Frenchification was speeded up by Napoleon, under whose government Alsace prospered. Yet, paradoxically, he was more tolerant of the Alsatian dialects than his revolutionary predecessors. At an official reception in Alsace he was to say: 'Let them speak their language, as long as their sword is French' (Petit 1993: 9).

Economic integration into the rest of France by the middle of the eighteenth century, as well as improved transport and communications and opportunity for social mobility, led to better knowledge of French and appreciation of its usefulness. It was considered indispensable to a full participation in the life of the nation, whether on a cultural, political or commercial level.

Despite such advances, by the end of the Second Empire proficiency in French could not be said to extend below the bourgeoisie. It was deemed the language of the elite. While the working classes and peasants may have had a greater understanding of French than before the Revolution, the everyday idiom of the populace was still an Alemannic or Franconian dialect. Literary production in the latter half of the century was primarily dialectal and the Church continued to adhere to German in all its services.

The Second Reich, 1870–1918

After the French defeat by the Prussian army, the annexation of Alsace–Lorraine by Germany was accepted by the National Assembly. This effectively put an end to any further development in the use of the French language, and to some extent cancelled out inroads already made in this direction. German became the official language and also that of education. French, as a foreign language, was available only to the minority who attended secondary school, and then only for an optional four hours a week.

School became obligatory in Alsace in 1873, under German law, and this reinforced the position of High German. No distinction was made between High German and the Alsatian dialects, so while French suffered, Alsatian did too. Both French and Alsatian became the symbols of resistance against Germany.

Increased economic prosperity led to greater acceptance of German rule, especially as Alsace was accorded progressively more autonomy, culminating in her becoming a quasi-*Bundesland* in her own right.

The Inter-War Period, 1918–1939

The Treaty of Versailles of 1919 saw Alsace reintegrated into French territory. Although the original intention was to respect Alsatian culture and identity, this proved illusory. The use of Alsatian was prohibited, and an influx of French civil servants led to the marginalisation of their Alsatian-speaking counterparts. The euphoria with which the French army had been greeted in 1918 was dissipated, and during the mid- and late twenties there were calls for a degree of independence and recognition of Alsace's right to bilingualism. The central government reacted strongly to particularist agitation which it perceived as having separatist, even anti-French, implications.

The Third Reich

After the capitulation of France to Hitler, Alsace was once again annexed to Germany, becoming part of Baden. While Alsatians were not considered citizens of the Third Reich, they were deemed members of the German people. A programme of Germanisation was put into effect. Linguistic policy included the banning of French and any reference to France, with Nazi posters proclaiming: 'Raus mit dem welschen Plunder'. Those caught expressing themselves in the Gallic idiom were subject to fines or imprisonment, with some even being sent to concentration camps. The ban on French extended to those items of vocabulary which had long been part of the Alsatian dialect. Proper nouns, whether the names of people or of streets, also had to be Germanised. Initially French was the target of language planning, but it was to become clear that, like other German dialects, Alsatian was to be replaced by High German, which had never been used in everyday speech in Alsace.

This aspect of Nazism may seem derisory when compared to all the monstrosities which it produced elsewhere.

Nevertheless, it allows for an understanding of the psycholog-
ical disorder created by the four years of Nazi presence in
Alsace. (Kretz 1994: 47–8)

1945 to the Present Day

Allied victory heralded Alsace's definitive return to France
and also a period of vigorous linguistic assimilation. The
annexation of Alsace during the war and the involvement of
its inhabitants in the German campaign, albeit under duress,
actually created the ideal terrain for the Frenchification of the
region. 'Nazism did more for the French cause in Alsace than
all the French patriots in Paris in the years up to 1939'
(Stephens 1978: 351). All too easily, especially in the media,
Alsatians were identified with Nazis and, as a result, 'because
of the German element of their identity, they feared they
would be assimilated with Germans' (Philipps 1978: 110).

After the war a concerted effort was made to eradicate German and Alsatian from Alsace. The slogan 'Out with the
French rubbish' was replaced by 'It's chic to speak French'.

Present-day policies are more favourable to regional idioms,
but do little to help regions which do not help themselves. In
relation to this, since 1968, when the René Schickele circle was
founded (now called *Culture et Bilinguisme*), there has been a
marked revival in interest in Alsatian. However, although initiatives for widening and/or maintaining the use of Alsatian
are in evidence, ranging from the introduction of Alsatian in
écoles maternelles and the support, by the clergy, for Alsatian
liturgy, these efforts affect the minority rather than the majority. A major problem is the failure to reach a decision as to
whether to promote German/French bilingualism or Alsat-
ian/French, and, if the latter, which form of Alsatian should be
the focus of attention. Such difficulties apart, in terms of shared
linguistic suffering, Alsace's vitality can only be viewed as
strong, having been subjected to attack from both French and
High German, and this, not only in the distant past, but as
recently as a few decades ago.

Economic Status

As French is the official language in Alsace it is naturally the
main language of communication in the working environment.

Academic achievement and economic progress are dependent on expertise in French. However, when asked to respond to the statement: 'Knowledge of Alsatian helps in finding a job', the overwhelming majority of those questioned in Zillisheim felt this to be true (see Table 3). Comments ranged from 'It can help' to 'It can be a plus'. However, just one respondent added an unqualified 'often' to his answer. Otherwise, a number of interviewees made such remarks as 'perhaps', 'sometimes', 'rarely'. One father felt the advantage was 'minimal' and described his daughter's situation in support of his view: 'My daughter is unemployed, although she speaks Alsatian'. In Southern Alsace 'Alsatian is not so important. French is spoken more and more in the area'. Other language varieties are more likely to be requested: 'Alsatian is not required very often. English and German are needed more often'. It is believed Alsatian can be an advantage but only 'in certain cases', 'for certain things', 'not systematically', 'for some people'. The knowledge of the local variety was not considered of value 'in France', 'in the interior' (i.e. in France, but outside Alsace), 'in the rest of France', but it was a point in a jobseeker's favour 'in Alsace', 'above all in Alsace'. Some interlocutors clearly limit the usefulness of Alsatian on the job market to 'the border area', 'the borders with Germany and Switzerland'. Indeed, it is those who commute across the border who are seen to benefit the most from speaking Alsatian: 'Cross-border commuters', 'It's helpful if you cross the border', 'In bordering countries'. In this case Alsatian could 'often' be helpful. Both Switzerland and Germany were named, but Switzerland figured slightly more often and, when both countries were indicated, Switzerland tended to be mentioned first. This can be explained by the proximity of

Table 3:   The Status of Alsatian

	Agree	No Opinion	Disagree
Alsatian helps in finding a job	81.4 percent	1.2 percent	17.4 percent
Alsatian is a dialect	96.3 percent	0.6 percent	3.1 percent
Alsatian is a separate language	37.3 percent	11.2 percent	51.6 percent
	French	German	Other
Of which language is Alsatian a dialect?	8.6 percent	60.1 percent	37.3 percent

Southern Alsatian varieties to Swiss German as noted by three informants: 'In Switzerland, as Swiss is close to Alsatian', 'Basle Swiss is Alsatian', 'In Basle, in Switzerland, Alemannic is still spoken, even if the official language is German'. If Basle is cited specifically here, this is because it is immediately across the border and, as a major town, is an obvious focus of employment.

The regional idiom is felt to be especially relevant to particular areas of work: 'In certain professions', 'In certain branches'. Amongst those listed were: 'Manual professions, craftwork, in business', 'There are firms which require it'. Professions which involve direct contact with the public were indicated, specifically health, administration and retail: 'If my husband, who is a doctor, were to employ somebody, he would require Alsatian', 'In certain professions, for example, nursing auxiliary', 'At the hospital, perhaps', 'In administration. Yes, for that, in relations with the clientele', 'At the counter. I have seen job adverts where Alsatian was required', 'At the counter, to speak to older people', 'Some jobs where there are old people, in shops'. As is evident from these examples, it is not just specific areas of employment in which Alsatian is of use, but more precisely, in relation to interaction with old people.

The situation is in flux. There are those who believe Alsatian is not a prerequisite for any career, although this was not felt to have always been the case as words such as 'no longer', 'not today' were used. If the local idiom is still an advantage, it is so 'less and less', 'Alsatian is less and less useful'.

Overall Zillisheim interlocutors share the view that Alsatian can be of help in acquiring a job, particularly in relation to its advantages in Switzerland and Germany, and this is an expression of a positive attitude to Alsatian in terms of its economic status. However, this perception is more negative in terms of Alsatian's status in the Alsatian job market, where it is generally agreed that the importance of being able to speak Alsatian is diminishing. In competition with French, Alsatian is losing economic status. However, on Swiss and German soil, it is seen as a bonus.

Social Status

Social status can be very closely associated with economic status, and can depend largely on it. A group's social status is considered to be a reflection of its self-esteem. In this research project, informants were asked to react to the statement: 'Being Alsatian is important to me'. The majority felt this to be the case, and some qualified the affirmation 'very important', 'more than important'. A great pride in being Alsatian was expressed: 'I am proud to be Alsatian', 'I am not ashamed to say it, wherever I am'. A love of Alsace is apparent: 'You love your region', 'I suppose like all those from a particular region, I love my region'. For some, identity was linked to place of birth: 'I was born here'. Others stressed the sense of belonging: 'I feel at home here', of which a part was the way people talked: 'We are at home here. Outside Alsace there are people who mock our accent, our idiom'. Not all interlocutors who expressed their agreement with the affirmation did so in such positive terms. Nevertheless, one interlocutor who did not feel too strongly about being Alsatian, stated: 'I wouldn't like not to be Alsatian any more'.

Amongst those who rejected the notion, some simply felt the idea was not important or were of the opinion that stating the importance of being Alsatian was too biased. Two interlocutors did not wish to emphasise their Alsatianness over and above their Frenchness: 'I am French, born in Alsace. I am not chauvinistic', 'We were born here. I spent the war years here. I would have liked to have been born somewhere else, especially because of some people with limited intelligence who think we are not true French people'. It appears, here, that an unwillingness to perceive being Alsatian as important is linked to a fear of being considered anti-French.

In general terms, strength of feeling regarding the importance of being Alsatian was high. This reflected attachment to Alsace itself or was considered a natural consequence of having been born in Alsace. This was true both for those who spoke Alsatian and those who did not.

Language Status

Language status is expressed by a community's esteem of its local variety. In the case of Alsatian in Zillisheim, this can be judged on the basis of reactions to the notions that 'Alsatian is a dialect' and 'Alsatian is a language' (see table 3). It should be underlined, at this point, that these two affirmations appeared separately in the list of statements on which respondents were requested to comment.

Any discusssion as to whether Alsatian is a language or not is considerably handicapped by common parlance; in the everyday French of Alsace the notion of Alsatian does not really exist. The local idiom is always referred to as *le dialecte* (the dialect). Lothar Wolf (1991: 224) sees this as Alsatian or German interference as the term *dialecte* 'belongs in Alsace to everyday language whilst elsewhere in France it is only part of scholarly vocabulary'.

He claims that elsewhere on French soil the word *patois* would be used. In view of these remarks, it comes as no surprise that 96.3 percent of Zillisheim respondents believe Alsatian to be a dialect. However, although in linguistic terms no variety is intrinsically better or worse than another, and the use of the term *dialecte* may just be a transfer of vocabulary from German, nevertheless, a series of commonly held prejudices continue to exist (Ott and Philipp 1993: 3). These include the belief that dialects are not suited to complex abstract expression. They are defined as more emotional than rational. They are viewed as detrimental to educational and professional success.

Despite the fact that Andrée Tabouret-Keller herself makes use of the word *dialecte* in her research, she nevertheless expresses her worries with regard to common usage in Alsace of *langue* (language) as opposed to *dialecte*. If French is described as a language, this underlines its status as the variety shared by an important community. In contrast, Alsatian is referred to as a dialect, which is merely the sum of various regional varieties. Set against each other in this way, language and dialect serve as indicators of a power struggle: in opposition to French as a language, Alsatian is *only* a dialect (Tabouret-Keller 1985: 11).

However, two-fifths of the Zillisheim interlocutors deem the local idiom to be a separate language, a considerably larger fraction than those who disagree with the idea that Alsatian is a dialect. This result indicates a positive appreciation of the regional idiom on the part of a significant proportion of the interviewees.

Those who were not inclined to describe Alsatian as a language used, in support of their view, the lack of a written code: 'It cannot be written', 'There are people who try to write it, but

no . . .'. It is true that there is some attempt to base a written
form of Alsatian on phonetic representation, but this was not
considered enough: 'It is not written. There is no orthography.
It's more phonetic', 'It's not a written language. There is a
phonetic way of writing it, but it is difficult to understand'.
One informant pointed out that (High) German was used as
the equivalent of Alsatian in written mode: 'German is used in
writing'. For one interlocutor, their regional idiom was not
deemed important enough to be a language: 'It does not have
that importance'.

The very fact that Alsatian can be written at all, in whatever
form, was seen as grounds to label it a language: 'It is spoken
and written'. Mutual cross-border intelligibility made Alsatian
worthy of the epithet *language*: 'We can get by in Germany, in
Switzerland'.

Whatever the seemingly factual, well-founded reasons for
deciding whether Alsatian is a language or not, it will be noted
that similar justifications are in evidence to support both a negative and affirmative response to the notion that Alsatian is a
separate language. In other words, the true situation is unim-
portant. The interviewees' answers reflect their personal perception of Alsatian. This serves to support the view that
labelling Alsatian a language demonstrates a positive attitude
towards it.

Conclusion

In terms of status, Alsace's ethnolinguistic vitality is considerably stronger than in relation to demographic and institutional
support factors. Thus, it seems reasonable to conclude that
Alsace and Alsatian's future is somewhat more positive than
that suggested by statistics relating to declining numbers of
Alsatian-speakers and the decrease in employment of the local
idiom. It reveals a certain will to survive which may result in a
more concerted effort to save Alsatian. However, if this proves
to be the case, it is debatable whether this will result in the
continued existence of a German-speaking minority in France.
Whatever the linguistic realities of the situation in that Alsace
lies in a Germanic linguistic area, historical events have led to
a distancing of Alsace from Germany. A significant proportion
of Alsatians themselves, strongly reject the notion that they

speak a German dialect. This is underlined by the question-naire responses, according to which, of those who considered Alsatian to be a dialect, over a third did not state *German* as the language of which Alsatian was a dialect (see table 3). At pilot stage, informants were requested to comment on the statement: 'Alsatian is a German dialect'. A positive response would almost be formulated as the researcher said dialect, only to be withdrawn with the remark: 'Oh no, not German'. Nevertheless, the category *other* includes 15.7 percent who describe Alsatian as Germanic, 6.5 percent a mixture of French and German and 3.9 percent Alemannic. It is the idea of pure German which is not totally accepted. Perhaps it would be better to consider Alsace a special case, a region inhabited by, in the words of one interlocutor, 'tricolour storks' rather than French German-speakers.

References

Appel, R. and Muysken, P., *Language Contact and Bilingualism.* London, 1987.

Converse, J. M. and Presser, S., *Survey Question: Handcrafting the Standardized Question-naire,* Beverly Hill, 1986.

Giles, H. and Coupland, N., *Language: Contexts and Consequences,* Milton Keynes, 1991

Hedges, B., 'Sampling', in *Survey Research Practice,* eds. Gerald Hoinville and Roger Jowell, Aldershot 1985, pp. 55–89.

Hoffmann, C., *An Introduction to Bilingualism,* London, 1991.

Kretz, P., *La langue perdue des Alsaciens. Dialecte et schizophrénie,* Strasbourg, 1994.

Moser, C.A. and Kalton, G., *Survey Methods in Social Investigation.* London, 1979.

Ott, J. and Philipp, M., 'Dialekt und Standardsprache im Elsaß und in germanopho-nen Lothringen', in *Deutsche Sprache* 21 (1993), no. 1, pp. 1–21.

Petit, J., *L'Alsace à la reconquête de son bilinguisme. Nouveaux Cahiers d'Allemand.* Stras-bourg, 1993.

Philipps, E., *L'Alsace face à son destin. La crise d'identité,* Strasbourg, 1978.

Salmon, G.-L., ed., *Le français en Alsace. Etudes recueillies par G.-L. Salmon. Bulletin de la Faculté des Lettres de Mulhouse, Fascicule XIV. Actes du colloque de Mulhouse, (17–19 novembre 1983),* Paris, 1985.

——, ed., *Bulletin de la Faculté des Lettres de Mulhouse, Fascicule XVII. Variété et variante du français des villes. Etat de l'est de la France. Alsace – Lorraine – Lyonnais – Franche-Comté – Belgique. Actes du colloque scientifique international de Mulhouse, (16 et 17 novembre 1988),* Paris, 1991, pp. 221–28.

Schwengler, B., *Le syndrome alsacien, d'Letschte?,* Strasbourg, 1989.

Stacey, M., *Methods of Social Research,* Oxford, 1969.

Stephens, M., *Linguistic Minorities in Western Europe,* Dyfed, 1978.

Strauß, D., 'Aspects of German as a Minority Language in Western Europe', in *Minor-ity Languages Today. A Selection of the Papers Read at the First International Conference on Minority Languages Held at Glasgow University, 8–13 September 1980,* eds. E. Hau-gen et al., Edinburgh, 1985.

Tabouret-Keller, A., 'Classification des langues et hiérarchisation des langues en Alsace', in *Le français en Alsace. Etudes recueillies par G.-L. Salmon. Bulletin de la Faculté des Lettres de Mulhouse, Fascicule XIV. Actes du colloque de Mulhouse, (17–19 novembre 1983).* ed. Gilbert-Lucien Salmon, Paris, 1985.

Vassberg, Liliane M., *Alsatian Acts of Identity. Language Use and Language Attitudes in Alsace.* Clevedon, 1993.

Wolf, Lothar, 'Réflexions sur la description de variations géographque d'une langue', in *Bulletin de la Faculté des Lettres de Mulhouse, Fascicule XVII. Variété et variante du français des villes. Etat de l'est de la France. Alsace – Lorraine – Lyonnais – Franche-Comté – Belgique. Actes du colloque scientifique international de Mulhouse, (16 et 17 novembre 1988),* ed. Salmon, G.-L., Paris, 1985, pp. 221–28.

CHAPTER 4

South Tyrol: Rethinking Ethnolinguistic Vitality

Anny Schweigkofler

The German-speaking minority of South Tyrol in Northern Italy has often been referred to as a 'model for the resolution of minority conflicts' (Feiler 1996: 287)[1] and as a 'success story' (Langer 1988 in Baur/Dello Sbarba 1996: 201).[2] But what does success for a language group at risk imply? It certainly includes any sort of improvement of status and enhanced collective identity, but it also means a change in the inter-ethnic relations with the majority. In my article, features of this 'success story' will be outlined in the context of sociopolitical issues concerning the majority–minority relationship.

Terms like 'ethnicity', 'language' and 'identity' are fundamental in discussing issues of linguistic minorities. Here, however, I refrain from defining each notion separately, since I view them as integral elements of one single structure. To identify such a structure, Giles/Bourhis/Taylor's notion of *Ethnolinguistic Vitality* (1977) provides a good starting point. 'Vitality' connotes energy and the capacity for progress, which are certainly relevant for the notion of success. However, the researchers' definition reads as follows: 'The vitality of an

---

1. Feiler's article about South Tyrol has the title 'South Tyrol – Model for the Resolution of Minority Conflicts?'
2. Langer's essays are quoted from: S. Baur and R. Dello Sbarba's collection *Alexander Langer, Aufsätze zu Südtirol/scritti sul Sudtirolo (1978-1995)*, Meran/Merano 1996. The subsequent references do not give the editors' names, they refer to the year when the article was written and to the page number of the collection in 1996.

ethnolinguistic group is that which makes a group likely to behave as a distinctive and active collective entity in inter-group situations' (Giles/Bourhis/Taylor 1977: 308).

'Distinctiveness' and 'collectiveness' are investigated by analysing factors of status, demography and institutional support. The higher the economic, social and socio-historical status of the ethnic group is perceived, the higher is the vitality of this group. The same applies to the demographic distribution and number of group members as well as to the extent to which the group receives representation in the various institutions (e.g. mass media, education, religion) of a region, nation or community. After Giles/Bourhis/Taylor, other researchers (cf. Husband/Khan 1982, Allard/Landry 1986, Labrie/Clément 1986 and Young/Bell/Giles 1988) analysed the above-mentioned factors, discussing especially their usefulness and taxonomic validity. Apart from its instrumental character it is worthwhile to look at the ideology behind the concept of ethnolinguistic vitality. It implies that a linguistic group in danger has first and foremost to concentrate on improving its own status, influence and power. The concept favours all the elements which distinguish a minority from other groups (distinctiveness) and which encourage a linguistic group to understand itself as a homogenous entity (collectiveness). The constant struggle for survival against the out-group (the majority) builds up a certain identity: moments of reaction against the outsiders, and against the experience of oppression and limitation determine the in-group's identity (Bhabha 1997: 123).

However, distinctiveness and collectiveness evoke a fairly ambiguous process. Being perceived and perceiving itself as different from the out-group(s) necessarily involves mechanisms of uniformity working inside the in-group: Vladimir Wakounig (1997: 50) points out that in such circumstances 'individual behaviour is judged solely on the grounds of its contribution to ethnic consciousness' (my translation).

Eighty years of minority status show different stages in developing an identity along the line of a distinctive inter-group behaviour and perception of autonomy. In order to structure a brief historical overview for the German minority of South Tyrol, I will use the model of a 'five stage campaign for language equality' that Colin Williams uses to analyse the situation of Welsh in the UK (Williams 1994: 104).

Stage one, labelled 'idealism', embraces the construction of a vision, stage two comprises the period of 'protest', when sections of the population agitate for a reform in the promotion of the lesser-used language. Williams defines stage three as 'legitimacy', when the minority language becomes generally accepted and language rights are exercised in selected domains. At stage four ('institutionalisation') the language is represented in 'key strategic agencies of the state' (Williams 1994: 105), whereas at stage five the use of the language is extended to an optimum range of social situations. At this last stage of 'parallelism and normalisation' equal status between the majority and the minority language is achieved. In Giles/Bourhis/Taylor's terms, a high degree of ethnolinguistic vitality marks the inter-group situation.

South Tyrol is a province in Northern Italy bordering on Austria along the line of the watershed. This geographical line comprising the highest peaks of the Alps dividing the direction of the rivers was taken as a reason for splitting South Tyrol from the Austrian regions of North and East Tyrol in 1919 (*Wasserscheiden-These*).

Under Mussolini's fascist regime the mainly German-speaking population was expected to become Italian. The dictator's plan of Italianising the German area embraced immigration of Italians from other parts of the peninsula and industrialisation of the larger cities. Since Mussolini realised by the end of the 1930s that this plan would fail, he agreed with Hitler on resettling the German-speakers who wanted to keep their German culture and language in the Third Reich. This so-called *Option* was offered to the people in 1939. All those who declined could stay on condition that they would become Italian, adopting Italian language and culture. Due to the Second World War, this plan could only partly be carried out: most of the inhabitants who 'opted' for Germany (86 percent) did not emigrate (Feiler 1996: 289–90).

Recalling Williams's stage one ('idealism'), I group together the period between 1919 and 1939 along with the late 1940s and the early 1950s:[3] significant were Michael Gamper's network of secret German classes (*Katakombenschulen*) of the 1920s as well as the founding of the Südtiroler Volkspartei (SVP), the

---

3. I excluded the problematic relationship between the *Optanten* and the *Nicht-Optanten* after the second half of 1939 as it would require a more detailed discussion.

most influential German political party. The Treaty of Paris in 1946 aimed to protect the German minority. By the end of the 1940s and early 1950s it was clear that this legal basis could not guarantee the fulfilment of the promises given by the Italian state.

The growing awareness of being overrun and forgotten led to the mass protest rally of 1957 in Bolzano/Bozen. At this stage two ('protest') the struggle to maintain the language and culture mobilised people to show their anger. The bomb attacks of the late 1950s and early 1960s radicalised the situation and led to Austria – since 1955 a fully sovereign state – taking the South Tyrol question to the UN General Assembly, which marked a crucial step towards stage three ('legitimacy').

In 1972, the *New Statute of Autonomy* came into force, comprising measures to ensure the equal rights of the Italian and German inhabitants of South Tyrol (*Autonomous Province of Bolzano/Bozen*). The legal basis was provided in order to institutionalise the language at stage four. Two major clauses were designed to guarantee the protection of the Ladin[4] and German minorities: the proportional system (*Proporz*) and the declaration of membership of one of the three ethnic groups (*Sprachgruppenzugehörigkeitserklärung*).

On the basis of the percentage of people declaring their membership of the different ethnic groups, a certain proportion of public posts is allocated to each group. The 1991 census shows the following distribution: Germans 67.9 percent, Italians 27.6 percent and Ladins 4.4 percent out of a total of about 430,000 inhabitants (Autonome Provinz Bozen 1995: 116).

Due to this system of apportionment the Germans and Ladins were given the opportunity to enter the public administration sector, which led to the formation of a German class of civil servants. Until the early 1970s the public sector was occupied almost entirely by Italians, who today still form the majority of the urban population, whereas the rural lives of the Germans and Ladins were traditionally linked to agriculture as the main source of income. The setting-up of an extensive provincial authority on the one hand, and the growing importance of tourism as the new driving force of the local economy

---

4. The Ladins are, with 18,000 members, the third and smallest ethnic group of the province. For a good overall picture see Zappe (1996).

on the other hand, helped the Germans and Ladins to over-come a thirty-year-long hiatus in their cultural and educational life (cf. Langer 1988/1996: 136).

The financial boost in a sector where the groups predomi-nantly involved were the minorities (Germans and Ladins), and a balance in the sector of public administration hitherto dominated by Italians, could also have been the starting point for a redefinition of inter-ethnic relations. Alexander Langer, a South Tyrolean journalist and politician, who died in 1995, describes the period between the mid 1970s and the early 1980s as *Sternstunden* (great moments), when the Germans were strong enough and the Italians did not yet feel weakened (Langer 1986/1996: 180). It was also a time of active inter-eth-nic movement directed towards a bilingual society. In this period, the search for a new identity based on the idea of autonomy for all three ethnic groups could have replaced the old paradigm of the 1950s and 1960s of a German identity dominated by the struggle for survival (*kampfbereite Identität*). There might also have been the chance of asking what the Italians' identity as South Tyroleans included and how it has been constructed in the previous decades. Langer describes the situation of the Italians in South Tyrol as follows: after the Second World War, they were busy putting down roots, because in those days most of them had their relatives some-where else in northern Italy. The Italians were recent immi-grants; they did not have any kind of settled relationship with the territory (Langer 1988/1996: 137f.).

It is these factors, even today, that account for the weaker position of the Italians in South Tyrol. In Manuela Zappe's research study about the sociocultural, sociolinguistic and eth-nopolitical attitudes of South Tyroleans[5] in the early 1990s, the interviewees underline this lack of a genuine local Italian iden-tity. The indigenous Germans and Ladins are rated higher cul-turally than the Italians with their mixed origins. Even though the Italians are judged as not having developed a specific South Tyrolean identity they are perceived by the Germans as a unity. The fact that they speak the same language unites them and labels them as the 'others'.

Not only the Germans but of necessity also the Italians have internalised the slogan propagated by the main political party

5. Manuela Zappe collected data by interviewing opinion leaders of all three ethnic groups.

of the German minority (SVP), originally coined when talking about the school system: 'The clearer we make the distinction between us, the better we will get on with each other.' (Langer 1988/1996: 352 – my translation).

Along this rigid separation policy, the relationship between Italians and Germans was, and unfortunately still is, dominated by the struggle for power (*rapporti di forza*). Langer uses the symbol of the pendulum to describe the dilemma in which the ethnic groups are trapped. The society is divided into two completely separate cultures. The pendulum swings from one extreme to the other: it establishes the 'here' and 'there', the 'us' and 'them'. It is the continuous movement 'against each other' (*Gegeneinander*): an advantage for one side automatically implies a disadvantage for the other side (Langer 1985/1996: 115ff).

Initially, the German minority saw their enemy in the Italian government, whereas since the development of the autonomous status the Italian inhabitants of the province have been categorised as the opponent (cf. Langer 1984/1996: 172). Positions and identities are fixed and homogenised at both poles. Any kind of deviance within the unity of one pole endangers its strength. We might also see this strict assignment of positions as a strategy of power which gives the German politician control over the out-group, as well as over the in-group (cf. Wakounig 1997: 4). This would partly explain the overwhelming and unbroken success of the SVP, founded in 1945 as the collective party (*Sammelpartei*) for all the German-speakers, and still unchallenged in its position as the main political party of the province.

In 1981 the SVP introduced the compulsory declaration of membership to one of the three ethnic groups (*Sprachgruppen-zugehörigkeitserklärung*). Alexander Langer (1995/1996: 115) speaks in this connection of a 'constraint to ethnic unambiguity' (*Zwang zur ethnischen Eindeutigkeit*): *In gabbia per sempre* (in a cage forever). The pendulum swung again, and in 1985 the MSI (Movimento Sociale Italiano) – a neo-fascist party – became a major party on the provincial Italian political scene: one-third of the Italians in the capital Bolzano voted for the neo-fascists. The frontiers were clearer than ever; the unity within the German-speakers and 'their' party was a duty. This explains why any movements for or towards a bilingual and multicultural society are bound to fail: they are associated with lack of identity. Thus, the real 'enemies' in such a society are not the ethnic groups themselves – they have an assumed, allocated, perceived identity -, but those who attempt to find their own way between the clearly defined borders. The punishment for this search for an autonomous way beyond the 'poles' is the refusal of recognition. As the decision about the language/ mother tongue determines ethnicity and identity, one can only have one mother tongue which automatically decides which side the person belongs to: 'Vermischung' (mixture), 'Mischehen' (mixed marriages), 'gemischte Schulen' (mixed schools) are expressions used to describe ethnic ambiguity.

The German term *zweisprachig* (bilingual) is only used in a neutral, technical sense, in connection with the certificate for the bilingual proficiency exam (*Zweisprachigkeitsprüfung*). In all other circumstances the term 'bilingual' (e.g. bilingual school, bilingual family) is replaced by the term 'mixed' (*Vermischung, gemischtsprachig*), which perhaps expresses more overtly the consequences Germans fear when thinking about language and ethnic contact. For a minority – no matter which stage of institutionalisation and recognition was achieved – *Vermischung* conjures up language decay which equates with ethnic apocalypse. This might also explain the unbiased use of the terms 'bilingual'/'bilingualism' (ital. bilingue/bilinguismo) by the Italians. Their struggle for the introduction of the immersion programme as a new second-language teaching method in Italian schools reflects the will to improve the bilingual competence of the Italian-speaking South Tyroleans. In immersion, children of the linguistic majority (that is, the German-speakers in South Tyrol) are partially taught through the medium of a second language. Immersion is – by definition – directed at the majority (Baker 1996, Johnson and Swain 1998). As the German and the Italian schools are separated in South Tyrol, the introduction of such a programme only affects Italian schools. The debates concerning the setting-up of the programme were fuelled by German politicians who feared the application of this programme to German schools. The consequence would be that some subjects would be taught in German and some in Italian. Even though immersion as described above never affects the minority's but only the majority's schools, and nobody seriously proposed the idea of adopting immersion in German schools, German opinion leaders are eager to emphasise the potentially 'dangerous infiltration' of the German education system. To concentrate on maintaining a German mono-ethnic island provokes, on the one hand, the constant accusation that the Italians' knowledge of German is unsatisfactory, but on the other hand prevents the introduction of a new programme which should improve the German teaching in Italian schools. With debates of this kind, language becomes a fetish, accessible exclusively to the members of the in-group. In Manuela Zappe's study some Italian interviewees conclude that the politicians of the SVP argue against the Italians adopting a new model of improving their German because it would allow them to integrate into the local culture (cf. Zappe 1996: 208). The outgroup is not meant to share the same culture as the in-group.

Returning to Williams' 'five stage campaign for language equality', my outline of the South Tyrolean case stopped at stage four with 'institutionalisation'. The ethnic minority is about to reach stage five of 'parallelism and normalisation'. The developments of the last twenty-five years can hardly be summarised under the headline of a success story, even though they will meet the requirements of Giles/Bourhis/Taylor's concept of ethnolinguistic vitality: the vitality is mainly judged by the distinctive behaviour of the ethnic group and their feelings of being a collective entity.

The current situation in South Tyrol contradicts the validity of this concept, even though it becomes evident only at stage five. 'Parallelism and normalisation' require a redefinition of ethnolinguistic vitality: it has to be made dependent on the individual's will to find an identity beyond the clear boundaries of the ethnic groups, possibly starting from the so-called *Mischkultur*, which in other contexts is already accepted as multicultural society. Inter-ethnic behaviour should be guided by the underlying concept of Taylor's 'politics of recognition' (Taylor 1994) where the crucially dialogical character of human life builds up an identity. Langer's ideal of a *Gesamtsüdtiroler* is part of a society where ethnicity no longer predominates over democracy, and where the leading slogan is: 'The more contact we have, the better we will get on with each other' (Langer 1986/1996: 181 – author's translation). In his discussion of the status of minorities in a multicultural society, Vladimir Wakounig (1997: 4) observes that ethnic minorities very rarely develop a strategy to cope with the differentiation and the pluralisation of ideologies.

Despite this sobering diagnosis, the results of a survey about South Tyrol carried out by the Italian researcher Marco Baldi (1998) allow a fairly optimistic perspective: they indicate that South Tyrolean society is about to reach a new phase, with a more 'intelligent relationship between the three linguistic groups' that may well overcome their strict separation, and open the way for new and more challenging areas of discussion. Almost 38 percent of the population are satisfied with their own status. They identify with the provincial government and the territory. Inter-ethnic relations are not seen as a problem at all, though that may only partly be true . The only problematic aspect of this group is the fact that people live predominantly in small villages in the countryside where the inter-ethnic contact is fairly restricted. About 28 percent of the interviewees were labelled as 'undecided': they are satisfied with their situation, but they also think that something must be done to improve inter-ethnic relations. They are more open towards immigrants and amenable to the values of a multicultural society. Yet only time will tell if this generally high percentage of positive reactions will affect the political scene as well as cultural life.

References

Baker, C., *Foundations of Bilingual Education and Bilingualism*, Clevedon, 1996.

Bhabha, H.K., 'Verortungen der Kultur', in *Hybride Kulturen: Beiträge zur anglo-amerikanischen Multikulturalismusdebatte*, ed. Elisabeth Bronfen, Benjamin Marius, Therese Steffen, Tübingen 1997, pp. 123–48.

Baldi, M., 'Die Sprachgruppen in Südtirol', in *FF – Südtiroler Illustrierte*, 7 March 1998, pp. 10–12.

Baur, S. and Dello Sbarba, R., *Alexander Langer: Aufsätze zu Südtirol 1978 – 1995. Scritti sul Sudtirolo*, Meran/Merano, 1996.

Dello Sbarba, R., 'Foto di gruppi con sorpresa', *FF – Südtiroler Illustrierte*, 7 March 1998, pp. 18–19.

Feiler, M. 'South Tyrol – Model for the Resolution of Minority Conflicts?', *Außenpolitik*, vol. 47, no. 3 (1996), pp. 287–99.

Giles, H., Bourhis, R.Y. and Taylor, D.M., 'Towards a Theory of Language in Ethnic Group Relations', in *Language, Ethnicity and Intergroup Relations*, ed. Howard Giles, London, 1977, pp. 307–43.

Johnson, R. K. and Swain, M., *Immersion Education: International Perspectives*, Cambridge, 1997.

Südtirols Autonomie, ed. Autonome Provinz Bozen, Bolzano/Bozen, 1995.

Taylor, C., 'The Politics of Recognition', in *Multiculturalism: Examining the Politics of Recogniton*, ed. Amy Gutmann, Princeton, 1994, pp. 25–73.

Wakounig, V., 'Der Zwang zur Einigkeit: Wieviel Pluralität verträgt die Minderheit?', *STIMME – Zeitschrift der Initiative Minderheiten*, no. 25/IV (1997), pp. 4–5.

Williams, C.H., 'Development, Dependency and the Democratic Deficit', *Journal of Multilingual and Multicultural Development*, vol. 15, nos. 2 and 3 (1994).

Zappe, M., *Das ethnische Zusammenleben in Südtirol*, Frankfurt am Main, 1996.

PART TWO

German Minorities in Central and Eastern Europe

CHAPTER 5

Poland's German Minority

Karl Cordell[1]

A Bitter Legacy

Upper Silesia is unique in contemporary Poland in that it contains a sizeable German minority, although there is no consensus as to its number. Despite the ethnic cleansing of 1944–49, the repatriation programmes between 1950 and 1990 when an estimated total of 1,372,188 ethnic Germans left Poland (Marshall 1992: 131) and easy access to a united Germany since 1990, over half a million Germans remain; primarily in the voivodeships (provinces) of Silesia and Opole, with a large majority of them residing in the Opole voivodeship (Kroll 1994).

The successive waves of emigration to Germany have resulted in there being something of a demographic imbalance among the German population, as it is primarily those born since 1945 who have availed themselves of the opportunity to leave. Another distinctive characteristic of the German community is that it is largely rural in character. At the end of the war, the large towns and cities were emptied of Germans who were in turn replaced with (Polish) survivors of the Soviet deportations from pre-war eastern Poland. These people together with migrants from *Wielkopolska* thereby came to

1. The author would like to extend his thanks to the many people in Poland and Germany who have spared time over the past few years to talk to me about this subject. A special vote of thanks goes to Andrzej Jablonski, Tomasz Kamusella, Bernard Linek and Friedrich Petrach.

form the new administrative and tertiary class in urban areas of Upper Silesia (Sakson 1993: 1). In terms of their occupational status, a large majority of Upper Silesian Germans are employed either directly or indirectly in the agricultural sector, in small firms, or are indeed self-employed (Rogall 1993: 4).

In order to understand past, present, and future of the Germans of Upper Silesia, it is necessary to identify the reasons why they have remained in such numbers in the region, how they perceive themselves, what the nature of their contemporary relationship with the Polish state and population is, and what the future holds for them.

The History of the Upper Silesian German Community

Turning to the first question, the answer would seem to be that German Upper Silesians strongly identify with their *Heimat*. It has been argued that identification with *Heimat* is the single most important factor in this case. Attachment to place of birth, a belief in collective origin, a particular set of cultural orientations and customs all contribute to the creation of a sense of identification with *Heimat*. The reasons for the prevalence of such identification have already been indicated. The Germans of Upper Silesia were never fully accepted during the period of German rule as full members of the *Volksgemeinschaft*. Their Catholicism, Slavic origins, and dialects combined with a certain parochialism served to differentiate them from other members of the *Deutschtum* (those who adhere to German culture and way of life).

Today representatives of the German community are apt to point out that Silesia left the Polish orbit in 1335 and from 1526 under various guises remained part of the Holy Roman Empire of the German Nation, until the Prussians helped themselves to it in 1742. Whereas these statements are incontestably true, the implication that the people of the area have been German nationals since 1335 is not. Pre-modern empires, kingdoms, principalities, bishoprics and the like were not equivalent to nation-states. Neither did the rulers of such entities seek to create ethnically homogenous nations.

Even under the Prussians, Upper Silesia remained something

of a backwater until the onset of the industrial revolution in the nineteenth century. Although the Prussian political elite sought to create a German nation in their own image, this was only achieved in an uneven fashion, and at the price of alienating key communities such as Catholics. Prussian nation-building policies in effect were counter-productive in Upper Silesia, and instead reinforced identification with the *Heimat* and served the cause of Polish nationalism which itself was Catholic, and wished to see Upper Silesians returned to their 'true' national group. Upper Silesia later came to be the touchstone of conflicting Polish and German claims, which culminated in three Polish uprisings, the Second World War, and the ethnic cleansing of the period 1945–49. Indeed the Nazis had provoked further estrangement from Germany by categorising the majority of German-speaking Upper Silesians as Third Class Germans, precisely because they were deemed to be insufficiently Aryan. Poland therefore inherited a group of people who spoke a mixture of German and German West– Slavic dialects, and as such were distinct from the remainder of the German nation.

In Pursuit of Homogeneity: Polish Minority Policy 1945-1990

The Fourth Partition and the Nationalities Question

In his desperate need for new allies following the German invasion of the Soviet Union in June 1941, Josef Stalin was forced to reappraise his attitude toward the Polish question. This reappraisal had three major short-term ramifications: first, Moscow established diplomatic relations with the Polish government-in-exile in London. Secondly, as a result of this rapprochement, hundreds of thousands of Poles were released from imprisonment in the Soviet Union and transported via the Middle East and Africa to the United Kingdom (UK). Thirdly, the Soviet Union began recruitment into Soviet-based Polish armed forces from among those Polish prisoners who were either forbidden to travel to the UK or who for whatever reason decided to throw their lot in with the Soviets.

Inevitably alongside this dual military power grew a dual civil power. As relations between the London government and Moscow worsened, so the political profile of Soviet-backed, communist-led forces was raised. Via a combination of faits accomplis and military muscle between 1944 and 1948 a neo-Stalinist regime was established in Poland. Not only was a new political system created, but Poland was territorially shifted westwards. However this westward shift in no way solved the problem of identity in Poland. It simply served to change the focus of Polish nationalism firmly toward the now potentially huge German minority. As early as 1943 it had become clear that Poland would be compensated for material losses incurred as a result of German and Soviet aggression and for territorial losses to the Soviet Union, via a westward expansion. The only questions were how far west Poland would extend, and what the fate of Germans living within post-war Poland would be.

Answers to the former question were arrived at during the closing months of the war and ratified at the Potsdam conference of July–August 1945. Poland's western border moved all the way to the Oder–Neiße line, and it was also decided that in post-war Poland nation and state should as far as possible be rendered coterminous; a decision which was popular with a majority of Polish politicians. Just how many people were expelled as a result of these decisions is a matter which is still hotly disputed. In 1944 there may have been as many as twelve million Germans within territory that came to be included in post-war Poland. Putting wartime resettlers, refugees and soldiers to one side, there were around eight million citizens of pre-war Germany and the free city of Danzig, together with around one million Germans who had been citizens of the pre-war Polish Republic. Of this nine million, approximately half fled beyond the Oder–Neiße line as the war drew to an end.

As to the fate of the remainder, as shall be shown below, and contrary to popular mythology in Germany, it is untrue to say that all Germans were forcibly expelled from post-war Poland. However, it is equally untrue to pretend, as did successive communist governments in Poland, that those Germans who left Poland after the war did so in an orderly manner in accordance with the terms of the Potsdam Agreement. What in fact occurred was a combination of mass flight, deportations to the Soviet Union and mass expulsion beyond the new border, which regardless of whether people wanted to leave or not, involved the re-establishment of former German concentration camps, organised and random acts of brutality, and mass pauperisation. Just how many Germans died or were killed during this time is to this date a matter of both conjecture and dispute, but a figure of around one million may approximate to the truth.

As for those not expelled from People's Poland in cities such as Wroclaw, Legnica, Walbrzych and Koszalin, skilled workers primarily engaged in the mining and metallurgical industries were often allowed to remain. Initially stateless, they received German Democratic Republic (GDR) passports after 1950, and thereafter were granted cultural and educational autonomy as well as designated minority status. By the late 1950s, there were sufficient numbers of Poles available to fill the posts occupied by Germans, and the vast majority were allowed to leave for Germany if they so desired.

Just how many of the approximately 250,000 eligible for emigration at that time actually left is as usual a matter of conjecture. It is clear that the overwhelming majority did decide to leave. However, it is also clear (as a glance at the Wroclaw telephone directory indicates), that an unknown number did decide to stay on. Evidence on motivational causes is fragmentary, but the comparative poverty of Poland seems to have played a major part in helping people make up their minds (Zimmer 1996). Those who remained were inevitably subjected to greater assimilatory pressures; although German cultural societies intermittently continued to function. In fact, the society in Walbrzych has maintained a continuous existence since 1957.

The 'undoubted' Germans from 'The Recovered Territories' were not alone in remaining in Poland. Most ethnic Germans who had been citizens of pre-war Poland either fled as the Red Army approached or were subsequently expelled. Yet, once again there were exceptions. Those from this group who successfully completed the 'rehabilitation procedure' (i.e. those who had been subjected to forced labour, spoke Polish and were clearly no threat to anyone), were offered their Polish citizenship back. Again, records are fragmentary, and no one is sure how many opted to remain in Poland as Poles. Whatever the case, the most important point is that those who reacquired Polish citizenship were now treated as Poles, and were expected to behave as such. For example, they were encouraged to Polonise their names, or indeed re-Polonise them if the Germans had Germanised them in 1939. Having said that, by 1960 the vast majority had opted for emigration. Those of mixed descent from within and without the borders of pre-war Poland were also allowed to stay on condition of Polonisation, but as usual there is no comprehensive data on the numbers affected.

From the End of Expulsion to the End of Communism: The German Minority in Poland from 1950 to 1990

The task now is one of explaining where all today's Germans come from. In order to provide an answer, some obvious facts need to be acknowledged first; namely that modern nations are relatively new constructs, that state and nation are rarely wholly congruent, that the borders between Germany and Poland have rarely been fixed and indeed have often been blurred, and that in the 1940s, as in the 1930s, ethno-nationalist irrationalism was the order of the day in much of central and eastern Europe.

With all of these factors in mind it is now possible to identify the provenance of the majority of Germans in today's Poland. Overwhelmingly, they stem from Upper Silesia, with smaller numbers stemming from Lower Silesia and the former Prussian areas of Ermland and Masuria. Together with the Kashubes of Pomerania, they formed a group of people whom the Germans claimed as German, and the Poles claimed as Polish. In Kashubia, Masuria, and Ermland formerly German groups were, following a 'verification procedure', collectively reclassified as Poles. An indeterminate number of people of mixed descent were also allowed to remain. Before dealing with these various groups, the question must be asked what the communist authorities hoped to achieve from pursuing such policies. This situation came about precisely because of the factors mentioned in the previous paragraph. As the Slav inhabitants of these areas came under increasing German influence, so many of them began to adopt elements of German culture. This was particularly true in those areas subject to industrialisation. The Germans deemed them to be capable of Germanisation, and as the Polish national movement gathered strength in the latter part of the nineteenth century, so these people were claimed as Poles. Unsurprisingly, the results of these countervailing pressures appear to have been mixed, not to say confusing, especially for members of the target groups. Some opted for Germany, others for Poland, whilst others resolutely refused to opt for either, sometimes declaring themselves to be either Czech or Moravian, or even assuming multiple and sometimes transient identities. The complexities of the situation were ill understood in either Poland or Germany, and are still not widely known today. This was true before the rise of Hitler, during the Third Reich, when they were classified as Third-Class Germans (*Volksliste Drei*), and after 1945 when in Poland (other) Poles regarded them with suspicion. In Germany, they are increasingly regarded as Poles who have taken advantage of Germany's generous definition of what constitutes an ethnic German in order to help themselves to the benefits of a life in Germany. Interestingly enough, this view is often shared in Poland, where it is not uncommon to hear those who emigrated during the 1980s and 1990s be described as *Volkswagendeutsche* (Volkswagen Germans or economic migrants), an obvious play on the word *Volksdeutsche* (ethnic Germans resident outside Germany).

In part the communists were hoping to gain greater legitimacy. By pursuing a policy of ruthless nationalism, the communists hoped to gain a wider degree of popular support. Formerly German-owned property and land could be redistributed to people who themselves had lost everything. By expelling the bulk of the remaining Germans, the communists could also go some way to at last establishing a Poland which was ethnically homogeneous and free from 'fifth columns'. This objective had been partially secured by the mass murder of Jews by the Nazis and the return of former Soviet territory to the Soviet Union. In a sense, the communists were therefore simply completing a particularly vicious cycle.

Why then did the Polish nationalists seek to 'return' certain groups to the Polish nation? Clearly, in the industrial basin of Upper Silesia economic considerations played a part. However, it is more important to examine the doctrine of nationalism as employed by the incoming communist authorities. The communists were bereft of any deep-seated legitimacy. Given that any material benefits resulting from socialist reconstruction would not be apparent for some years, it made sense for the new authorities to broaden the base of their support by incorporating the demand of the pre-war right for the creation of an ethnically pure state. After all, German and Soviet policies had already begun the task; the Polish communists now saw it as their mission to complete it.

The way in which this task was 'accomplished' in East Prussia and Upper Silesia is of crucial importance in aiding our understanding of the contemporary situation. In theory, and in a curious parallel with wartime German policies, the task was first to identify the Germanised Slavs, separate them from ethnic Germans, who were largely to be expelled, and then to implement policies which would encourage greater identification with Poland. So much for theory. In reality the policy was badly implemented and probably was not capable of exact implementation in the first place.

These people resided in areas that were subjected to countervailing nationalist pressures. For good measure, the Czechs had also claimed parts of Upper Silesia, along with the inhabitants. Nationality was not fixed to the degree it was elsewhere in Poland, and national identification was not necessarily coterminous with language. Indeed, many Upper Silesians lacked a working knowledge either of *Hochdeutsch* or standard Polish, and were fluent only in a variety of localised German–Polish creoles.

In the autumn of 1945, in the aftermath of war, with refugees, deportees, and the homeless and unemployed filling the streets, the Rehabilitation/Verification Commission attempted to begin its work. The result was a disaster. Outsiders with little local knowledge, but possessed of a communist/nationalist agenda, attempted to separate 'real' Germans from Germanised Slavs. In practice, this involved trying to ascertain the ancestral provenance of those being verified, deciding whether a surname was indigenous or German, and whether or not an individual had a sufficiently pro-Polish attitude.

Anyone with a score to settle had a field day in denouncing his or her enemies. As usual figures vary, but in Upper Silesia, by the end of 1947 it is estimated that around 850,000 people had been 'positively rehabilitated/verified', in some cases against either their knowledge or will (Buchofer 1975: 70). Those who stayed did so for a variety of reasons. In many cases people did not identify particularly closely with Germany, and were willing to give Poland a chance. Some believed that by becoming Polish they would have recently plundered and confiscated property returned. Others decided to sit it out in the belief that either the border would once again be pushed eastward or that communism in Poland would prove to be ephemeral. Their disappointment with the reality of the 'rehabilitation/verification process' and life in communist Poland more than anything else explains the existence of two interrelated phenomena of post-1945 Polish politics. The first of these phenomena is that of the *Spätaussiedler* (late [i.e. post-1970] resettlers). The second is the German minority in contemporary Poland. What unites both groups is the fact that they are overwhelmingly drawn from groups of people whom the Poles claimed as Germanised ethnic Poles in 1945, and who were the targets of (forced) re-Polonisation campaigns. Their existence as either *Volksdeutsche* in Poland or *Spätaussiedler* in Germany serves to indicate the extent to which both (forced) Polonisation and 'really existing socialism' failed to promote close identification with the Polish nation and state.

Although the numbers facing the 'rehabilitation/verification process' in former East Prussia were smaller, the result was even worse. There a greater percentage of the affected population opted for emigration, and generally speaking earlier than in Upper Silesia. This was particularly true in Masuria where the Germanised Slavs were Protestant. In the late 1940s, in addition to pressure from the communists, they found themselves subjected to renewed attempts by the Catholic Church to turn them away from 'German' Christianity. As for the Kashubes, whose language is actually not of Germanic origin, that element which identified with Germany also opted for emigration at an early stage. Those who remained for the most part quickly came to terms with their Polish identity, although since 1990 there has been an attempt to recreate a specifically Kashubian identity. Having thus identified the factors which created the German minority in Poland, the remainder of the chapter will concentrate on the role of the Germans of Upper Silesia, because today that is where ninety per cent of this minority resides.

A Changing Environment: Poland after 1990

With the rise and eventual triumph of Solidarity in Poland came the project finally to establish the notions of civic society and of individual civil and collective human rights. Fundamental to this reappraisal of the relationship between state and society was a reassessment of nation and citizenship in Poland, and a move away from the idea that Polish society was almost exclusively comprised of ethnic Poles. Thus, as Solidarity moved toward the attainment of political power, it had to confront the position of indigenous ethnic groups and national minorities in Poland. Apart from anything else it would be impossible finally to jettison the legacy of Yalta, without acknowledging all of the human consequences that had stemmed from it. The role of the first post-communist prime minister Tadeusz Mazowiecki was particularly important at this time. Not only was he instrumental in repairing Polish–German inter-state relations, he was also supportive of the attempts of the German minority to organise itself both politically and culturally (Bingen 1994).

When it came to the position of ethnic Germans, such a reappraisal also fairly obviously contained an element of *Realpolitik* on the part of Solidarity. It was inevitably intertwined with relations between Poland and united Germany and a definitive recognition of Poland's western border. The first post-communist government in Poland became actively engaged in the 'Two-plus-Four' negotiations on German unification. After much soul-searching on both sides and not a little disagreement, two treaties eventually emerged which sought to redefine bilateral inter-state relations, and in addition sought to promote reconciliation between the two peoples. The first of these treaties was the German–Polish Treaty of 14 November 1990. This treaty finally granted to the Poles recognition of Poland's western border by the government in Bonn in international law, and not merely in accordance with the norms of international law as had the Warsaw Treaty of 1970 (Johannes 1994). The second of these treaties was the Treaty on Good Neighbourly and Friendly Cooperation of 17 June 1991 and is that which most directly concerns us. The basic trade-off was that in return for definitive German recognition of Poland's western border, Poland would not stand in the way of German unification and would undertake to recognise the existence of an indigenous German minority. In return the German government would further reduce its support for, and would further distance itself from, those elements among the *Landsmannschaften* who demanded the right of return to their places of origin and/or compensation from the

Polish government for material and emotional harm suffered as a result of their expulsion. Of greater importance however, was the fact that Germany agreed to act as Poland's de facto ambassador with regard to Polish membership of the European Union (EU) and NATO.

In the treaty of 1991 on bilateral cooperation Poland recognised that an ethnic German minority resided in Poland and granted official recognition to that minority. The inability since then of parliament to pass a Law on National Minorities has contributed to a situation where no single ministry has overall responsibility for minority questions. A Commission for National and Minority Rights was established in 1988, within the Ministry of the Interior. With the completion of the first phase of the post-communist transition in 1990, the Commission was transferred to the more appropriate Ministry of Culture, and was upgraded to the status of Bureau in 1992. To complicate matters further, the Ministries of Education and Foreign Affairs quite obviously become involved in the affairs of ethnic minorities from time to time. Thus it was noticed as early as 1995 that a negative consequence of a laudable endeavour was to muddy accountability and to encourage buck-passing (*Dialog* Nos. 2/3 1995).

Since 1989, the objectives of Polish governments towards Germany have been varied. At one level they wish to foster good-neighbourly relations with their German counterpart. They have recognised that in order to achieve this objective some concessions have to be made with regard to the minority question. Successive governments have also been keen to facilitate Poland's entry into such organisations as the EU and the Council of Europe. Just as importantly, they have sought definitively to break with past political practice and promote the growth of civil society within Poland. This ideal is of particular importance in the context of German–Polish relations, where for years the Federal Republic had been portrayed by successive communist governments as the main enemy of the Polish nation (Bingen undated).

Germanness and German Identity in Upper Silesia

The self-perception of the Germans of Upper Silesia has clearly undergone something of a change in the last fifty years.

From being a people unsure of their national identity, large numbers now come to view themselves quite firmly as German. This even includes people whose parents thought of themselves as Polish, and who are descended from people who fought for the Polish cause during the Silesian uprisings at the end of World War One. This change in perception is in large measure a consequence of the chauvinism of the old communist party.

West Germany also played its part in cementing a German identity among large sections of Upper Silesian society. The old West German state actively sought to facilitate the emigration from former German territories and traditional areas of German settlement of those who under German law could be counted as ethnic Germans. The West German government was signalling that it felt itself morally responsible for the fate of these communities, and regarded those who wished to declare for the Federal Republic as Germans first and (in this instance) Upper Silesians second, and not the other way round. The activities of the *Landsmannschaften* and *Vertriebenenverbände* (Associations of Expellees and Refugees [from Eastern Europe]) must also be mentioned within this context. To this day they consistently lobby Bonn (and increasingly Warsaw) on behalf of Germans in Upper Silesia and elsewhere, and have over the years sought to maintain links between themselves and their compatriots in Poland.

Regardless of the interminable debates about numbers, a claimed total of 420,000 adults are currently affiliated to the *Verband der deutschen sozial-kulturellen Gesellschaften in Polen* (Association of German Friendship Circles in Poland, [VdG]). Of these, almost 200,000 are to be found in the Opole voivodeship, and 75,000 in the Silesian voivodeship. The rest of the membership is scattered throughout the country, with the next biggest concentrations to be found in Lower Silesia, Masuria and Ermland. In recent years the greatest area of growth has been Pomerania. There are other smaller German organisations, throughout Poland, and some individuals remain unorganised.

Only around one-third of the claimed total membership actually pays its membership dues. This in turn raises a whole host of questions, such as why the initial rush of enthusiasm, and why the equally sudden waning of interest? Inevitably, answers to these questions are complex, and space does not permit of anything other than a cursory examination. In Poland the years 1989–91 were a time of hope, especially for groups which had previously been marginalised. Given that the Germans of Upper Silesia did not officially exist until 1989, it is reasonable to assume that their hopes and expectations were possibly the greatest among any similar group in Poland. Unfortunately, their knowledge of geo-political realities and of Germany had been mediated by three equally unrepresentative sources: the communist media, *Landsmannschaft* activists, and contacts with relatives in Germany. Consequently their expectations of what was possible were unrealistic, and the progress that has been made since 1989 is sometimes lost sight of.

Whatever the reasons for the decline in participation, there is nothing like one million Germans in Poland, despite occasional claims to the contrary from the *Landsmannschaft Schlesien.* Poles who could theoretically lay claim to adherence to the *Deutschtum* are not Germans by virtue of the fact they choose not to be. The same applies to those who designate themselves as Mazurs, Kashubes or Silesians, just as it does to people of mixed descent who have opted for a Polish identity. Neither are there any official figures available, as the national census omits questions concerned with nationality/ethnicity. However, there is no evidence to support the claim of one million, just a rather dubious theoretical construct. Whatever the case, out of this definitional tangle it is normal for German academics to offer a figure for the community in the region of 500,000 (Bingen 1994). Polish academics tend to offer figures of between 350–400,000. For example, Dr Zbigniew Kurcz of the Department of Sociology at the University of Wroclaw, estimates the number of Germans to be around 350,000 on the basis that only those who regularly participate in the affairs of the German societies in Poland possess a German consciousness and can therefore be counted as Germans.

The Task of the Minority Today: Securing German Identity, Language, and Culture

The response of the emerging leadership of the German community in Upper Silesia to the wider process of political change in Poland was to press forward with a series of political and cultural demands. As early as 1988 Johann Kroll and others attempted to register a *Deutscher Freundschaftskreis* (German Friendship Circle) with the courts (Kroll 1994). Although their initial attempt was unsuccessful, they met with positive results when, in January 1990, such societies were registered in Katowice. With the treaties of 1990 and 1991 any remaining legal obstacles to the registration of German cultural societies were removed. The immediate consequence was that a plethora of such societies appeared throughout Poland, even in such cities as Radom and Gdansk, where the German population had been reduced to a mere remnant of its pre-war size. The objective of the societies in Upper Silesia as elsewhere was to secure the support of both governments for a series of activities which were designed to maintain the collective existence and cultural cohesion of the German community.

These societies operate in a majority of Poland's sixteen voivodeships. Their activities are co-ordinated by a ten-person national executive, which is turn is led by Friedrich Retrach. Following legalisation, they set themselves a number of tasks. At one level these centre on taking steps which are designed to preserve the German language. This is especially the case in voivodeships and cities such as Poznan, where the German population is small, elderly and scattered. Community centres and libraries have been established, and a range of ancillary organisations such as 'The Association of Silesian Farmers', which has 3,500 members, have come into existence.

The German language is disseminated through both the printed and broadcast media. There is a German-language press in Poland, and in the Raciborz, Opole and Katowice voivodeships there are now weekly radio broadcasts in German, including German language lessons, which can now also be heard in the Masurian city of Olsztyn. In Opole, where the greatest number of Germans live, there is also a fortnightly German-language TV programme (*Schlesisches Wochenblatt* 11 April 1997). Indeed, in the Baltic port city of Szczecin, although there are no radio or TV broadcasts in German, one of the public libraries now stocks a range of fiction and non-fiction for the local German community.

Another key objective is that the practice of ensuring that the religious clergy of (Upper) Silesia is bilingual, begun in the nineteenth century and terminated by the Nazis, be restored, and that religious services be conducted partially in German where such demand exists. For decades the Catholic church in Poland and in particular the current primate Cardinal Glemp, sided with the government in its claim that, whereas there may be 'autochthons', there were no Germans in Poland. The problem of liturgical language was particularly sensitive. German Upper Silesians are deeply religious, and the right to hold services either wholly or partially in their mother tongue was one of the original demands of the activists in the late 1980s. By 1991 and mainly thanks to the endeavours of Bishop Nossol of the Silesian diocese, and despite opposition from Cardinal Glemp, the situation had changed and such church services are once again a regular occurrence. In addition to masses in Polish, bilingual services are available in over two hundred parishes in Upper Silesia, and priests are once again required as far as possible to be bilingual, as they were throughout Silesia before the Second World War. Similarly, Bishop Nossol was instrumental in gaining permission for bilingual services to be held for the Moravian, Ukrainian, and Armenian communities of Upper Silesia (Kandzia 1995).

In the educational sector, three kinds of activities can be distinguished. The first concerns the provision of education for the German minority as a minority within the state school system, and as such is seen to be of primary importance (Kroll 1994). The second comprises those which are designed to promote Polish-German understanding, and are not necessarily aimed at the German minority itself. The third comprises a series of cultural activities sponsored by the *Bund der Vertriebenen* (Federation of Expellees [BdV]) and the VdG, which aims to inform both members of the minority and Poles of the cultural inheritance of formerly German areas of Poland.

Politically, the German community in Upper Silesia has sought to translate its numeric preponderance in the rural areas into political muscle. In 1990 the German minority entered the political arena. Its objective was to complement the work of the non-political associations and achieve national and local representation for the Germans of Upper Silesia, and on behalf of the smaller German communities scattered around Poland. It met with immediate success in the October 1991 elections when seven of their candidates were returned to the *Sejm* (Lower House of Parliament) and one to the Senate.

Given the multiplicity of parties which adorned this first post-Communist *Sejm*, the role of smaller parties was of importance in coalition formation and the maintenance of governments. However, the total vote for German minority candidates has fallen with each successive general election, as has the number of individuals paying subscriptions to the various *Deutsche Freundschaftskreise* (German Friendship Circles). At the general election of 1997, voter participation was lowest in precisely those electoral districts where the number of ethnic Germans was highest. This in turn provoked a furious debate among German activists as to why this was the case. At the time of writing, a thorough review of organisational structures, objectives, activities and membership lists is being undertaken. At one level, the German minority and its political leadership can be characterised as conservative. However given the nationalist tendencies of the Polish right, the minority finds itself most comfortable with the liberal post-Solidarity Freedom Union (UW). Given the narrow base of its constituency, i.e. the Germans of Upper Silesia, and the fact that the VdG operates as both political party and interest group, it defies straightforward classification (Sakson 1993: 3).

Prior to the general elections of 1997, the VdG used both houses of parliament as a means of publicising its grievances, and in reality confines itself to a rather parochial range of issues. Not only did the VdG lose its seat in the senate in these elections, it lost two of its four seats in the *Sejm* (it had already lost three in the 1993 elections), and with them the privileges accorded to political parties. Given that the number of emigrants has rapidly declined since 1993, it would appear that apathy has set in among large numbers of the German minority. Its two remaining representatives Henryk Kroll and Helmut Pazdzidor, lobby various parliamentary institutions including the Parliamentary Committee for National and Ethnic Minorities (Kroll is actually a member of this committee), and the relevant sections of the Ministries of Interior and Culture on behalf of their constituents. Significant gains have been made in recent years, although the Germans claim that areas of discrimination still exist. It has been claimed that, because (collective) minority rights – which guarantee equality before the law to all ethnic minorities in Poland – have not yet fully been enshrined within Polish law, the various minorities do not necessarily receive equal treatment (*Dialog* Nos. 2/3 1995).

Given that a draft Law on National Minorities was at last laid before parliament in the autumn of 1998, that issue may finally be near a resolution.

What has not come any closer to a resolution is the dispute on how many Germans actually live in Poland. However, the results of the regional and local elections held in October 1998 may help to shed some light on the matter. In 1998, a law on the reform of regional and local government was passed. The original plans envisioned the abolition of the Opole voivodeship and its merger with the neighbouring Upper Silesian voivodeship. Unsurprisingly this caused outrage within the ranks of the VdG, which recognised that its representation on the *Sejmik* (regional parliament) of such a voivodeship would be minimal.

Aided by the government's reliance on opposition votes to get the legislation through, and by a cross-party campaign at the local level, the VdG succeeded in ensuring the continued survival of the Opole voivodeship. Their strategy seems to have paid dividends, in that following the elections to the Sejmik, they have emerged as the second strongest party in the voivodeship with thirteen seats, just one behind the fourteen of the Democratic Left Alliance (SLD) (Gazeta Wyborcza 23 October 1998). In the coalition talks that will now follow, the major Polish parties are faced with a choice, either of entering into discussion with the VdG, or of forming a coalition of 'Polish parties' whose sole commonality would be national provenance. Having said that, given that the AWS leadership has issued instructions that under no circumstances will coalitions with the SLD be allowed, a German Minority–AWS–Freedom Union coalition seems to be the most likely option (*Gazeta Wyborcza* 14 October 1998).

Success at the *Sejmik* level was also repeated at the level of the *powiaty* (counties) and *gminy* (communes). The VdG has taken control of a large number of *gminy*, mainly in the south and east of the voivodeship, and also the *powiaty* of Kluczbork, Krapkowice and Strzelce Opolskie. For the first time ever it has also obtained representation on the Opole City Council. However, there were also setbacks. In the Silesian voivodeship, each branch of the VdG was left to make its own decision on whether it contested the elections on their own, or in alliance with a Polish party. That most ran candidates on a variety of 'Polish lists' is encouraging. What was less encouraging for the

VdG is that whether or not such indivduals stood on the VdG
or on for example, the (UW) list, German candidates did
poorly. Although there will be German representation in cities
such as Katowice and Gliwice, nowhere in this voivodeship
does the VdG control any *powiaty*.

The leadership of the VdG has pronounced itself to be
happy with the results in Opole Silesia (*Schlesisches Wochenblatt*
16 October 1998), and on the surface they have every right to
be, especially after their poor showing at the previous two general elections. However, the voting returns indicate that the
VdG has greatly exaggerated the number of Germans in that
voivodeship and probably elsewhere in Poland. The VdG
achieved 21 percent of the vote in the Opole voivodeship,
which has an overall population of some 600,000. We therefore can crudely estimate that around 120,000 of the total elec-
torate is German. To that number young people of under
eighteen must be added, and it has to be considered that not
every declared German feels obliged to vote for the VdG.
Whatever way one looks at the figures it is clear that claims of
there being as many as 500,000 Germans in Poland are in fact
difficult to substantiate, and the estimates of the scholars such
as Kurcz are probably much closer to the truth.

Conclusion and Outlook: The Future of the German Minority in Poland

For decades, the position and existence of the Germans in
Upper Silesia and other parts of Poland dogged bilateral relations between Warsaw and Bonn. The two sides eventually
established formal diplomatic relations in 1970, with one of
the fruits of this tentative rapprochement being that over
550,000 people claiming adherence to the *Deutschtum* were
allowed to leave Poland between 1970 and 1988. The changed
political climate in Poland from 1988 resulted in official recognition by the government that Poland did in fact possess an
ethnic German minority. However, it is also necessary to note
that the fall of communism prompted a further exodus of designated Germans from Poland to Germany, and that this exodus, coupled with the changed political climate in Poland,
prompted a rethink in Bonn of policy toward (the future of)
this minority.

The pattern of migration to Germany has, temporarily at least, been broken. Despite the uncertainty over exact numbers, the German community appears now to be the largest ethnic minority in Poland, and certainly is the best-organised (Sakson 1993: 7). However, this does not mean that the political leadership among the German community is necessarily happy with either the attitude of or level of support it receives from Berlin. There are also complaints that the wider population of the Federal Republic has insufficient interest in the fate of the Germans of Upper Silesia. In a sense such feelings demonstrate the impact of years of isolation from Germany, and the existence of a community which finds it difficult to comes to terms with the fact that the experiences and orientation of post-war Germans, and particularly post-war West Germans, are very different to those Germans who have remained in Poland (Bingen 1994). Thus the community leaders claim they are receiving insufficient financial and material support from the federal government. For its part the federal government sees itself as a facilitator of aid, and rarely involves itself in issues that it considers to be solely within the competence of the Polish state. It has also made it crystal clear to the nationalist fringe, which inevitably inhabits various of the German societies, that any activities which might lead to disturbance in Polish–German relations, or within Polish society, will not be tolerated (Kroll 1994).

Despite the progress of the past few years, the hubris of distrust still lingers, as was shown in the thorny issue of pension rights of former members of the German armed forces living in Poland. Although a bilateral agreement had been initialled in 1975, the question of pension rights for those who served in the German armed forces up until 1945 was settled only in the autumn of 1995. This settlement, for which time spent as a prisoner-of-war or in the *Landarmee* or as civilian forced labourer (either in Poland, Germany or the Soviet Union) is not taken into account, has proven to be something of a disappointment for many members of the minority. Quite simply, they regard it as insufficient compensation both for their years of military service, and for the subsequent discrimination they had to endure because of it. In addition, one encounters complaints that the German minority does not enjoy the same privileges as the Ukrainian and other minorities in Poland. This is a claim which both the Polish and German governments refute, and have jointly stated that in their opinion the treaty of 1991 conforms to the United Nations' Charter on Human Rights, the Closing Act of the 1975 Helsinki Agreement, the Paris Charter for a New Europe of 1990, and the Copenhagen Document on the Human Dimension of 1990.

In the late 1980s and early 1990s the 'Grand Design' of the VdG was to develop (Upper) Silesia as a bridge between Poland and Germany on the one hand and Western Europe and Eastern Europe on the other (Sakson 1993: 19-20). Although bilateral cooperation has improved out of all recognition, there is no sign that Silesia is about to become some kind of 'Super-Euroregion'. Although under Article 24 of The Basic Law, German *Länder* are empowered to transfer functions to Euroregions, the idea that in the short or even medium term, Polish voivodeships will acquire similar rights is pure fantasy. The success of such grandiose schemes is of course contingent upon Polish admission into the EU and a continued strengthening of the EU's regional policy. Leaving the vagaries of the latter to one side, one can say that not only is the dependency upon a continued strengthening of the Polish economy essential, it is necessary to devise and implement a specific programme aimed at radically restructuring the economy of Upper Silesia. As if that were not enough, such designs are inevitably predicated upon the process of constitutional reform. Given the ambiguities of the situation, current constitutional provisions do not fully entrench Poland's assent to the obligations it has assumed through membership of such organisations as the Council of Europe. German (Upper Silesian) anxieties are therefore understandable, if at times exaggerated.

It is important to acknowledge that gains have been made in Upper Silesia over the past few years. The German minority now has its own voice in both national and local politics in Poland. Its existence is no longer denied by the Polish state, and both the Polish and German governments have sponsored a range of initiatives aimed at preserving the distinct nature of this society. It must be noted that there is a tendency on the part of the VdG and its affiliates to look to Berlin rather than Warsaw in this respect, and to lobby Berlin through the *Landsmannschaften*. Given the latter's pre-occupation with the property rights of expellees and refugees, this is a situation that neither government is altogether happy with. However, this has not led to real disruption to either inter-state relations or inter-communal relations which at present are good.

The greatest change has perhaps been in the matter of citizenship and ethnicity. What has happened in Poland since 1945 is the creation of a German community in Upper Silesia which is more certain of its identity. This has come about not because of the success of German nation-building strategies, but because of the failure of Polish equivalents. Given the authoritarian nature of the communists, Stalinist methods were bound to be employed in the post-war years. Because of that experience, it is pointless to talk about 'missed opportunities'. The failure of communist authoritarianism shows that you cannot force upon people an identity which they reject. What has been encouraging is that since 1989 the presence of a declared and substantial German minority has not proven to be the major political issue in Poland that some feared it might become. However, their 'discovery' did come as something of an initial shock to a people who had for decades been told that virtually no Germans resided in Poland. Yet there has been a halting but steady rapprochement between Germans and Poles in Poland since the downfall of the PUWP.

The incorporation of the Germans and their main organisations into the new Polish political culture demonstrates that there is increasing acceptance that Poland as a state is host to a number of national minorities. Both sides have made concessions. The greatest of these concessions has been to recognise that not every citizen of a state has ipso facto to possess the nationality of the titular nation. Citizenship thus becomes detached from nationality, and acknowledgement of German nationality does not debar someone from membership of Polish society. Given the terrible legacy of German–Polish relations in the twentieth century, the continued toleration and flourishing of a German minority in Poland is the best indication of the strength of Polish liberal democracy.

References

1. Books and Articles

Ash, T. Garton, *In Europe's Name,* London, 1993.

Bingen, D., Deutsch-Polnische Beziehungen nach 1989: Themen und Tabus. Undated Conference Paper.

Buchofer, E., *Die Bevölkerung Oberschlesiens Zeit* 1945 in, *Oberschlesien nach dem zweiten Weltkrieg*, ed. E. Bahr, Marburg, 1975, pp. 65-75.

Kuechler, M., 'Germans and 'Others', German Politics, Vol. 3, No.1, 1993.

Marshall, B., 'Migration into Germany: Asylum Seekers and Ethnic Germans', *German Politics*, vol.1, no. 1, 1992.

Rogall, J., 'Die deutsche Minderheit in Polen heute', *Das Parlament*, 26 November 1993.

Sakson, A., 'Die deutsche Minderheit in Polen: Gegenwart und Zukunft', *Bundesinstitut für ostwissenschaftliche und internationale Studien*, Bonn, 1993.

2. Interviews

Dr Dieter Bingen of the *Bundesinstitut für ostwissenschaftliche und internationale Studien*, 8 November 1994.

Fr Wolfgang Globisch of the Silesian Diocese, 9 November 1995.

Dr Berthold Johannes of the German Foreign Office in conversation with the author, 25 October 1994.

Ms Klaudia Kandzia of *Bund der Jugend der deutschen Minderheit*, 9 November 1995.

Mr Henryk Kroll, Member of the Polish Parliament, 16 November 1994.

Dr Christoph Liedtke of the Foreign, European and Development Section of the Free Democratic Party, 25 October 1994.

Dr Andreas Zimmer of the German Consulate in Wroclaw, 26 October 1996.

3. Periodicals
Dialog
Gazeta Wyborcza
Schlesische Nachrichten
Schlesisches Wochenblatt

CHAPTER 6

The Carpathian Germans

Lucy P. Marcus

Ethnic Germans in the Carpathian Mountains of today's Slovakia and Ukraine can trace their origins back to the earliest German colonists in Central Europe. By the end of the twelfth century the ancestors of the few remaining Carpathian Germans had established their first settlements in the northern part of the Carpathian arc. They settled along the entire stretch of the Carpathian Mountains in what are present-day Slovakia and Ukraine. The three main territories in which they lived were in the south-east in the area of Bratislava, in the so-called *Hauerland* in central Slovakia, and in the region of Zips towards the east of the mountain chain in the border land with today's Ukraine.

Through the centuries, their number grew, and by 1938 there were between 150,000 and 200,000 Carpathian Germans (Krejci and Machonin 1996: 31; Stone and Strouhal 1992: 99; Reimer). According to the 1930 Czechoslovak census, Germans in Slovakia made up 4.7 percent of the population in the Slovak part of the first Czechoslovak Republic. This figure still included the eastern Carpathian region with about 18,000 ethnic Germans (Reimer). Their number was drastically reduced at the end of the Second World War, with a mere 0.1 percent recorded in the 1961 Czechoslovak census (Krejci and Machonin 1996: 53) symbolising the obvious and dramatic decline. The last Czechoslovak census of 1991 gave the number of Carpathian Germans in Slovakia at 5,900, while unofficial estimates assume their number to be about

15,000 (Reimer). This has been indirectly confirmed by a 1993 estimate of the German government giving the number of ethnic Germans in Slovakia at between 10,000 and 20,000 (*Bundestagsdrucksache* 12/6162). In the early 1990s, it was estimated that the Ukrainian part of the Carpathian Mountains, annexed by the Soviet Union in 1945, contained about 3,000 members of the Carpathian ethnic German community (Reimer). Some further 30,000 Germans are still living in the southern parts of Ukraine (Eisfeld 1993: 48). At the end of the decade, resettlement programmes have led to an increase of the ethnic German population in Ukraine to almost 40,000 (Heintze below).

From the First Settlements to the First Czechoslovak Republic

For almost one millennium, the Carpathian region in today's Slovak Republic was part of the Kingdom of Hungary. The first German migrants arrived in the area after King Bela IV had issued an invitation to them. When German settlements started after 1100, colonists began to settle in already existing mining towns or created new ones by themselves (Kirschbaum 1995: 51). Apart from the monarch who had sought to bring German mining specialists to his country, Germans were also invited by local aristocrats in the Carpathian Mountains to develop vineyards and wine production (Makkai 1990: 29). As in most other cases of German colonisation in Central and Eastern Europe, the settlers enjoyed significant privileges, including exemption from tax payments for a pre-determined number of years. These privileges did usually not cause problems with the local population. The locals benefited from the arrival of the colonists, because, gradually, some of the social and 'political' privileges (elected local officers and councils, market rights, right to property transactions) were extended to them. The town council of Nitra, for example, came to accept equal representation of the German, Slovak, and Hungarian sections of the population by the middle of the sixteenth century (Kirschbaum 1995: 65). Old and new sections of the population furthermore were active in different sectors of the economy so that no competition and rivalry could develop (Kirschbaum 1995: 55f.). Thus, by the early twentieth century, an almost 200,000-strong German community had developed in the southwestern and central parts of Slovakia.

The eastern part of the Carpathian region, in contrast, had a much more complex history full of conflict and wars. The area was originally settled by the ancestors of today's Ruthenian population and by Magyars. Romanians and Jews arrived in the fourteenth century. The first Germans that settled in the eastern Carpathian region arrived in the twelfth century following an invitation from King Geza II. Their original settlements were destroyed during the invasion of the Mongols. Despite the fact that successive Hungarian kings continued the policy of inviting settlers from other developed regions, including Germans, Slavs and Romanians, the area remained isolated and underdeveloped. The invasion by the Mongols in the thirteenth century was followed by that of the Crimean Tatars in the fifteenth and sixteenth centuries and by that of the Ottoman Turks in the sixteenth century. All the invaders devastated the area and prevented greater economic and social development. Constant border hostilities with the Turks until the early eighteenth century, and a civil war between pro- and anti-Habsburg Magyar aristocrats that lasted until the 1720s, extended these unfavourable conditions for proper colonisation further. Even though local landowners realised that in order to make their lands productive there was a need for settlers with appropriate skills and motivation, it was not until the last quarter of the eighteenth century that more serious, and especially more successful, steps were taken in this direction. In 1775, the Austro–Hungarian Empress Maria Theresia ordered the recruitment of about 100 skilled workers to maintain the large forests of the northeastern part of the Carpathian mountain chain and to prepare them for colonisation. Together with their families, approximately two hundred people arrived from Upper Austria in October 1775 and settled in a small village that they named Deutsch-Mokra. Settlers continued to arrive in the following years and quickly outgrew the capacity of the village. In 1815, some colonists moved further to the south where they founded a new German settlement, Königsfeld. While the first Germans to arrive worked primarily as woodcutters and charcoal-makers, soon more skilled and higher qualified settlers were attracted, too (Reimer). Increasingly, Germans were not making a living in the agricultural sector or in forestry, but rather worked as engineers and skilled workers in the local mining and chemical industries.

Apart from Upper Austrians, people from Galicia, Bohemia, and Slovenia migrated to the region in the following decades adding to the ethnic mix of the local population. As a result of the various waves of migration, an ethno-linguistically mixed, but not assimilated, local population had developed in the eastern Carpathian mountains by the middle of the nineteenth century, of which ethnic Germans were one component. Because of the relative isolation of the villages and the dominance of the first settlers from Upper Austria, their traditions and customs prevailed over time, as did their dialect and architectural style. While no major inter-ethnic tensions had occurred by then, Magyarisation attempts after the Austro–Hungarian compromise in 1867 began to change the situation.

Local aristocrats continued to recruit new ethnic German settlers from Bavaria and eastern Lorraine until 1880, and other Germans arrived on their own initiative, mostly in small groups. Nevertheless, the policy of Magyarisation threatened to forcibly assimilate large sections of the ethnic German population. This, and the economic and political decline of the area, resulted in several thousand Carpathian Germans emigrating before the beginning of the First World War, primarily to the United States.

From the Foundation of the First Czechoslovak Republic to Its Destruction

At the end of the First World War, a number of new states were created out of the former Austro–Hungarian Empire. The treaties of Versailles in 1919 and Trianon in 1920 diminished the territory and population over which Austria and Hungary retained sovereignty, resulting in the independence of Romania, the Kingdom of Yugoslavia (initially, the Kingdom of Serbs, Croats, and Slovenes), and Czechoslovakia. Part of the Austro–Hungarian legacy that all these states carried on, was the multinational character of their population. In Czechoslovakia, the more than three million Germans were the numerically largest minority group making up almost one quarter of the entire population of the new country. This was

primarily because of the vast and populous German settlements in the *Sudetenland* in the Czech part of the country. In
Slovakia, the ethnic German community was outnumbered
almost five to one by Hungarians, due to the territorial and
population gains Slovakia had made in the Treaty of Trianon
that changed the borders of Hungary.

In contrast to the Sudeten German minority in the Czech
part of the newly independent country, ethnic Germans in Slovakia were not at the centre of either domestic or foreign political interest in the inter-war period. The increasing
radicalisation of the Sudeten Germans after 1933 and the official response by the Czechoslovak state and by Germany
affected them to some degree. However, the major ethnic conflict line in Slovakia was between Slovaks and the recently
acquired Hungarian population in the south of the country.
The Germans living in and around the capital Bratislava as
well as in their traditional settlement areas in central Slovakia
were generally well integrated. Over the centuries after their
initial migration, ethnic Germans had assumed crucial positions in the country's economy, many of them working as
engineers in machine building, mining, or in the chemical
industry. While the economically active section of the German minority was, for the most part, bilingual, community
activity was generally conducted in German, which was also
the language of everyday communication. The local administration was partly bilingual in a majority of rural German settlements and the minority maintained functioning community
structures, including schools, cultural facilities, and German or
part-German print media. Many German-speakers, particularly in Bratislava, were Jewish and contributed significantly to
the rich cultural life of the minority in the inter-war years.

The north-eastern part of the Carpathian Mountains, an
area of almost five and a half thousand square miles, was
annexed to the new Czechoslovak state and for the first time
organised as a separate administrative unit – the province of
Podkarpatska Rus. Promises of autonomy that had been made
in 1919 in the wake of League of Nations attempts to protect
the multiple national minorities that came into being as a
result of border alterations all over Central and Eastern
Europe were only fulfilled for a short period after 1938, and
even then only as a result of pressure exercised by the signatory states of the Munich Agreement.

There had been more than 60,000 ethnic Germans in the area in 1910, making them the third-strongest regional minority group after Ruthenians and Hungarians. By 1921, their number had decreased to about one-sixth of the pre-war figure. Apart from casualties suffered as a consequence of the war and emigration, the decline must also be seen in the context of the large number of Jews who had recorded their nationality as Germans in Austro–Hungarian censuses before the foundation of the Czechoslovak state, because Jewish was not a choice available on the census form. Even though many of them never really identified with their 'declared' ethnic group in cultural or national terms, German seemed the most logical choice because their mother tongue was either German or Yiddish. After 1919 they registered as Czechoslovaks, but continued to speak German. Their impact on the German minority was similar to that of the German-speaking Jewish community in the southwestern and central parts of Slovakia. Because of the relatively large number of Jewish German-speakers, cultural institutions of the ethnic German community survived even in the bigger cities of the region where the actual number of ethnic Germans was less than 5 per cent of the local population. By 1930, there were some 13,000 ethnic Germans living in the eastern part of the Carpathian Mountains, and even the increase of the German population to just fewer than 18,000 by 1940 was still a far cry from the pre-1914 figures. Most of them resided in the rural parts of the region, concentrated in two main areas – about 12,000 lived around Munkatsch and some 4,000 in Theresienthal (Reimann) – where twelve villages had a German majority.

The Munich agreement of 1938 also affected the Slovak part of Czechoslovakia. Germany and Italy decided in November 1938 that Hungary would regain large parts of the Hungarian-populated south of Slovakia, an area totalling more than ten thousand square kilometres and containing over 800,000 inhabitants, including almost a quarter of a million Slovaks (Kirschbaum 1995: 181). As a result of the (Germany-prompted) Slovak declaration of independence and subsequent secession from Czechoslovakia in March 1939, Hungary could also regain the rest of the eastern Carpathian Mountains, including all the major German settlements, after it had already been 'awarded' the southern section of the area in 1938, which was inhabited mostly by ethnic Hungarians. Slovakia also lost some territory to Poland and Germany.

Divided History – Carpathian Germans in Slovakia and Ukraine after 1945

After the end of the Second World War, Slovakia became part of a Czechoslovak state again. The eastern parts of the Carpathian Mountains, however, were annexed by the Soviet Union and became part of the Republic of Ukraine in 1991, when the former Soviet Republic gained its independence in the course of the breakup of the USSR.

Slovakia: From the Expulsions to the Breakup of Czechoslovakia

After the Second World War and the expulsion of large sections of the German minority from Slovakia, the ethnic German community in the eastern parts of Slovakia virtually vanished. In the central and southeastern parts of the country, ethnic Germans also suffered a great deal during the period of expulsion and 'organised' population transfer. According to the Czechoslovak census of 1950, of the almost 3.5 million ethnic Germans in Czechoslovakia in 1937, only 165,000 were left. Emigration from Slovakia to Germany continued after 1950 at a much reduced level,[1] so that census data compiled at the beginning of the 1990s showed that more than 5,600 people regarded themselves as German by ethnic origin, yet only 4,200 stated their mother tongue was German as well (Ondrejovic 1993: 9). Unofficial estimates assume that between 10,000 and 20,000 Germans are still living in the country.

After the openly repressive retaliation policy against ethnic Germans was generally phased out at the end of the 1940s, it took until 1953 before they could regain their citizenship

1. Between 1950 and 1995 just over 100,000 ethnic Germans left Czechoslovakia as a whole, more than half of them between 1964 and 1970. In contrast to other Central and Eastern European countries, there was no major upsurge in emigrants after 1989. Cf. the annual breakdown of Czechoslovak German immigrants in *Infodienst* 91 (1997: 2–5).

rights. Legal guarantees for their protection as a minority were only in force after 1968; their implementation, however, was often less than satisfactory. In general, between 1950 and the late 1980s, the German minority suffered from discrimination and assimilation pressure for two reasons. One was the carefully preserved memory of the German involvement in the breakup of Czechoslovakia in 1938/39. The second was the political activism of the expellee and refugee organisations in the Federal Republic. Finally, one result of the expulsions and deportations of the 1940s was that the few remaining members of the minority have lived rather dispersed, thus not warranting their own schools. German has therefore only been taught as a foreign language, but as such it is relatively common in the Slovak education system (Ondrejovic 1993:13). Consequently, the everyday language of most ethnic Germans in Slovakia is Slovak. There are also some bilingual Slovak–German families and even a few trilingual Slovak–German–Hungarian ones (Ondrejovic 1993: 11).

This generally unfavourable situation was not improved by the foundation of the Cultural Association of Citizens of German Nationality in the Czechoslovak Socialist Republic in 1969. Not only was it controlled by party and state, but the only source of 'native' German information in the Slovak part of the country was the East German Cultural Centre in Bratislava (Ondrejovic 1993: 13).[2]

The issue of the expulsions and problems related to it, like the restitution of property and settlement rights for expellees in their former homelands, delayed any significant improvement of the situation of the German minority in Czechoslovakia as a whole after the 'velvet revolution' of 1989. However, this began to change gradually after the conclusion of the German–Czechoslovak treaty in 1992.

Improving Conditions in Independent Slovakia after 1992

The dissolution of Czechoslovakia in 1992 affected the Carpathian Germans in Slovakia in a variety of ways. First, the German minority 'problem', similar to the situation in Romania, became more or less marginalised in the face of

2. On the perception of the *Sudetendeutsche Landsmannschaft* in Czechoslovakia and the Czech Republic, Kimminich (1996: 33–6).

growing ethno-political tensions between the Slovak govern-ment and the large Hungarian minority in the south of the country. Second, the dissociation of the Carpathian Germans from their kin-group in the *Sudetenland* in the now Czech Republic made the existence of an ethnic German community in the country appear far less threatening. Historically, the role of the Slovak Germans was perceived as less negative in the developments leading to the Munich Agreement of 1938. In the post-war period, the *Karpatendeutsche Landsmannschaft* took a less aggressive stance than its Sudeten German counterpart. Furthermore, similar to other Central and East European countries, the Slovak government recognised the 'value' of the German minority it hosted for the rapprochement with West-ern Europe. Because of the small size of the remaining Ger-man community, Slovakia was prepared to make a number of concessions, as it gave the Slovak government an opportunity to demonstrate the good intentions in its minority policy.[3]

Recent cooperation with Germany on issues related to the minority is generally good (*Bundestagsdrucksache* 12/6162: 36). With the beginning of the academic year 1993, German has been introduced at primary school level in four schools, and since 1994–95, there have been bilingual German–Slovak classes in another six schools (Mohlek and Hoskova 1994: 133). A Carpathian German Association in Slovakia, founded in 1990, can operate without restrictions and is, together with a German-language newspaper – *Karpatenblatt* –, partly funded by the Slovak state budget (Mohlek and Hoskova 1994: 139). The monthly with a circulation of 2,5000 copies receives further support from the German Federal Ministry of the Interior. Other joint Slovak-German projects include the Museum of Carpathian German Culture in Bratislava, which was founded in 1997. In addition, German aid has been forth-coming since 1990 in the form of equipment, consulting ser-vices, interest-free loans for companies operated by ethnic Germans or employing them, and in the form of sponsored places in qualification and vocational training courses for members of the minority (*Deutscher Ostdienst* 9/10/1998).

However, it is important to note that the assimilation of Carpathian Germans in Slovakia has progressed very far.

---

3. Slovak minority policy has often been criticised for the discrepancy between pub-lic statements in the international arena and its domestic implementation. Cf. Heintze in this book.

There are no longer any major compact German settlements in the country, and functioning community structures that would be essential for the survival of the minority as distinct ethno-cultural group hardly exist. Unless there is a concerted effort by the two governments and the ethnic German community in the near future, the minority will become completely assimilated in the medium to long term. This process has also been accelerated by the unfavourable age structure of the Carpathian German community, within which almost half of its members are beyond their sixtieth year (Ondrejovic 1993: 9).

Ukraine: From Deportation to Resettlement

Facing the advance of the Soviet Red Army in 1944, most of the ethnic German inhabitants of the future Ukrainian part of the Carpathian Mountains were evacuated by the German *Wehrmacht* to either Germany or Austria. Those who did not leave suffered severe repression at the hands of the Red Army and the new Ukrainian authorities. Many were killed in special detention camps or deported to forced labour camps in Siberia. Even though openly anti-German violence had ended by the end of decade, the following period of discrimination and forced assimilation denied the few ethnic Germans in the area all rights to their identity, and resulted in their almost completely vanishing as a distinct ethno-cultural group. After the 1960s some of the formerly resident German population returned from Siberia, and by 1970 the number of Germans in the Carpathian Ukraine had grown back to some 6,000 (Reimer). According to the last Soviet census in 1989, however, their number had declined again by some 2,500.

A Future in Ukraine?

The end of communism in the Soviet Union lifted most of the restrictions previously imposed on cultural activities of the German community. After gaining its independence, Ukraine recognised the 'value' of the German minority in the context of its bilateral relationship with Germany, its transition efforts to democracy, and its ultimate goal of closer ties with the West.

For historical reasons, the major focus of the Ukrainian government has been on the German minority in the southern parts of the country, where (including the Crimea) almost half a million Germans lived prior to the beginning of the Second World War. About 100,000 of them were deported immediately after 1941. Most of those who remained were deported after 1945 (Eisfeld 1993: 49). Thus, the 1989 Soviet census recorded less than 38,000 ethnic Germans on the territory of the then Ukrainian Socialist Soviet Republic.

The new openness of the country after 1989 resulted in the German organisation 'Rebirth' (*Wiedergeburt*) being legalised as early as 1990. In cooperation with the German government it directed its efforts at the restoration of traditional ethnic German settlements in southern Ukraine. The inception of the German–Ukrainian Fund in 1992 was part of the joint German–Ukrainian project to (re-)create a six hundred kilometre-long belt with compact German settlements to become the home of more than a quarter of a million ethnic Germans from all over the former Soviet Union. The German federal government committed 20 million Deutschmarks to the fund in 1992 and another 32 million in 1993. Economic problems in Ukraine and the long unresolved citizenship issue delayed the start of the programme and its ambitious aims have not been achieved by the turn of the millennium.

Although it did not directly profit from the resettlement programme, the Carpathian German population benefited nevertheless from the generally more favourable attitude of the Ukrainian government after 1990. Members of the German community can freely use their language and practice their particular lifestyle as far as it is still alive, or revive it according to their needs. In this, they are supported primarily by the *Karpatendeutsche Landsmannschaft* of their former fellow countrymen who had migrated to Germany or Austria after 1944. Despite the fact that there are no particular limits as to the preservation, expression, and development of their German identity, the degree to which assimilation has progressed and the small size of the community make it almost certain that the German population in the Ukrainian part of the Carpathian mountains is unlikely to reconstitute itself as a distinct ethno-cultural group.

Conclusion

Carpathian Germans have one of the longest histories among all ethnic German migrant communities in Central and

Eastern Europe, reaching back to the twelfth century. On the territory of today's central and southwestern Slovakia, they integrated well and developed a flourishing community life through the centuries. In contrast, German settlers in the northeastern part of the Carpathian Mountains suffered from invasions and prolonged warfare, and a more stable and prosperous community life could only develop from the late eighteenth century onwards.

After the Second World War, Carpathian Germans found themselves in two countries – in the recreated Czechoslovakia and in the Ukrainian Socialist Soviet Republic. Subjected first to expulsion and deportation, they continued to suffer from discrimination and assimilation pressures until the late 1980s. By then, the decline of the two communities had progressed so far that post-communist reforms improving the situation of minorities have, probably, to prevent them from being eventually becoming completely assimilated.

References

Bundestagsdrucksache 12/6162.

Deutscher Ostdienst.

Eisfeld, A., 'Zwischen Bleiben und Gehen: Die Deutschen in den Nachfolgestaaten der Sowjetunion', in *Aus Politik und Zeitgeschichte*, no. 48, 1993, pp. 44–52.

Infodienst Deutsche Aussiedler, no. 91, 1997.

Kimminich, O., 'Völkerrecht und Geschichte im Disput über die Beziehungen Deutschlands zu seinen östlichen Nachbarn', in *Aus Politik und Zeitgeschichte*, no. 28, 1996, pp. 28–38.

Kirschbaum, S.J., *A History of Slovakia. The Struggle for Survival*, London 1995.

Krejci, J. and Machonin, P., *Czechoslovakia, 1918–1992. A Laboratory for Social Change*, London 1996.

Makkai, L., 'Transformation into a Western-type State, 1196–1301', in *A History of Hungary*, ed. Peter F. Sugar, Bloomington 1990.

Mohlek, P. and Hoskova, M., *Der Minderheitenschutz in der Republik Polen, in der Tschechischen und in der Slowakischen Republik*, Bonn, 1994.

Ondrejovic, S., *Minderheiten und Kontaktsprachen in der Slowakischen Republik. Ein enzyklopädischer Überblick*, Bratislava und Bielefeld, 1993.

Reimer, T., *Carpathian German Homepage*, http://pw1.netcom.com/~ycrtmr/slovakia.htm.

Stone, N. and Strouhal, E., *Czechoslovakia: Crossroads and Crises, 1918–1988*, London, 1992.

CHAPTER 7

The Ethnolinguistic Vitality of German-speaking Communities in Central Europe

Patrick Stevenson

Locating Ethnolinguistic Communities: Language Ecologies and Communities of Memory

The idea of the German language has long had a powerful and compelling influence on the ways in which otherwise highly disparate social and ethnic groups in the centre of the European continent have imagined themselves. The construction of national identities amongst German-speaking peoples has repeatedly depended crucially on this linguistic 'bonding', and the ideological mobilisation of 'the German language' has been a constant feature of attempts over at least the last 200 years to establish the nature and extent of 'Germanness' (Stevenson 1993; Coulmas 1985, 1997).

However, language as a central component of identity formation has been, and continues to be, important not only in the process of constructing an inclusive sense of nationhood within states dominated numerically by German-speakers, but also in the project of maintaining external membership of the German cultural tradition by ethnic German minorities, especially in Central and Eastern Europe. Until 1989, this project seemed to a large extent like a lost cause: German-speaking minority populations received little, if any, institutional support and they were generally not succeeding in reproducing themselves. Since then, the opportunities for a revitalisation of these communities have ostensibly increased, but (as other chapters in this book show) this issue has occupied different positions in the democratisation agendas of different states in Eastern Europe.

Furthermore, academic interest in these ethnolinguistic minorities over the last ten years has understandably focused on the one hand on their possibilities of collective regeneration and relocation within the radically redefined geopolitical setting of the new version of *Mitteleuropa*, and on the other hand on the broader implications of these developments for theories of language and nationalism (see, for example, Mar-Molinero 1994). In this context, questions of identity formation are typically discussed in generalised terms in relation to large-scale socio-political phenomena and the macro-sociological categories of the sociology of language. For example, Földes (1992: 94–95) points out the more than threefold increase in what he refers to as 'Bekenntnis-Deutschen' (self-declared Germans) in the 1990 census in Hungary compared to the previous one ten years earlier: while the number of those giving German as their 'mother tongue' rose from 19,072 in 1980 to 21,893 in 1990, this increase was far outstripped by the rise in the number of those declaring their 'nationality' as German (from 5,252 in 1980 to 17,421 in 1990). Clearly, it is one thing to acknowledge that your mother tongue (whatever this term is taken to mean) is not the dominant language of state authority, but it is quite a different matter to declare allegiance to an extraneous and historically antagonistic nationality. Furthermore, for many people the relationship between language and ethnicity is apparently not only not self-evident but also negotiable.

Földes is no doubt right to explain these changing patterns of behaviour in terms of Hungarian–Germans' responses to the repressive policies imposed on them after 1945 and of the more recent democratisation and pluralisation of Hungarian society in the 1980s (although Gal 1993 shows that changes in census-taking policies and census design make a more complex and more subtle analysis necessary). However, his conclusions on shifts in patterns of identity formation amongst

Hungarian–Germans are reached by extrapolating from a range of influences (including the effects of urbanisation in diluting the predominantly rural strongholds of German-speakers) and are applied globally to the 'ungarländisches Deutschtum' (the Hungarian–German population):

> On the one hand, there was a levelling of ethnic-cultural-linguistic differences through political power as a result of the conception of an egalitarian society (levelling from the outside) [. . .], on the other hand, there was a certain psychological resignation or passivity in relation to the effort of otherness, above all due to an often justified fear of the serious conflicts that otherness gives rise to (levelling from within). (Földes 1992: 104–5; my translation – P.S.)

Generalised analyses such as these may or may not be valid on the level of surface outcomes, but they reveal little or nothing about the underlying processes and their meanings. Therefore, broad-brush assessments of social trends need to be complemented by more fine-grained empirical research that focuses on the micro level of personal experience and the interpretation of individual biographies within a framework that still permits a coherent synthesis without ironing out specific differences (a good example of this is Ulla Fix's Leipzig project on linguistic biographies of East Germans: see, for example, Fix 1997b). In contrast to Földes's 'top down' approach to identity formation, this approach emphasises the exploration of ways in which identities emerge or evolve 'from below'. However, it is not a question of ignoring macro features of social change in favour of the micro, nor of merely characterising the former as the context or scene in which the latter are performed. The aim is rather to integrate individual changes in behaviours and practices with large-scale socio-political and economic changes in terms of the mediating effects of changes in values and beliefs (as opposed to a direct cause and effect model).

In this chapter, I shall show how this approach can contribute to an assessment of the ethnolinguistic vitality of minority communities. I shall focus in particular on the German-speaking minorities in the Czech Republic and in Hungary, exploring the connections between macro- and micro-sociolinguistic aspects of their recent history, and analysing the self-perceptions of individual German-speakers and their experience of accommodating themselves in and to their new political and cultural environment.[1] For this kind of analysis, it is not the absolute number of German-speakers nor their proportion of the total population within a particular state that is significant (for statistical information of this sort, see Nekvapil 1997a, Nekvapil and Neustupny 1998 and *National and Ethnic Minorities in Hungary* 1991); we shall be concerned here not with the size of these communities, but with their nature.

On the one hand, the very notion of homogeneous ethnolinguistic communities may be construed as no more than a convenient fiction (see Stevenson 1997), but on the other hand, we have to be able to account for the fact that while individual experiences are unique, people make sense of them in terms of what they have in common with the experiences of others. For this purpose, and in the present context, a more narrowly defined concept of community is required, such as what Fix (1997a) calls *Erinnerungsgemeinschaften* (communities of memory). These self-constituting groupings can be particularly significant in periods of major social change in guaranteeing social and cultural continuity, for common memories are not simply 'shared knowledge' but 'collective experiences'. For example, it is not merely being a Protestant and being committed to the Union with Great Britain that makes someone a Loyalist in Northern Ireland, but the memory of the Battle of the Boyne that is evoked in the ritual call to 'Remember 1690!'. Although this decisive victory of the Protestant King William III over the Catholic former King James II took place over 300 years ago, it remains fresh in the minds of all Loyalists: they do not merely know that it occurred, they 'experienced' it in just the same way that the young West Berliners interviewed by Jürgen Beneke shortly after the fall of the Wall had experienced the post-war years: '"We", said a 22-year-old trainee, "we had to work hard for 40 years too, you know"; "we couldn't just travel all over the place either", said another trainee, all of 19 years old.' (Beneke 1993: 226; my translation – P.S.), or the middle-aged Czechs, who responded to our questions about their German compatriots by saying:

1. This analysis is based on semi-structured ethnographic interviews, some of which were conducted in 1995 as part of a larger project on linguistic minorities in Central Europe, others derive from a project currently being carried out by Jiri Nekvapil of Charles University, Prague. The former were conducted in German but the extracts here have been translated into English for the benefit of non-German-speaking readers.

'Germans? What Germans? We got rid of them after the war', or the Hungarian–Germans of all ages who 'remember' the 1941 census as 'the unjust bureaucratic excuse for the deportations of the post-war years' (Gal 1993: 348).

As these examples suggest, this conceptualisation of community is bound to ideas of historical, geographical and social space. Ethnolinguistic minorities understood as 'communities of memory' therefore need to be situated in an environment that is less tidy than the purely politically defined state. For this reason, Einar Haugen thirty years ago proposed an ecological approach to the study of multilingual societies, which would not only take into account all essential elements of the structure and development of a linguistic community but would also acknowledge their interdependency (Haugen 1972). More recently, the creolist Peter Mühlhäusler has taken up Haugen's ecological approach in relation to language change, language shift and linguistic imperialism in the Pacific region (Mühlhäusler 1996). Here again the emphasis is on the necessity of a holistic conception of the object of study, including all relevant features of its social and physical environment, and conventional social constructs such as community, society and network are replaced as sites of communicative action by the concept of the 'habitat'.

The concept of language ecology and especially the notion of the habitat are useful for the study of Germanness in contemporary Europe for a number of reasons. On the one hand, for example, the habitat is a historical and dynamic concept, which has to do with geographical and social space but is not bound to political borders. We can therefore say, in Mühlhäusler's terms, that all Germans and all German-speakers in Central Europe inhabit a 'disrupted habitat', and the effects of this disruption make it impossible to study one set of inhabitants in isolation from the others. On the other hand, the ecological metaphor emphasises the reciprocal relationship between linguistic and non-linguistic practices, and it offers a possibility of viewing the relationship between macro and micro phenomena in a different light, such that events and actions on the micro level are conceived as individual or collective responses to changes in the macro conditions of the overall speech ecology.

One way of illustrating this is through the ethnographic approach of the American anthropologist Susan Gal, which (implicitly) combines the idea of the *Erinnerungsgemeinschaft* and the foregrounding of effects of changes in the communicative environment (or habitat) on speakers' perceptions and practices. In various places, Gal has argued that the sociolinguistic investigation of majority/minority relations can be inadequate and even misleading if it (a) relies on apparently universal criteria (e.g. dichotomies such as status and solidarity) and thereby overlooks the fact that ideas about language are embedded in specific cultural discourses (Gal 1987: 637–8, 1995: 93), and (b) interprets patterns of language use as a static indicator of the minority's position in its immediate political context:

> Patterns of language use are not simply a reflex of the [minority] group's political and economic position; they are part of a group's actively constructed and often oppositional response to that position (Gal 1987: 650).

She goes on to contend that

> [Recent studies argue that] patterns of linguistic variation that express status or solidarity not only co-ordinate interpersonal relations, they also provide evidence about the workings of 'symbolic domination' or 'cultural hegemony' in social life. [. . .] This analytical move [. . .] conceptualises the use of a nonauthoritative variety not simply as a way of expressing different interpersonal meanings, but as a type of social practice that constitutes 'resistance' to the dominant values and institutions of a society (Gal 1993: 337).

and therefore argues in favour of a dynamic approach, which she characterises as the 'recontextualisation' of the opposition between the majority and minority languages (Gal 1995: 94). According to this model, social and political change generates changed perceptions of the relationships between the respective languages, which then promote changes in linguistic practices (such as language choice) and forms of identification (such as language allegiance). Fundamental to this approach is the possibility for speakers to contest the established relationship between dominant and minority languages and to develop individual forms of resistance to linguistic hegemony, which in turn depends on how individual members of a community interpret their social context. The aim of the analysis is therefore not simply to establish and explain general trends (such as language maintenance or shift), but to construct a dynamic picture of multiple and often contradictory responses to changes in the geopolitical setting.

Explorations in Border Country: German-speakers in Hungary and the Czech Republic

In this section, I shall explore the process of the recontextualisation of the oppositions between contact languages in a particular historical and geopolitical frame: *Mitteleuropa* in the 1990s. The segments of this 'disrupted habitat' that I shall focus on here are the German-speaking communities in Hungary and the Czech Republic, but the interpretation of the interviews on which the discussion will be based takes account of the overall language ecology which the speakers inhabit. The common point underlying both studies is the evaluation of the German language by its speakers in these communities and the role attributed to it in their attempts to redetermine their position in their changed circumstances.

Hungary

Individual evaluations of Hungarian and German and of their relationships to each other depend very heavily on personal experiences of the last 60 years. When we explored perceptions of the connections between minority language and group identities with our interviewees, the responses ranged from the complete rejection of any such links to the emphatic assertion of their fundamental importance. However, the assertion of a close tie between language and ethnicity was not necessarily a simple, taken-for-granted expression of local, historical continuity: there often appeared to be more complex rationales. In her research in Hungary, Gal received similar reactions and she distinguishes between two distinct meanings of these responses depending on the prevailing political and economic conditions: she argues that before 1990 this assertion constituted an act of resistance to the symbolic domination of state authority, while after 1990 it was an expression of a wider cultural identification (Gal 1993, 1995). For some speakers, at least, the relationship between Hungarian and German has therefore been 'recontextualised' twice since 1945: before the war, German was perceived neutrally as a marker of ethnicity in a multiethnic society, but it then became first a local symbol of internal resistance to the language of state authority, and later a transnational resource in the global political economy of the new Europe. However, these changes in perception are relativised by the memories of the collective past, and there are conflicting views on what it means to be a German speaker in Hungary:

> 1 Because of the political events [i.e. post-1945] there will never be as many who are prepared to declare themselves as are actually there [i.e. 'Hungarian–Germans'], not even today. Here in Hungary, in central Europe, you can never know what's going to happen tomorrow. The bad experience following the census in 1941 left such deep scars that many people will never do it again, expose themselves. [Ms B., Budapest]

> 2 And this attitude in the local communities in the past, if you were in such a small minority as my parents were in the village, you had to keep your mouth shut, because 'you're fascists, aren't you?' – things have changed since then, that doesn't happen any more. On the contrary, people are queuing up for these German classes which are being set up because of the minority, even from the Hungarian side, because they know that with the special nationality classes [i.e. curriculum taught in German] a Hungarian child can learn German just as well. [Ms H., Budapest]

The infamous census of 1941 plays a critical role in the collective memory of German Hungarians. Respondents were to declare not only their mother tongue but also, for the first time, their nationality, with the result that 'not only the counting itself, but also the political activity preceding it, had the effect of forcing a change in respondents' understanding of what it meant to be speaking a language. [. . .] Language choice was no longer a local matter, but one with much broader political significance' (Gal 1993: 345). The most devastating effect of this broader political significance was that individual census returns were used as the basis for drawing up lists of those to be deported after the war: i.e. not just those who were known to have been members of the *Volksbund der Deutschen in Ungarn* (Association of Ethnic Germans in Hungary), many of whom had joined the SS, but also those who had declared German nationality in the census. Ms B. and Ms H. participate in the same community of memory, but their constructions of the present draw on this group membership in quite different ways. For Ms B. the handeddown memory of the consequences of declaring German nationality in 1941 is still so powerful that it has not been expunged by the collapse of the context that would have made this minority allegiance potentially dangerous. However, Ms H. clearly detaches the painful experiences of the past from the present, and the changed status of the German language plays an important part in this process.

Furthermore, as Ms F. implies, this reformulation of the relationship between 'the German language' and 'German-speakers' is closely linked to the contrast between the local German dialects (the traditional mother tongue and the speech form generally associated with Hungarian–German ethnicity) and standard German (which is seen as a second language and as the prerequisite for access to the international German-speaking community):

> 3 (The speaker spent most of her pre-Kindergarten years with her maternal grandparents, who spoke only German dialect; her mother is bilingual, her father is a monolingual Hungarian speaker:) That led to complications in the family, so my mother decided that we should learn Hungarian at home. (She now speaks only Hungarian with her mother:) Because she's ashamed of speaking German to me ever since I've been learning standard German, because she's just afraid to. She speaks to me in dialect, but then I can't reply in dialect, and that bothers her, and so she switches straight away into standard German. She can do it, she tries to, but she doesn't stick to the dialect. [. . .] My grandparents don't even speak dialect to each other any more, because Hungarian is much easier for them, because in all their public dealings they only use Hungarian. [. . .] (Her younger sister never spoke German dialect with their grandparents, but is learning (standard) German now:) She's making the effort now, because she wants to go to Germany. She does understand quite a lot, but not because my grandparents spoke German to her, but through television. She watches the satellite programmes a lot, so it's got nothing to do with the minority. [. . .] I'm encouraged to speak German, even with my parents, because they want to learn German. My father's 50 now but he's beginning to learn German and he's taking it really seriously. [Ms F., Pécs]

Within this family there are at least two sets of oppositions in terms of the relative evaluations of languages: between Hungarian and German dialect, and between German dialect and standard German. Both of these oppositions illustrate, as Gal puts it, 'the classic form of hegemony': in each case, one language variety (Hungarian in the former, standard German in the latter) is 'felt to be authoritative even by those who don't know it or fully control it' (Gal 1993: 353). Furthermore, this complex and dynamic pattern of attitudes and practices within a single family shows very clearly what remains invisible when the relationship between language and ethnicity is reduced to general trends. It is precisely this degree of detail that is essential in any serious assessment of the ethnolinguistic vitality of a minority community.

Czech Republic

As with the Hungarian–Germans, the expulsion of the majority of the German-speaking population from Czechoslovakia after the war remains the decisive historical event in the collective memory of the Czech population as far as the relations between German and Czech speakers is concerned. German-speakers of the middle and older generations are often defensive in this respect, and stress the suffering and injustice they experienced after the war. For example:

> 4 (The speaker's mother converted to speaking Czech to her after the war:) You see, my mother was desperately afraid that a moment might come when someone comes and takes her to a camp. It was a terrible time. [. . .] I wasn't allowed to do the Matura [school-leaving certificate, qualification for university entrance.] Not just because I was a German, but because we lived in our own apartment house, and a caretaker wrote to my school that we were bourgeois, that we were enemies of the working class, and I wasn't allowed to do the Matura [Mrs M., Prague; born 1933].

However, here too the underlying pervasive bitterness and resentment between the two 'communities' have to be set against the many specific differences between individual biographies. Some younger informants, for example, are conscious of living through their own phase of an inherited conflict:

> 5 My father only told me I was of German origin 3 years ago, because he didn't want me to have problems. Because he wasn't able to study at university, for instance, because he was a German. [...] My grandfather died in the concentration camp, but as a German. My grandmother was able to stay here and she hated the Germans. [Interviewer: Was she a Czech?] No, a German, too. And she didn't want my father to learn German, because the conditions were bad for people here, and she wasn't sure, perhaps my father would emigrate. [. . .] I live in a very communist village, and 10 years ago my father built a very beautiful house , and then a lot of anonymous letters came, saying he had been in the Hitler Youth, but he was 4 years old at the end of the war. [Mr P., Prague; born 1974]

But while some dogmatically and defiantly assert their German ethnicity:

> 6 (Interviewer: When did your family come to Czechoslovakia?) The family comes from Czechoslovakia, because this country doesn't belong just to the Czechs, but to *us* too. [. . .] We live in Czechoslovakia, but we feel we are members of the German people. [Ms K., Prague; born 1958]

others are evolving hybrid identities:

7 I don't know myself how I should feel. If someone asks me whether I'm a German or a Czech, I can't give an exact answer. [. . .] If you say: 'I feel like a German', then people would say: 'Well, go to Germany then.' [. . .] I am a German from Bohemia. [Mr P., Prague, born 1974]

Ms K., whose parents were of the generation that grew up during the Second World War, implicitly acknowledges her Czech *citizenship* while explicitly distancing herself from 'the Czechs' by asserting her right to declare herself a member of the German *nation*. Mr P., on the other hand, who was a teenager in 1989, is much less secure in his ethnicity and is still trying to position himself. In this process of relocation, language choice can play a significant part, and for some German-speakers the regular, conscious use of German constitutes what Le Page and Tabouret-Keller (1985) call an 'act of identity':

8 (The speaker has recently begun to speak German to her mother again:) The reason for that was really this German friend who comes from Berlin, and that I returned to my German identity, so to speak. That had such an effect on me that I now speak almost exclusively in German with my mother. [Ms H., Prague; born 1962]

As Jiri Nekvapil (2000; see also Nekvapil 1997b) shows, the relationship between language and ethnicity is clearly a salient issue for ethnic Germans in the Czech Republic and they frequently address it in his interviews without necessarily being prompted to. He also argues that while the relationship between 'ethnic category X' and 'language x' is not necessarily self-evident, it is typically considered to be so. This can have serious consequences for those whose ethnicity is not (for them) language-based (see also extract 5 above):[2]

9 And after the war, when they were searching who collaborated, they found that my father wrote into the census documents 'Czech nationality' and 'German mother tongue', and this was a hundred percent truth, but with those after-the-war supercommunists that was a fault indeed, because how could a Czech have the German mother tongue, you know? [Mr S., Liberec]

This declaration was clearly seen as a violation of an axiomatic relationship between language and ethnicity, and as a subversive act. The firm popular belief in the necessary association

2. Extracts 9–11 are adapted from Nekvapil (2000). I am using the English versions of the interview extracts given there (the originals were mostly in Czech) but, as with my own data, I have used a greatly simplified transcription method in order to facilitate reading by those unfamiliar with the procedures of conversation analysis.

between language and ethnicity is reinforced by the reported behaviour of opportunists whose ethnicity was not fixed but contingent upon circumstances:

> 10 Nowadays there are those again that claim German nationality towards, you see, Federal Germany. Or some relations who were Germans for a while, then Czech for a while, depending on where the wind was blowing. In 1938 they were Czech, they might have been partly of German origin, the grandmother and so on, then the border country was occupied after the Munich treaty, right, and from then on they were super-German. They served in the Army, they were SA, and so on, and then in 1945 they turned Czech again and took an active part in the national committees and so on, when an old lady came and asked if they could interpret and so on, right, they could not, they did not know how to. [Mr B., Novy Bor]

The presupposition underlying the question 'how could a Czech have the German mother tongue?' is that 'Germans speak German' and 'Czechs speak Czech', but clearly the converse appears to apply too – use of 'language x' necessarily implies membership of 'ethnic category X', and in extreme cases this can result in the choice of silence:

> 11 (*Interviewer*: How did it work with those bands,[3] when did you have to wear them?) We should have worn them all the time, but when we were running around at home you wouldn't wear them. But when you went out shopping, then we simply had to put them on, if you didn't you got a fine. You see, you must understand, just as the Jews had to wear stars during the war, you see, so we wore bands after the war. Everyone knew, and well but we took it off sometimes too, when we much wanted to for the cinema, because if you're fourteen, fifteen then you might feel like going to the cinema, don't you, so we took it off sometimes too, and we just wouldn't talk and went to the cinema. [Mrs H., Krkonose Mountain region]

Today, of course, the language ecology of the Czech Republic and the whole of Central and Eastern Europe is completely different from the post-war period, and German enjoys a very high social value through its substantial market share in terms of communication in international trade in the region. However, the indigenous German-speaking population remains highly marginalised. A command of German (i.e. standard German) as a second language brings status and enhanced prospects on the job market, but to declare German as your

---

3. For a short period immediately after the Second World War, Germans in Czechoslovakia were required to wear armbands bearing the letter N (for Nemec, the Czech word for German).

mother tongue is still considered politically suspect. An essential distinction is therefore drawn between the instrumental value of German as an international language and the affective or symbolic value of German as a marker of ethnicity:

> 12 In the Czech Republic there are now 50,000 people with German nationality. They're mainly the older generation. But the younger generation now, these bank managers, from various . . . this Skoda–Volkswagen Group. The younger generation without, you might say, the tradition from the old days, is coming and bringing the German language. And also the reason for people to learn German [Mr G., Prague; born 1948].

Mr G. is careful to confine his attribution of German ethnicity amongst the indigenous population to the older generation, to which he does not himself belong, and reinforces this by identifying a younger generation with German ethnicity but which apparently consists of non-Czechs. These young, socially mobile outsiders are not weighed down with the baggage of the past ('the tradition from the old days'), and if one of the special gifts they bring with them is the German language this is somehow different from the German language that is already there: and above all they supply a motivation for learning German, which the aim of sustaining a local German ethnicity does not. The long process of assimilation (or 're-ethnicisation' of 'Germans' as 'Czechs') is probably too far advanced to be arrested by the instrumental revaluation of the German language. Nevertheless, it could be argued that the relationship between German and Czech has been recontextualised under radically changed social and political conditions in much the same way as the relationship between German and Hungarian. From being a native symbol of resistance to the dominance of the state language, German has been rebranded as a valued import associated with inward investment and therefore with individual prosperity and social mobility.

Conclusions

Language is a crucial factor in the processes of political and economic globalisation, and even within the regional context of European markets the ever increasing hegemonic dominance of English appears to be attested by, amongst other things, the English-only policies for executives of German companies such as Siemens. However, the German government in particular continues vigorously to promote the export of the German language, especially in Central and Eastern Europe, where it is far from conceding defeat to English (see Ammon 1991, chapter 13). At the same time, German industry is investing heavily in this region, both in terms of capital and human resources. The presence of the German language in Eastern Europe therefore appears to be secure for the foreseeable future, and its value in terms of cultural capital has clearly been greatly enhanced in the 1990s. However, there is no direct relationship between this value and the status of the German-speaking minorities in countries like Hungary and the Czech Republic. Their members may, of course, profit economically from their ability to operate in German in the job market, but this advantage is not peculiar to them, and there is no evidence that the prestige attached to the German language will bring any collateral benefit for the promotion of German ethnicity amongst the indigenous populations.

A number of factors strongly suggest greater prospects for the revitalisation of the German minority in Hungary than of their counterpart in the Czech Republic. The principal ones are the more deeply embedded cultural ties with Germany, and, more especially, with Austria, the greater number of German-speakers, the geographically more concentrated German-speaking population, and the constitutional recognition of the rights of ethnic and national minorities. However, my main aim in this chapter was not to calibrate the vitality of these minority groups, but rather to show how members of ethnically, geographically, socially and politically marginalised German-speaking communities in Central Europe are relocating themselves under the changed social circumstances post-1990, particularly in relation to others, whether these be the dominant population of the state in which they live or that of another state in whose cultural heritage they believe they have a stake. In this sense, while the cataclysmic events in the aftermath of the Second World War had a devastating and probably irreversible effect on the status and validity of the German language as an indigenous ethnic and cultural marker in these countries, and on the internal coherence and integrity of their 'German-speaking communities', these same events and their consequences constitute a crucial component in the formation of 'communities of memory'. However, the shaping of these communities is not a homogenising process: as I have tried to show in this chapter, it is necessary to explore individual narratives, and the relationships between them, in order to construct a coherent account of the different ways in which the process of reconfiguring identities is taking place.

References

Ammon, U., *Die internationale Stellung der deutschen Sprache*, Berlin, New York, 1991.

Beneke, J., "Am Anfang wollten wir zueinander . . .' – Was wollen wir heute? Sprachlich-kommunikative Reflexionen Jugendlicher aus dem Ost- und Westteil Berlins zu einem bewegenden Zeitthema', in *Wer spricht das wahre Deutsch?*, eds Ruth Reiher and Rüdiger Läzer, Berlin, 1993, pp. 210–38.

Coulmas, F., *Sprache und Staat*, Berlin, New York, 1985.

—— 'Germanness: language and nation', in *The German Language and the Real World*, revised edn, ed. Patrick Stevenson, Oxford, 1997, pp. 55–68.

Fix, U., 'Die Sicht der Betroffenen: Beobachtungen zum Kommunikationswandel in den neuen Bundesländern', in *Der Deutschunterricht* 1997, pp. 34–41.

—— '*ERKLÄREN* und *RECHTFERTIGEN*: Die Darstellung der eigenen sprachlich-kommunikativen Vergangenheit in Interviews', in *Deutsche Sprache* 2/97, pp. 187–94.

Földes, C., 'Überlegungen zur Problematik der Identität bei den Ungarndeutschen', in *Germanistische Mitteilungen* 35/1992, pp. 93–106.

Gal, S., 'Codeswitching and consciousness in the European periphery', in *American Ethnologist* 14(1987)4, pp. 637–53.

—— 'Diversity and contestation in linguistic ideologies: German-speakers in Hungary', *Language and Society* 22/1993, pp. 337–59.

—— 'Cultural bases of language use amongst German-speakers in Hungary', in *International Journal of the Sociology of Language* 111/1995, pp. 93–102.

Goebl, H., Nelde, P., Stary, Z., and Wölck, W. (eds), *Kontaktlinguistik*, vol. 2, Berlin, New York, 1997.

Haugen, E., *The Ecology of Language*, Stanford, 1972.

Le Page, R. and Tabouret-Keller, A., *Acts of Identity*, Cambridge, 1985.

Mar-Molinero, C., 'Linguistic nationalism and minority language groups in the "new" Europe', *Journal of Multilingual and Multicultural Development* 15(1994)4, pp. 319–28.

Ministry of Foreign Affairs, *National and Ethnic Minorities in Hungary*, Budapest, 1991.

Mühlhäusler, P., *Linguistic Ecology: Language change and linguistic imperialism in the Pacific region*, London, 1996.

Nekvapil, J., 'Tschechien', in *Kontaktlinguistik/Contact Linguistics/Linguistique de contact*, vol. 2, eds. Hans Goebl, Peter Nelde, Zdenek Stary and Wolfgang Wölck, Berlin, New York, 1997, pp. 1641–9.

—— 'Die kommunikative Überwindung der tschechisch-deutschen Polarisation: Deutsche, deutsche Kollegen, Expatriates und andere soziale Kategorien im Automobilwerk Skoda', in *Sprache, Wirtschaft, Kultur,* eds. Steffen Höhne and Marek Nekula, München, 1997, pp. 127–45.

— 'On non-self-evident relationships between language and ethnicity: how Germans do not speak German, and Czechs do not speak Czech', *Multilingua* 19(2000) 1–2, pp. 37–53.

— and Neustupny, J., 'Linguistic communities in the Czech Republic', in *Linguistic Minorities in Central and Eastern Europe*, eds Christina Bratt Paulston and Don Peckham, Clevedon, 1998.

Stevenson, P., 'The German language and the construction of national identities', in *Das unsichtbare Band der Sprache*, eds. John Flood, Paul Salmon, Olive Sayce and Christopher Wells, Stuttgart, 1993, pp. 333–56.

— 'The dynamics of linguistic and cultural identification in the central margins of Europe', *Sociolinguistica* 11/1997, pp. 192–203.

CHAPTER 8

Bilingualism among Ethnic Germans in Hungary

Peter Hans Nelde

Compared to standards in many other countries, such as Finland, Sweden, Belgium, Luxembourg, or Canada, bilingualism in Hungarian schools for students with a language other than Hungarian as their mother tongue hardly exists. Oversimplifying the situation of the German minority, one could say that all bilingual classes from kindergarten to university are in fact monolingually Hungarian with German as a second language.

Background

Hungarians with German as their mother tongue live principally in six linguistically defined territories in various Hungarian *komitats* (Hungarian administrative unit). With around 200,000 German-speakers, this minority is numerically the strongest in the country. Apart from ethnic Germans, Hungary is also a host-country to Croat, Serb, Slovene, Slovak, Romanian, and Roma minorities, many of whom live in border-regions adjacent to their mother countries. Balanced and favourable minority legislation was put in place after 1990 to allow these minorities and their members to preserve and develop their cultures and languages.

Concern about the fate of the several million strong Hungarian diaspora in neighbouring countries like Serbia, Croatia,

Slovenia, Austria, the Czech and Slovak Republics, Ukraine, the Russian Federation, and Romania has strongly sensitised the Hungarian state towards a fair treatment of its own minorities, not least since this can be seen as a precondition for ensuring a favourable attitude of the neighbouring countries towards the Hungarian diaspora. Similar to Western Europe, Hungary has thus discovered the cultural wealth of its minority populations – a wealth on which it also hopes to capitalise economically and politically by bridging the gap to neighbouring states via the promotion of minority languages and cultures. German, as the most important minority language, thereby plays a special role which is not only defined with an eye towards the future but also has important historical components, all of which explains the increased interest the authorities in Hungary display vis-à-vis German and the Germans.

First Example: Instead of Field Research

There are hardly any German-speaking media in Hungary. The German paper *Neue Zeitung* has only a small circulation; there are only a couple of hours of German broadcasts per week on the radio; and on TV, Studio Fünfkirchen/Pécs has half an hour every two weeks and extremely limited funds. In addition, no larger town in Hungary is German-speaking. Thus, in the early 1990s, when the country was in the midst of transition after its velvet revolution, the only way to gather information on the preservation and change of patterns of language use among the German minority was to conduct interviews in those villages in which a majority still speaks German. For a preliminary investigation, the villages Tscholnok/Czolnok near Budapest and Schomberg/Somberek near Fünfkirchen/Pécs were chosen.[1] The following are the results of this preliminary investigation.

Both villages, which are considered German-speaking, are in

1. Both villages are well-suited for a comparison. Although different local varieties are spoken, the number of German-speakers is about equal, both contain a relatively large number of consciously German-speaking families, and both are roughly equidistant from the next major town (Budapest and Fünfkirchen/Pécs, respectively).

fact bilingual as there are monolingual Hungarians alongside Hungarians of German origin, who speak Hungarian and German.

The degree of bilingualism differs from generation to generation. While Hungarian language capabilities are relatively poor among the oldest generation, the reverse is the case for the youngest, who very often have nothing but a few German idioms.

The knowledge of German among the middle generation, especially among the younger members, is mainly passive so that, in view of the domestic and educational encouragement of parts of the young to speak German, a generation break becomes obvious. At best, the middle generation uses German at home, but it does not play any significant part in their professional lives anymore.

As almost everywhere in a predominantly rural environment, the mother tongue is primarily used in a local dialect. This way, German (dialect) is no longer competing with (standard) Hungarian. Rather, it has become some kind of complementary language diglossia to emphasise particularity and distinction in contact with speakers of another language.

Because of a past in which persecutions and forced resettlements threatened the very existence of the German minority in Hungary, a systematic survey of ethnic Germans in Hungary is hardly possible today. Similar to East Belgium and the eastern part of France, the German minority in Hungary suffers from a collective neurosis (Quix 1981: 231) and has not yet been able to overcome the post-war repression of its cultural and linguistic life.

Individual interviews with 'privileged' witnesses, such as businessmen, engineers, or foremen, allow a less pessimistic picture to be painted of the linguistic functions the German language still serves. These interviewees benefited from their knowledge of German. Typical statements testifying to this were: 'I have to travel abroad on a regular basis to collect machines because I speak German.' 'I am responsible for the translations of operation manuals, which in our company are almost exclusively in German.' 'I am travelling a lot on business, which gives me many advantages. But German was a precondition for this job.'[2]

2. All quotes were recorded in Tscholnok/Csolnok.

Bilingual signs to emphasise the German character of a village, such as on house walls or shop windows, very often have a prestige function only. Enquiries regularly revealed that the *Dentist* or *Fleischer* spoke only Hungarian and were mostly ethnic Hungarians rather than ethnic Germans.

Second Example: Bilingualism at School

Formerly, so-called nationality classes existed, in which students were taught in their native language. These have been gradually replaced or complemented over the years by 'bilingual' classes. According to Hungarian school statistics of the 1980s, between 200 and 300 kindergartens, primary, and secondary schools educated more than 30,000 youngsters in Hungarian and German (Szende 1987: 28). In addition, there are three sixth form colleges/highschools in Budapest, Frankenstadt/Baja, and Fünfkirchen/Pécs in which German is also used as a language of instruction in two subjects. These quantitative data, however, are not very indicative of the situation at large. Teachers very often are not of ethnic German origin, nor do they have German as their mother tongue. The schools usually exist in places where German is not or not any more the medium of everyday communication. Students at these schools often do not have German as their mother tongue. Since 1989/1990, German has had to compete with other western languages, such as English and French, and has in some instances lost its leading position.

This places all those involved – teachers, parents, and students alike – in a difficult dilemma, namely whether to teach it as a first or second language. What is more, the distance between the very different local varieties and standard German is hardly likely to pass unnoticed in the way classes are conducted. For the majority of the 'Magyarised' students, this is, however, hardly a relevant problem.

To summarise, it has to be concluded that there are nowhere continuous classes from pre-school to high school level in which members of the German minority can enjoy instruction in German only, while there are a number of schools which use German as the language of instruction in selected subjects.

Third Example: German as First Language in the Schools of Raab–Ödenburg/Györ–Sopron and Eisenburg/Vas

In order to exemplify and validate these general observations, two of the *komitats* with local education authorities for German kindergartens and primary schools were selected for a more qualitative study. Because of its geographical proximity to Austria and the historically based bilingualism of its two major towns – Raab/Györ and Güns/Köszeg –, the *komitat* of Raab-Ödenburg/Györ-Sopron could have been assumed to provide favourable conditions for bilingual education. In addition, the *komitat* Eisenburg/Vas in western Hungary was chosen, which is also inhabited by members of the Croat and Slovene minorities.

For a better understanding of the school situation 'on the ground', I will first provide some examples from the post-1990 period. The school inspectorates in the west Hungarian *komitat* obviously have little contact with sixth form colleges with German classes because there are no special local authorities for the German minority. Thus, these classes are run directly by the Ministry of Education or the *komitat* institute. Members of the local education authority responsible usually do not belong to the German minority, nor are they requested to speak German.

Teaching conditions in the individual villages differ greatly and depend strongly on whether or not there is a German-speaking minority in the village at all. Therefore, it is difficult to compare even neighbouring villages to each other.

At two pre-schools (Agendorf/Agfalva and Wandorf/Bán-falva) and at three primary schools (Agendorf/Agfalva, Brennberg/Brennbergbánya, and Wandorf/Bánfalva) in the *komitat* of Raab-Ödenburg/Györ-Sopron, German has to be taught as the first language. While the percentage of German-speakers in Agendorf/Agfalva is around 25 percent,[3] it is about twice as much in Wandorf/Bánfalva. Because of the administrative incorporation into Ödenburg/Sopron, monolingual

3. All percentage figures quoted are estimates stemming from observation and need socio-linguistic verification. They are merely given as orientation. (I am extremely grateful to Mrs. Marti Siluou who – as an expert on bilingual schools in western Hungary – provided me with the necessary local data. P.N.)

Hungarian students from there are allowed to participate in the German classes in Wandorf/Bánfalva. Therefore, the percentage of native German students has decreased to under 20 percent.

A much more encouraging example is the border village of Brennberg/Brennbergbánya, one of the most German villages in the whole of Hungary. Here it is still possible to hear students speaking German during break, so that the few native Hungarian-speakers have to accommodate to this, thus ensuring an almost completely monolingual German environment. Because of small numbers of native German-speakers among students, and the merger of classes with native Hungarian-speakers later on in their educational career, this initial advantage is certain to be lost again.

In the *komitat* of Eisenburg/Vas native German classes are offered at two pre-schools (Großdorf/Vaskeresztes and Pernau/Pornóapáti) and at five primary schools (Güns/ Köszeg, Oberschilding/Felsöcsatár, Oberzemming/ Felsöszölnök, Raab-fidisch/Rábafüzes, and Roggendorf/ Kiszidány). However, none of these villages are predominantly German, nor is the teacher who teaches pupils German as their first language a native speaker of German. The ethno-linguistic composition of the areas from which the schools draw their students reveals anything but the picture of a linguistically favourable set of conditions for native German classes. Only two of the villages have a strong or medium-strong German majority – Großdorf/Vaskeresztes with 80 percent German-speakers and Pernau/Pornóapáti with 53 percent. Here, however, only pre-schools exist so that students later on have to go to schools drawing from ethnolinguistically more heterogeneous areas with a smaller German share in the total number of students. Thus, to the linguistic contact between German and Hungarian, contact with Slovenian and Croatian is added. The village of Roggendorf/Kiszidány is predominantly Croatian (about 70 percent) and has a regional primary school, which is attended by 18 percent of students from the neighbouring Deutsch-Roggendorf/Kiszidány, who expect to be taught and learn German as a first language at a minority school in a Croatian village, where the language of instruction is Hungarian.

Similarly confusing is the situation in the predominantly Croatian Oberschilding/Felsöcsatár with its 65 percent Croatian majority. However, here the German-speaking students benefit from the enlarged area from which the school draws its students, as the villages of Großdorf/Vaskeresztes and Pernau/Pornóapáti with their German majorities alter the ethnolinguistic structure of the classes in favour of native German-speakers.

Closer to the Slovenian border, the share of ethnic Slovenes increases to up to 70 percent in Oberzemming/Felsöszölnök. Moreover, in this border region between Hungary, Slovenia, and Austria there is a relatively high proportion of Roma, too. There and in Sankt Gotthard/Szentgotthárd ethnic German students from the surrounding villages come into contact with the Slovenian language.

Less colourful, but therefore more problematic is the situation in Güns/Köszeg, where native Hungarians are taught German as a first language. The formerly German community Schwabendorf/Köszegfalva has long become part of the larger town and the percentage of ethnic Germans has decreased to just a few percent so that these classes are actually no longer visited by native speakers of German. This example, however, demonstrates the good will of the otherwise rather inflexible school authorities. Yet at the same time, it makes obvious the difficulties students and their parents face when they actively wish to express their membership in a minority community. It is, therefore, hardly surprising that many ethnic German parents are afraid their children could be overwhelmed in such minority classes and would be unable to enjoy the full benefits of social upward mobility in a monolingual and monocultural society. Thus, many parents voluntarily let the opportunity pass to have their children educated multilingually.

Last Example: A Comparison

Although the above is merely a preliminary investigation limited to a small number of issues of a complex matter without sufficient empirical evidence to generalise, some concluding remarks are nevertheless possible.

The German minority in Hungary has participated in the construction of the state and the political and administrative process, thus historically enjoying equal status with the majority population. The consequences of the Third Reich have left deep marks on the ethnic group which are impossible to overcome within only a few generations. The majority of ethnic Germans work in the agricultural sector. The percentage of members living in urban environments is small and more likely to be assimilated linguistically. Today the German minority participates actively in the regional and national political process in Hungary. Generally prepared to integrate, the members of the minority enjoy their rights in a modest way and without exaggerated ethnic self-confidence. Upward social mobility requires full command of the majority language so that the younger (urban) generation increasingly replaces German with Hungarian as their first language. The mother tongue is usually not standard German but some local variety of it. As a consequence of this, ethnic Germans do not have an easy time in learning German at school, while simultaneously the focus on standard German at schools makes it more difficult for members of the Hungarian majority to communicate with members of the German minority in their mother tongue. Legally, the culture and language of the German minority are protected to an exemplary degree, in practice, however, not all good legislative intentions are realised. Full integration into Hungarian society and bilingualism in fact depend on the (native-like) command of Hungarian and only secondarily on the occasional use of German. If this is not to lead into a monolingual Hungarian society over the next few generations, the everyday use of German must be intensified and the number of areas in which it can be sensibly used as a means of communication must be increased. In a country dependent on international trade like Hungary, there is obviously a market for German which could be more easily served by ethnic Germans with a native command of the language than by Hungarians who have to acquire it as a second language in a costly and time-consuming process.

As the example of Belgium highlights, the survival of a minority language when confronted with a stronger majority language can only be secured when three areas are exclusive domains of the minority language – local administration, education, and work place (Nelde 1987: 143–15). Even if this seems rather illusory right now for ethnic Germans in Hungary, awareness of alternative concepts of bilingualism is necessary. If German is downgraded to domestic use only, it becomes a merely folkloristic asset and loses its potential for economic and cultural bridge-building in Europe.

References

Nelde, P.H., 'Bilingualism in Western Europe: An Approach toward Investigating Unprotected Minorities', in *Aspects of Multilingualism*, eds. E. Wanda et al., Uppsala, 1987, pp. 143–52.

Quix, M.P., 'Altbelgien-Nord', in *Kulturelle und sprachliche Minderheiten in Europa*, ed. P. S. Ureland, Tübingen, 1997.

Szende, B. (1987), 'Das Bildungs- und Erziehungswesen der Ungarndeutschen', Globus 1/1987, pp. 3–7.

CHAPTER 9

Ethnic Germans in Romania

Richard Wagner

Historical Background

In 1990, the first year after the end of Ceaucescu's dictatorship, one hundred and ten thousand ethnic Germans from Romania left the country for their ancestral home Germany. Although on a considerably smaller scale, this emigration continues until the present day. In Romania itself, about 50,000 ethnic Germans are left – a far cry from the 800,000 members of the German minority in the 1930s or even the approximately 400,000 Germans living in Romania in the immediate post-war period. The fact that emigration, in contrast to the period prior to the end of the Second World War, increased so dramatically over the past five decades, has its reasons in the political developments after 1945 and their long-term consequences.

Before the First World War, ethnic Germans from Romania went to America as labour migrants. They intended to make enough money to secure for themselves and their families a livelihood in Romania and regarded their regions – the Banat and Transylvania – as their *Heimat* to which they returned once enough money had been saved. For them, it was not citizenship that counted, but regional affiliation and ethnic belonging, which, in turn, was firmly rooted in the region in which they had been living for generations. In the 1920s and 1930s, the young went to German universities and also returned home, bringing with them the 'ways of the mother country', including national socialist ideology.

The ethnic German population of Romania consisted, and still consists, of two large groups – Transylvanian Saxons and the Banat Swabians. Until 1919, they did not have a common history, and it was only the territorial reorganisation of the wider region after the collapse of the Habsburg Empire that assigned their settlement areas to the newly created Romanian state. This required the two groups to constitute themselves as a new entity as well as to establish themselves in the political spectrum of inter-war Romania. National socialism became an influential player and found willing advocates and followers among the ethnic Germans who were well aware of their national affiliations that distinguished them from their fellow countrymen.

The involvement of the ethnic Germans in Romania in the crimes of national socialism was particularly strong, but is, until today, considered a taboo by the minority itself. Even though recruitment to SS units unquestionably came about under pressure from the traditional village community, the high number of recruits remains an equally indisputable fact. Despite them not being German citizens, the leadership of the ethnic German community in Romania staged their own recruiting shows, such as the *Tausend-Mann-Aktion* in 1940. In 1943, an agreement between Hitler and the Romanian dictator Antonescu regulated the transfer of ethnic Germans from Romanian to German army units. The German community itself developed its internal structures throughout the Antonescu dictatorship, eventually became a 'state' within the Romanian state, and conducted the policing and political monitoring of minority members.

This significantly affected the fate of the group in the immediate post-war period. About half of the ethnic Germans had fled with the withdrawing German army and did not return to Romania once the war had ended. Those who had stayed were, in contrast to, for example, Poland or Czechoslovakia, not expelled, but faced the even grimmer reality of deportation to forced labour camps in the Soviet Union and the confiscation of all their property and land. While the principle of collective guilt and collective punishment dominated official Romanian policy in the first years after the end of the war, in the 1950s, ethnic Germans saw the gradual restoration of their status as an acknowledged minority.

Ceaucescu and the Ethnic Germans of Romania

In the 1960s, the general euphoria of the early years of Ceaucescu's 'national communism' in Romanian society had a positive impact on the situation of minorities as well. Ethnic Germans were allowed to revive their ethnic and cultural traditions, and their cultural institutions, schools, and media also benefited from the process of de-Stalinisation. Yet, the resulting hope was short-lived.

Soon afterwards, Ceaucescu began to establish his 'family dictatorship' and carried through with his programme of forced industrialisation that eventually led to the economic collapse of Romania. In order to stay in power, Ceaucescu increasingly played the nationalist card, and this inevitably had adverse consequences for ethnic minorities. The issue of bilingual place names, which had been banned from the late 1970s on, is just one of many anti-minority policies the regime used to hold on to its power.

Hungry for money, Ceauscescu exploited the desire of ethnic Germans in his country to migrate to the Federal Republic when, in 1978, he concluded an agreement with the then federal chancellor Schmidt to allow the emigration of 12,200 people annually for the initial price of 8,000 Deutschmarks each, payable by the German government. A well-organised emigration bureaucracy extorted further sums of money from those intending to leave. The rapid deterioration of the economic and political situation in Romania in the 1980s, the famine, the plan to eliminate traditional rural structures by way of 'systematisation', the growing nationalism of the Romanian public, and the fear of harassment by the Securitate secret police made emigration to Germany an increasingly attractive option for an ever greater number of ethnic Germans in Romania.

The toppling of the Ceaucescu regime in 1989 came too late to prevent the mass exodus of the German minority. The emigration process had already left its mark on the group – urban and rural communities of the minority had been dissolved, the infrastructure of the minority, which continued to exist, lacked the essential staff to be run properly, and in most German-speaking schools, more Romanian children were registered than German ones.

The German Minority after the End of Communism

The peculiarity of the Romanian situation, in contrast to, for example, Poland, Hungary, or then Czechoslovakia, was that the mass movement that had overthrown the Ceaucescu regime remained without any organised structures or leadership. Thus, it became marginalised very soon, while inside the communist apparatus a palace revolt took place inspired by reform communists around Ion Iliescu, who exploited the developing power vacuum for their own purposes. The initial popular opposition movement took several more years before it developed political structures and could become a serious contender for power in the still fragile process of democratisation.

Obviously, this situation did not promote any real confidence in substantial changes in Romanian society that would have given the German minority an encouraging perspective in the country. Rather, the common perception among minority members in 1990 was that a window of opportunity had been opened that should be used as quickly as possible, because nobody could foresee how long it would remain open. In addition to this general uncertainty, Romanian nationalism, already existing under Ceaucescu, began to flourish in post-communist Romania. Extreme nationalist organisations like *Vatra Romanescu* (Romanian Home) and *Romania Mare* (Greater Romania) were formed. Tensions between the Hungarian minority and Romanian nationalists in Neumarkt/Tirgu Mures in Transylvania erupted in violence. In the summer of 1990, the post-communist government shipped busloads of miners to the capital to 'deal with' the extra-parliamentary democratic opposition that had established a permanent protest camp in the university square. Thus, there were sufficient reasons to leave the country, not only for ethnic Germans, but also for members of the Hungarian minority who migrated to their mother country and for 'ordinary' Romanians as well, many of whom left for Western Europe seeking political asylum.

At the same time, the remaining members of the German community in Romania made efforts to reorganise themselves under these new conditions. They formed their own interest group, the Democratic Forum of Germans in Romania, which has become active not only in the territories traditionally inhabited by the German minority, i.e., the Banat and Transylvania, but also in places where smaller numbers of ethnic Germans have come to live as a result of internal migration over the past decades. The dispersion of the German community throughout Romania, however, has also resulted in a further weakening of the minority, as it now no longer has a political and/or cultural centre. The various organisations represented in the Democratic Forum deal with a variety of issues affecting the minority, including the distribution of aid from the German and Austrian governments.

Politically, the Democratic Forum has never been a homogeneous organisation. As most political ideologies relevant in contemporary Romania are in one way or another represented in the Forum, the organisation had to focus its activities on matters important to the ethnic community of Germans as a whole. Participation in Forum activities by far exceeds the number of ethnic Germans left in Romania. This is a result of the privileged position ethnic Germans have acquired over the last two decades. In the eighties, they received packages from friends and relatives in West Germany and had a very real chance of emigration. While packages sent from Germany continue to play a part in their social standing in the 1990s, a more valuable benefit of being a member of the German minority is probably the less restrictive visa regulations for travel to Germany. Thus, the common perception that being German means to be privileged, has led to a surprising increase in the number of people who registered their nationality in the last census as German to about 120,000. However, the registration of one's nationality is a voluntary act and there is no burden of proof on the part of the individual.

Despite this increase in membership, the German minority has become too small for the Democratic Forum to play any politically significant role. Without any real chance of winning a seat in elections to any one of the two chambers of the Romanian parliament, the German community, alongside other small minorities like the Ukrainians, Serbs, Roma, Armenians, Bulgarians, Turks, and Poles, benefits from a regulation in the Romanian constitution that guarantees ethnic minorities at least one seat in parliament. This, however, does not necessarily increase the political power of any of these minorities; rather, they must be wary not to be used as a figleaf for other deficits in Romanian minority policy. This danger has long become a reality, as the Romanian political scene is dominated by the conflict between the Hungarian political parties, which represent a minority with almost two million members, and the major Romanian parties. Even after the election victory of the democratic opposition in 1996 and the participation of ethnic Hungarians in the governing coalition, this situation has not fundamentally changed. The Hungarian–Romanian confrontation provides the arena for everything that is relevant for minority policy. Smaller minorities, if they are considered at all, become mere objects of manipulation and power politics. Only recently, the Romanian parties suggested, in the context of the restoration of the Hungarian-speaking University in Transylvania, that a multicultural university be established instead – a pitiful attempt to disguise a fundamental anti-Hungarian attitude by instrumentalising the presence of other ethnic groups in the country.

Just as the ethnic Germans who decided to stay in Romania founded their own organisation to deal with cultural, economic, and existential problems of the minority, those who left the country and settled in Germany have had their representative organisations throughout the post-war period. These so-called *Landsmannschaften* representing the interests of their members from the various German settlements all across Central and Eastern Europe are organised in Germany in the *Bund der Vertriebenen*, the Association of Expellees. Since the collapse of communism in Romania, the *Siebenbürger* and *the Banater Landsmannschaft* can act officially in the country, and the main focus of their activity is humanitarian in nature, providing support for cultural activities and care for the over-aged population of ethnic Germans in Romania. In Temeswar/Timisoara in the Banat, for example, the *Adam-Müller-Guttenbrunn-Haus*, a combination of cultural centre and care facility for the elderly, has been financed. In a joint effort with the German federal government, schemes for the establishment of small businesses were funded. For example, agricultural projects in which Germans and Romanians work together were supplied with credits for the purchase of equipment and grains. These efforts, however, can only bring partial relief in a chaotic economic situation in Romania. Partly caused by the heritage of the Ceaucescu dictatorship, but partly also due to the delay of essential economic reforms in much of the first half of the 1990s, the economic crisis has caused widespread poverty, especially among the older generations, and thus particularly affects the ageing German minority.

Culturally, German schools and German-speaking media continue to exist and are, for the most part, funded by the Romanian government. The schools have gradually become inter-cultural institutions in which mostly Romanian children learn German. The media – newspapers, daily radio and weekly television broadcasts – satisfy primarily the remaining ethnic Germans' demand for entertainment.

An important aspect in the relationship between minority and state, the deportation to the ex-Soviet Union and the forced resettlement of farmers from the Banat to the Baragan, has recently been treated in public with care and sensitivity. Documentation about the fate of those affected has been published, and former deportees to the Soviet Union have formed their own interest group.

Outlook

Viewed from the present day, the cultural and economic importance of the German minority in Romania lies in the past. Decades of emigration have deprived the minority of its potential to constantly renew itself, and to maintain an environment in Romania that would be favourable to the preservation and development of its distinct ethno-cultural identity. Ironically, with the necessary political will and legislative provisions in place for the first time since the demise of the Habsburg Empire, the overwhelming majority of the once flourishing ethnic German community has decided to seek a future in a 'homeland' only few of them have seen before emigration. There will probably be ethnic Germans in Romania for a long time, yet they will not be able to play a significant role in Romanian society similar to that before the Second World War.

References

Baier, H., ed., *Rußland-Deportierte erinnern sich. Schicksale Volksdeutscher aus Rumänien 1945–56*, Bukarest, 1992.

Schieder, T., *Das Schicksal der Deutschen in Rumänien*, Munich, 1984.

Sterbling, A., 'Die Deutschen in Rumänien zwischen Tradition und Moderne. Aspekte sozialer Mobilisierung nach dem Zweiten Weltkrieg', in *Minderheiten in Südosteuropa*, ed. Gerhard Seewann, Munich, 1992.

Wagner, R., *Sonderweg Rumänien. Bericht aus einem Entwicklungsland*, Berlin, 1991.

Zach, C.R., 'Totalitäre Bewegungen in der Zwischenkriegszeit: Rumänen und Deutsche in Rumänien', in *Rumänien im Brennpunkt*, ed. Krista Zach, Munich, 1998.

CHAPTER 10

The Unfortunate Minority Group: Yugoslavia's Banat Germans

Željko Šević[1]

Two million Danube Germans (*Donauschwaben*) have contributed to the history and development of the Danube region since the twelfth century, when the first German settlers arrived in the territories of today's Hungary and Romania. The Germans arrived much later in the Vojvodina (Northern Serbia), in the eighteenth century. In particular, they influenced the development of the Banat, a geographic region which is now divided between Yugoslavia and Romania. Today, Banat Germans are living predominantly in Romania, but a far larger number of them used to live in Yugoslavia's Banat. Banat Germans (*Banater Schwaben*) were the ethnic group which, at the time, made up almost half of the Vojvodina's population. On the eve of the Second World War, over half a million Germans were living there. Some sources state their exact number as 509,350 people (Weber, 1994).

In this chapter the rise and the fall of the German ethnic group in the Vojvodina will be analysed, i.e., the ethnic German population in the territories of the former Socialist Federative Republic of Yugoslavia and the now smaller Federal Republic of Yugoslavia. In the course of only one century the number of Germans living there decreased over 130 times, as a result of the many conflicts and crises the Balkans have experienced during the twentieth century.

Apart from published material, documents held in a number of Yugoslav archives and private collections have been analysed, and structured interviews with members of the German Club 'Donau' in Novi Sad were conducted for this study which consists of four parts – the settlement process of Germans in the Vojvodina from the eighteenth century until the First World War, the position of the German ethnic group in the inter-war period, developments during the Second World War, immediately after it, and until the 1970s, and, finally, the current position of the small German diaspora still living there.

Arrival of Germans in the Vojvodina and Developments Prior to the First World War

Germans reached Vojvodina during the wars with the Turks in the eighteenth century, but only a very small number of them remained there because the borders were constantly changing.[2] The first group of Germans, as far as accessible records go back, came to Pancevo and Zemun in 1717, and consisted of veterans, civil servants, soldiers, and craftsmen and other professionals supporting the army (Jankulov 1961). According to some other sources (Popović 1957), the first group of Germans reached Vojvodina in 1702, and settled in Varadin, a small town below the Petrovaradin fortress, now a borough of Novi Sad. In 1716 they established a small and exclusively German settlement outside the town itself.[3]

---

1. The author is very grateful to Dragan Gačić, Deputy Director of the Yugoslav Federal Archives in Belgrade, to historians Dr Gojko Malović (Yugoslav Federal Archives, Belgrade) and Zoran Janjušević (Institute for Contemporary History of Serbia, Belgrade), to Professor Milan Rešcánski, former Director of Education in Kikinda, to Mag. Aleksandar Šević (Economics Institute, Belgrade), to Edit Andrek, and to the members of the German Club 'Donau', especially to Andreas Bürgermayer, president of the Club, and to Mag. Gerhard Burbach.
2. It was not the first encounter of Serbs with the Germans. During the rule of the Serbian medieval king, Uroš (mentioned in Dante's *Decameron*) in the thirteenth century, the Saxons were the only miners in Serbia, and at the time Serbia had very developed mining. However, the traces of those immigrants were lost soon after Serbia was occupied by the Ottoman Turks in the fourteenth century. In Serbian and Turkish medieval documents the members of German communities were referred to as '*Saxones*' or '*Sassi*' (Jireček 1953: 256).
3. Those settlers who came to Zemun established a separate village called the '*Deutsche Stadt*'. Germans in Pančevo organised a settlement outside the city and named it '*Deutsche Pacsova*' (Popović 1957: 39).

Within two years, between 1723 and 1724, organised colonisation of Vojvodina by Germans began. Reports suggest that there were ten to twelve thousand of them, settling mainly in the cities. These first colonists were offered fairly poor accommodation and hardly any facilities necessary for a decent life. Later, the Habsburg monarchy changed its strategy and German settlers in Vojvodina were offered many facilities and privileges.

The German settlers were favoured over both the 'old' population and 'newcomers' from other nationalities. They were exempted from providing the necessary accommodation for the Army, and many other duties. If they were farmers, they were spared paying all taxes and fees for a period of ten years. If they were craftsmen, this tax-free period was extended by another five years. Together with some of the German groups, Spanish, Italians and French settlers arrived in Vojvodina. Alsatian French were settled in St Hubert, Soltour and Charleville. Today all these villages form Banatsko Veliko Selo.[4] However, all these groups were subjected to Germanisation and lost their national identity fairly soon after they arrived (Mitrović, 1982). Therefore, in the nineteenth century there was a strong Germanised population scattered all over Vojvodina and mixed with other nations: Serbs, Hungarians, Romanians, Slovaks, etc. While Germans in Srem and the Bačka were subjected to the feudal regime, Germans in the Banat never had feudal lords. Banat Germans were farmers and craftsmen, and the Habsburg monarchy provided them with the necessary security and economic assistance, so that their activities could flourish.

The situation radically changed *de facto* in 1867 with the Austro–Hungarian Agreement, and *de jure* in 1870 when the *Vojna Krajina* was abandoned. Vojvodina became an integral part of the Hungarian segment of the *dual* monarchy. Magyarisation became an official policy that was enforced by the now Hungarian-dominated public administration. The Germans ceased to be a favoured nation and were specifically targeted by the Hungarians in their attempts to assimilate other

---

4. According to the names that can be found in the churches' birth registers of the mid- to late-eighteenth century in the Velika Kikinda district, most of the Alsatian settlers were in fact French (their native language was French), but fairly soon they were Germanised. As early as the beginning of the nineteenth century, the Germanisation process was fully completed.

nationalities in Vojvodina. The fact that the Vojvodina's Germans were mostly Catholics, who shared churches with Hungarians, helped this assimilation process. Church services at the end of the nineteenth century were mainly in Hungarian. Facing the same threat of assimilation and feeling that they would share the same destiny, the Germans and Serbs started to co-operate.

According to documents available in the Yugoslav Federal Archives, the Vojvodina Germans became politically active in 1848. That year the Banat Germans held a Conference in Bogaroš and petitioned the Vienna Court to grant the Banat the status of an autonomous county. The Count who would have been the head of the Banat County would have had jurisdiction over all Danube Germans. This desire for autonomy was not satisfied. Some fifty years later, the Germans began to organise themselves politically on a more formal basis. In 1906 the Banat branch of the German People's Party in Hungary (*Ungarländischdeutsche Volkspartei*), was formed. However, the party was not particularly successful in the general elections in 1910 (Fanko, 1944; Biber, 1966).

There were a number of newspapers in the Banat, despite attempts from the Hungarian central and regional authorities to impede public activities of non-Hungarian ethnic groups. The Germans alternatively organised themselves in many 'economic associations', credit unions, co-operatives, etc. The beginning of the twentieth century was marked by the German national awakening. This has been credited to an almost forgotten German writer in the Banat, Adam Müller-Guttenbrunn, who, through his works, novels, and pamphlets, launched and promoted the idea of the German spirit 'under oppressive Hungarian rule' (Sepp, 1944: 44).

Towards the end of the First World War, deputies of the Danube Germans came together in Timisoara at a conference and demanded self-determination. Following Wilson's Fourteen Points, the Germans formulated a declaration requesting the inception of the 'Republic of the Banat.' However, the proposal passed unnoticed. Austria and Germany as defeated powers could not sponsor the idea, while the Alliance was not interested in solving the problems of the Danube Germans. The geographical area of the Banat was divided between the Kingdom of Serbs, Croats and Slovenes (from 1929 on, the Kingdom of Yugoslavia), Hungary, and Romania. As a consequence, the German population found itself in three, newly formed countries – Hungary, Yugoslavia, Romania.

Germans in Yugoslavia Between the Two World Wars, 1918–1941

In 1921, the newly created Kingdom of Serbs, Croats and Slovenes had 12,017,323 citizens of which 513,412 (or 4.21 percent) declared German to be their mother tongue. The largest number of Germans lived in the Banat, the Bačka and Baranja – 328,173; Slavonia and Srem – 122,836, and Slovenia – 38,631. There was also a small group of Germans in Bosnia (near Banja Luka) and in the Belgrade District (Biber, 1966). The new Yugoslav authorities did not have a special policy towards the German national group. In Vojvodina, where Germans together with Serbs had been subjected to Hungarian assimilation attempts in the late nineteenth and early twentieth centuries, the authorities looked at Germans favourably, wanting to attract them to the idea of a new country with equal opportunities for all citizens, regardless of nationality, race, religion, etc. In contrast, in Croatia and Slovenia the situation was different. Germans were seen as sporadic remnants of a past, in which they had been proponents of Germanisation. Needless to say, the new authorities in Croatia and Slovenia largely overreacted. All German societies, associations, and institutions were dissolved, property confiscated, and later given to similar Croatian and Slovene organisations free of charge (Biber, 1966). In professional and charitable organisations, in which Germans performed management functions, special commissioners were appointed (Biber, 1966). A similar policy was applied in Slavonia (now part of Croatia) and Srem. Local councillors in villages and cities with a German majority were replaced, and civil servants of German origin were dismissed at all levels without proper reason or explanation.

While mistreated in the newly established states, Germans in Vojvodina managed to capitalise on the positive attitude of the Yugoslav/Serbian authorities. They established their schools, newspapers and journals, and a wide range of German societies (*Dokumentation*, 1961). The German Economic and Cultural Society (*Deutscher Wirtschafts- und Kulturverein*) was incorporated in 1919 in Bečkerek (today Zrenjanin). In the same year, the German–Swabian Club (*Deutsch–Schwäbischer Klub*) was established in Novi Sad (*Neusatz*), the capital of Vojvodina. The German Club opened a printing office and incorporated a publishing house. In the autumn of 1919, the German daily *Deutsches Volksblatt* (German People's Newspaper) was launched and a big specialised German bookshop opened in Novi Sad (Biber, 1966). Following their success at the regional level, the Germans, thanks to their good relations with the Radical Party,[5] obtained permission to set up a national German organisation. The Swabian–German Cultural Union (*Schwäbisch–Deutscher Kulturbund*), an educational and charitable organisation was organised in June 1920 in Novi Sad. However, in 1924 the police authorities obtained proof that *Kulturbund* activities were not merely cultural and educational, but politically sensitive and revoked its licence. Although it was formally renewed only in 1927, the local organisations kept working, as local authorities were not particularly interested in enforcing the ban. However, the *Kulturbund* was forbidden again in 1929 when King Aleksandar I proclaimed his dictatorship and banned activities of all political, national and ethnic organisations (Šević and Rabrenović, 1999). In 1931 the Ministry of Internal Affairs reinstated the *Kulturbund* as a legal entity, but proscribed new rules. Now, many special sections were organised within the *Kulturbund*, including the Association of German Sport Societies (*Verband deutscher Sportvereine*), the Association of German Youth Groups (*Verband deutscher Jugendgruppen*), the German Association of Women (*Deutscher Frauenverband*), and the Association of German Medical Doctors (*Deutscher Ärtzteverband*).

Quite early in the inter-war period, Germans organised themselves politically. In December 1922, the Party of Germans in the Kingdom of Serbs, Croats and Slovenes (*Partei der Deutschen des Königreiches der Serben, Kroaten and Slovenen*) was founded. The party's main programme item was to introduce a special Constitutional Law that would formally regulate the

---

5. The Radical Party was one of the main political parties in the Kingdom of Serbs, Croats and Slovenes, especially until 1926, that is, until the death of its long-standing leader Nikola Pašić, regarded by many modern historians as the best Serbian politician ever, who led Serbia, as a prime minister, through the First World War and the relatively harmonious creation of the new Kingdom of Serbs, Croats and Slovenes.

position of Germans in the Kingdom, allowing them to open schools and to use their native language freely. In 1923 the Party won eight seats in the lower house of the national parliament (43,415 votes), in 1925 five (45,172 votes), and in 1927 six (49,849 votes). Usually two Germans were amongst the Senators in the upper house (Biber, 1966).

Germans paid particular attention to information and education activities. Apart from the daily *Deutsches Volksblatt*, which was published in 25,000 copies, there were thirty-five other publications in German, including four daily newspapers, eighteen weekly, three bi-weekly and seven monthly reviews, and three occasional journals (Biber, 1966: 40). The editorial policy was mainly neutral and moderate, so there was no conflict with the Yugoslav authorities which practised censorship, as a means of action against 'communist, chauvinist and other anti-popular propaganda' (Šević and Rabrenović, 1999). The Germans were also interested in establishing a credible educational system in German. The Yugoslav authorities pursued a very benevolent policy toward the German minority in Vojvodina, where the largest number of Germans lived. Therefore, they were allowed to organise their own schools, which Germans could not even do in Hungary before 1919 despite the supreme authority of the Habsburg monarchy. The system was developed for a number of years after the first formal act had confirmed the right to create German schools in 1922. That year the Royal Minister of Education and Religious Affairs issued a Decree ordering the creation of classes with teaching in German in all settlements that had more than thirty pupils of German nationality. In 1929, a law was passed which regulated education in German.[6] Parents could choose in which language their child would be educated. In German schools, all the subjects were taught in German, except history and geography in the fifth and sixth grades, which were taught in Serbo–Croatian. The government also ordered the establishment of a German Teacher-Training College, for which the teaching staff came from Germany. The college was established in Beckerek and in 1933 moved to Vrbas (*Dokumentation*, 1961: 26E). The Yugoslav Ministry of Education did not report the data on the number of classes taught in the Kingdom, but a survey published in 1932 suggests that there were

6. Cf. Yugoslav Federal Archives, holdings of the Royal Ministry of Education and Religious Affairs.

209 German schools, 790 classes with 41,069 pupils. Some 730 teachers taught in German (Biber, 1966).

Yugoslav Germans were mainly farmers and craftsmen with only some 15,000 people being employed in the industrial sector. Co-operatives played a very important part in the economic rise of the German minority. The biggest and most important co-operative was 'Agraria', established in Novi Sad in 1922. The co-operatives had a *de facto* monopoly on trade with Germany, and were generously supported by credits on favourable conditions from German financial institutions. In 1927, the Credit department of the 'Agraria' was transformed into a credit union, the Central Agricultural Credit Institution (*Landwirtschaftliche Zentral-Darlehens-Kasse*). It later initiated the incorporation of the Association of German Co-operatives (*Verband deutscher Kredit- und Wirtschaftsgenossenschaften*), which had 364 member organisations on the eve of the Second World War. Although Germans made up only a quarter of the population of the Vojvodina at the time, they controlled almost 50 percent of the Vojvodina's economy before the Second World War (Fanko, 1944). Mills and brickyards were under the complete control of Germans, while 80 percent of the Vojvodina's export products originated from companies and farms owned by the Germans (Fanko, 1944).

Unfortunately, from the mid-1930s, Nazi influence on the Yugoslav Germans was notable and permanently rising. A number of the Banat Germans supported the ideas launched by an organisation originally started in Romania – the 'National-Socialist Renewal Movement of Germans in Romania' (*Nationalsozialistische Erneuerungsbewegung der Deutschen in Rumänien*). In 1934, the Renewal Movement (*Erneuerungsbewegung*) was organised within the *Kulturbund*. However, until 1939 the German Nazi government did not encourage the separatist and nationalist ideas of the Yugoslav Germans (Biber, 1966). After the inauguration of the Cvetkovic government this policy changed. Chauvinist activities were encouraged and supported, members of the German minority were secretly armed and trained in Germany for sabotage actions, and the spynetwork 'Jupiter' was organised and supervised by the German *Abwehr*. Formal control over those illegal actions was exercised by a 'police attaché' at the German Embassy in Belgrade. In 1939, the organisation of *Kulturbund* was transformed according to the 'Führer' principle. Dr Sepp Janko was appointed as National Leader of the ethnic German population in Yugoslavia.

War and Post-War Developments: Grief and Retaliation

In the Second World War, Yugoslav Germans played an important role in organising and sustaining the German occupational regime in different parts of Yugoslavia. The situation in the Banat was fairly specific, as that region was under direct German rule, although formally the local governments in the Banat were under the control of the Serbian puppet government led by General Nedic. In mid 1941, the Banat's authorities proposed the expulsion of more than 50,000 Serbs from the region, but the German government objected, being aware that those people, if forced to Serbia as refugees, would certainly support the Communist Partisan movement. Simultaneously, an idea to create the Free State of Banat (*Freistaat Banat*) emerged, but was rejected again. This time Heydrich objected, authorising the local Gestapo 'to arrest proponents if necessary' (Wüscht, 1968). Since Yugoslavia was partitioned amongst Germany and its allies, the Germans in the Banat and Serbia became a new national group, while Germans in the independent state of Croatia, and Slovenia had their own 'national leaders'. During 1941 the Jewish population in the Banat was eliminated. Jews were either killed or sent to concentration camps to be exterminated. Jewish property was confiscated and usually distributed to the local Germans. In Croatia, there were reportedly conflicts between local German and Croatian authorities over the distribution of confiscated property. A number of Germans joined 'attack groups' (*Deutsche Mannschaften*), which had already existed before the Second World War in the guise of the German Sport Groups (*Deutsche Sportmannschaft*) (*Dokumentation*, 1961: 47E). During the war, a large number of Germans joined the newly formed SS-division 'Prince Eugen', which was created mainly from Banat Germans. During the war, several 'transit' concentration camps were set up in the Vojvodina. Labour camps were formed separately, but the mortality rate in both camps was very similar. In the Banat, local power was exercised by the resident German population with the regular German Army, and civilian authorities merely performing a supplementary role.

It is estimated that about 93,450 Yugoslav Germans actively participated in the Second World War as soldiers in either *Wehrmacht* or SS, that is 18.6 percent of all Germans according to a census of 1931. However, a vast majority of them supported the German army economically through different programmes. The support charge was set at 60 Reichsmark per head, including children (Janko, 1944).

Because of Germany's difficult political and military situation in 1943, the idea to organise the return of the Vojvodina's Germans to Germany emerged for the first time. Many senior SS officials, however, objected, and preparations for the evacuation began only in the summer of 1944. When the Red Army entered the Banat on 1 October 1944, it cut off the area from still German-held territories, thus making evacuation no longer possible. A couple of days later the evacuation from the Bačka began. On 10 October 1944, the Reich's Ministry of Foreign Affairs confirmed that 215,000 Yugoslav Germans could be admitted to, and accommodated in, the Reich. There were four convoys, the main one being more than 20 km long. The remaining Bačka Germans were included in an additional quota of 254,000 Germans from South-East Europe at the end of October 1944. When the Partisans entered the Bačka there were around 70,000 Germans left there. The new government allowed them to emigrate to Germany to join their families. The Partisan units had significant problems in taking over the Bačka, as it was defended by the 31st Grenadier SS-division, which included more than 17,000 soldiers who had lived in the Bačka before the beginning of the war. By that time, Germans from Croatia and Bosnia had already been evacuated in large numbers. The Germans in Slovenia were in the worst position as they were left on their own to organise evacuation, primarily because they were close to Austria and could get there within a few hours. Resistance to evacuation has not been recorded in either Yugoslav or German sources. Although it is usually claimed by German historians (*Dokumentation*, 1961) that Yugoslav Germans were banished from Yugoslavia forcefully, this was not the case. The majority of them left willingly, with the German Army towards the Reich. The flyer from 1944 signed by the *Volksgruppenführer*, Dr Sepp Janko, invited Germans to leave temporarily for Germany.[7] The German belief that evacuation was only temporary, could explain some of their behaviour (no resistance, large number of evacuees, etc.).

In a situation where the vast majority of Germans had left Yugoslavia, the Presidency of AVNOJ (Parliament) enacted the 'Decision on Transfer of Property of Non-present Persons and Sequestration of the Property Forcefully Taken by the Occupying Authorities'. By this decision all the property of the Third Reich and its citizens on Yugoslav territories became state property. The Decision included the property of war criminals, collaborators, and persons of German nationality, except those who had been members of the People's Liberation Army.

In legal terms, this was a rather ambiguous decision, which could, and was, very easily interpreted broadly. The decision *de facto* also covered the families of German soldiers who sent parcels to the front, thus 'supporting the occupier's war efforts'. In retrospect, this decision was simply a legal framework for the retaliation policy very widely advocated amongst the Allies at the time.

In late 1944, the Soviet Red Army entered Vojvodina and the first arrests of Germans began. People who had served in local authorities during the occupation were arrested along with prominent members of the *Kulturbund.* There were many cases of retaliation against the German minority. The Soviets were very brutal, particularly some special NKVD units that were freely roaming Vojvodina in late 1944 and early 1945. The newly established local government was involved in examining Germans and determining their guilt. They were assisted by OZNA (Department for the Protection of People), Tito's secret police. The Soviets chose many able-bodied Germans and deported them to forced labour camps in the Soviet Union, mainly in the Ukraine. The data on this are inconclusive. Historians speak about 30,000, while some survivors claim that at least 60,000 Germans were forcefully deported to the USSR. The survivors also claim that there was an agreement between the new Yugoslav authorities and the USSR on deportation of Yugoslav Germans to the USSR, but proper historical sources cannot be found to substantiate these claims. Men between 17 and 45, and women between 18 and 40 were

---

7. The originals of the documents can be found in the Archive of the City of Vršac and Vršac City Museum.

sent to the USSR on the same trains that took Jews to Germany. On the way there, many of the deportees died.

In October 1944 it was decided to isolate the remaining Yugoslav Germans in detention camps, similar to those organised in the US for Japanese nationals. It is very hard to establish the exact number of those camps. According to some sources there were more than forty camps of different types. Some of them were labour, others 'collection' camps. Some survivors claim that there were also hospital and children's camps (Magyar Szó, 1998). The camps were established in deserted German villages. Camps in Knićani, Bački Jarak and Gakovo had high mortality rates. It is assumed that ten to fifteen thousand people died in the camps. The precise number cannot be established, as the Yugoslav authorities treated Germans as foreign nationals, and were not interested in determining their exact numbers.[8]

Based on the appropriation decision, 637,939 hectares of land were taken from the ethnic German population. In the whole of Yugoslavia 1,500,000 hectares were confiscated, of which 59.7 percent belonged to Germans. Germans from Slovenia were expelled to Serbia and put in detention camps in the Vojvodina. According to survivors, all the Slovenian (Kočevo) Germans were forced to leave or were killed without trace.

However, the biggest problem on the ground was the lack of a clearly defined policy. Local commanders were free to impose even stricter rules. Particularly unfortunate for the German minority was that the Partisan units which were in the Vojvodina were the Fifth Krajina and Sixth Lička ka Proletarians Brigades, who came from the territories where Germans (especially the Seventh SS-division 'Prince Eugen') had committed many atrocities against the local civilian population. Full of grief and hatred, the soldiers often retaliated against detained Germans.

It is difficult to establish a correct number of losses amongst Yugoslav Germans. There are some estimations that 85,399 Yugoslav Germans lost their lives, 26,064 as Nazi soldiers and 59,335 as civilians. German estimates from the 1960s state that 48,447 died in the detention camps, 8,049 were killed

---

8. Based on the interviews conducted with the members of the German Club 'Donau' in Spring 1998 and conversation with Professor Reščanski in summer 1998.

immediately after the partisans entered the Vojvodina, while 2,599 died on the way to the Soviet Union in 1944/45.

It is very hard to understand the destiny of the Yugoslav Germans from today's perspective. The winners in the Second World War, Tito's partisans, retaliated not only against Germans, but also against all those who did not support their political programme. While the Germans were sent to the detention camps, non-communist-orientated Serbs were enlisted to the Army, and sent with little or no military training to fight the German Army in Srem at the end of 1944 and beginning of 1945, suffering huge losses. It is difficult to establish whether Tito's regime had a well-defined policy towards the 'German problem'. Evidently, the regime, as all the other communist governments, used public animosity towards Germans immediately after the Second World War, to sequester property and profit. The Germans were just one of many enemies of the 'people's rule', and as such they were subjected to organised state persecution. The suffering of Germans in Tito's socialist Yugoslavia immediately after the Second World War was the result of the clash with a totalitarian regime, rather than a conflict with the Yugoslav nations, particularly the Serbs. Many of the old Banat Serbs would even now praise their former German neighbours, especially for their punctuality and tidiness.

The Current Status of the German Minority

The detention camps were operated in Tito's socialist Yugoslavia between late 1944 and 1948. However, some survivors claim that they were allowed to leave camps only as late as 1953. The problem for the people who were liberated from the camps was that they had nowhere to go. Since they were in the camps, their property was (technically) abandoned. Thus, AVNOJ's sequestration decision was applied and their land and property confiscated in many cases. Some of them left Yugoslavia and went to Germany, while others remained in Yugoslavia and tried to build a new life. Highly qualified technicians were working in factories and were not sent to camps at all. According to some estimates, over 70,000 Germans consciously decided to become assimilated. Some 50,000 declared themselves as Hungarians, 10,000 as Croats,

Table 4:   The German-speaking Population in Yugoslavia, 1910-1991

Census year	1910	1921	1948	1961	1981	1991
Germans	323,918	335,898	321,821	11,423	3,808	3,873
Austrians	–	–	–	48	88	–

Source: Federal Office of Statistics

6,000 as Serbs, and some 3,000 as Slovaks (Magyar Szó, 1998). This is evident from the large increase in the Hungarian population in many post-1945 censuses. But again, the number of people who emigrated to Germany as Germans, making use of Article 116 of the German Basic Law, surpassed the total number of declared Germans in Yugoslavia, from which one can conclude that many declared themselves Germans only when they left Yugoslavia.[9]

Currently in the Federal Republic of Yugoslavia (Serbia and Montenegro) around 4,000 people declare themselves as Germans. After the breakup of the Socialist Federal Republic of Yugoslavia, small German minorities live in Slovenia (785 people) and Croatia (less than 500). In other former Yugoslav republics Germans cannot be regarded as a distinctive ethnic group. Changes in number of members of the German minority can be seen in the table above.[10] Interestingly enough, there were two results for the 1981 census – 3,808 persons declared themselves Germans, while only 1,878 stated that German was their mother tongue.

Many Germans left Yugoslavia, particularly in the 1960s, with other Yugoslav economic emigrants who were heading to Germany in large numbers. This was particularly the case for people who were highly educated and trained, and, at the time, in their twenties and thirties. According to personal statements of ethnic German emigrants, in the vast majority of cases they were very well received in Germany and given opportunities to integrate in their ancestral homeland.[11]

9. Based on interviews conducted with the members of the Deutsche Klub 'Donau' in spring and summer 1998 in Novi Sad.

10. Austrians were included as a separate group in the census in 1961 and 1981 on a Slovenian request, which wanted to segment the German national group in the Socialist Federative Republic of Yugoslavia. Most of the declared Austrians were living in Slovenia, and this way the total number of Germans living in Slovenia was administratively reduced.

11. Supra note 6.

Usually, *Aussiedler* from Yugoslavia distanced themselves from other people coming from Yugoslavia as guest-workers. There are two possible explanations. First, there was often a large education gap between these two groups. While the German returnees were usually well educated, other emigrants from Yugoslavia were, as a rule, unskilled labourers. But, there is also some evidence that German employers who were originally Yugoslav Germans preferred to employ Yugoslavians.[12] This is, however, very difficult to support as a general statement, since no systematic studies have been conducted on Yugoslav immigrants in Germany. Second, while the German 'returnees' came from the 'developed' parts of Yugoslavia (e.g., Vojvodina), the average Yugoslav economic emigrant came from the deprived areas in Bosnia, Croatia, or Kosovo. It has also been noticed that only some children would go to Germany, while others would stay with their parents in Yugoslavia. The older generation, as it may be expected, had been very reluctant to change their place of permanent residency. Family members who emigrated to Germany continued to support the family back in Yugoslavia.

A continuing problem with the status of the German minority was the lack of precise legal regulations, and continuous inconsistency in terms of official minority policy vis-à-vis the group. For instance, the Germans were deprived of their citizenship rights by laws enacted in 1945/46, but in the 1950s, with the liberalisation of the socialist regime in Yugoslavia, they could obtain, without any problem, a passport, which is a citizen's privilege. Also, from the 1950s onwards, Germans were regularly called to complete their national service, like any other citizen in Yugoslavia.

Problems emerged in the 1950s during the Trieste crisis, when some Germans refused to do their service in Slovenia,[11] and a wave of retribution was launched. While after 1948/49 the Germans were allowed to organise themselves in cultural associations and clubs, from 1953/54 that privilege was withdrawn. In Sombor, for example, there were special classes that were taught in German at primary and secondary school levels. During the Trieste crisis this practice was abandoned. The main problem in these cases was that neither the right to organise classes in German nor its subsequent cancellation were formally legalised. Simply, the local government allowed,

12. Ibid.

certainly with prior consent from the Republican Ministry of Education, German to be used as language of instruction in primary and secondary schools, and when the political situation changed, their attitude changed as well. In order to understand this situation it is necessary to know the basis of the classic socialist (read *Soviet*) legal system. The main sources of law were decisions of executive organs, and they were numerous but subject to politically motivated discretion. This is why a Soviet-like legal system can be simultaneously both over-regulated and causing legal insecurity.

After the Trieste crisis, many Yugoslav Germans fled the country, followed by a mass exodus in the 1960s. While there were sporadic cases of occasional German publications after 1948, from the mid-1950s they disappeared totally. As a dispersed, constantly diminishing ethnic group, Germans did not really try to organise themselves before the 1990s. Again, from the 1960s they were regarded as equal citizens, participated in the political process and civil society, and held public offices. They could join the army or police forces and became officers, mostly after the early 1980s, while prior to this it was very difficult to be admitted if anyone in the (larger) family had been a member of any other than partisan military units during the Second World War. There have been a number of officers, in both the police and army, who were Germans. But since socialist Yugoslavia applied a so-called national key for the senior positions, the Yugoslav nations (Croats, Macedonians, Montenegrins, Muslims, Serbs and Slovenes) and two major national minorities, Albanians and Hungarians, were the only ones who were normally appointed to the ranks of generals. It should be mentioned, however, that the officers of German origin were loyal to the country to which they swore an oath, before and after the Second World War. Some of them participated in the Yugoslav civil war (1991/92) as officers of, at that time, the Federal Yugoslav Army. Probably, the best example of German loyalty was Pavle Jurišic – Šturm, a General in the Serbian Royal Army, who commanded an army in the First World War. He was one of those prominent Serbian military commanders and national war heroes, who was involved in the defeat of the Austrian Army in 1914.

The recent German '*national awakening*' in Yugoslavia unfortunately coincided with the Yugoslav Civil War, and the breakup of the previous Yugoslav Federation. Official German government encouragement of Croatia's and Slovenia's secession in 1991 had negative repercussions for the public regard of the German minority in Yugoslavia. The Yugoslav public perceived German government actions as a new act against the Serbs, one of many in this century.[13] In this environment, the German Club 'Danube' (*Deutscher Klub 'Donau'*) was established in 1992 in Novi Sad, a city in which today 319 registered Germans live. In the six years of its activities so far, the Club succeeded in rising to over 500 members from all over the Vojvodina. It is registered with the Republican (Serbian) Ministry of Internal Affairs, as a cultural and educational charitable organisation. At this turbulent time, it also serves as a forum of Serbian–German friendship and cooperation, as many members, some one hundred of them, are not Germans at all.

The Club organises cultural events, has published a bulletin (*Die Nachrichten*) since 1995, and disseminates information about Germany. However, it seems somewhat marginalised by both Yugoslav and German authorities. From the day of its establishment, the Club had problems in finding an office for its headquarters. Currently, it operates from a private house on the outskirts of Novi Sad. Members come together twice a week, mainly to socialise. The intentional assimilation, practised or not in the past, contributed to the fact that most of the members are trilingual (German, Hungarian, and Serbo–Croatian), and not surprisingly some of them are more confident speaking Hungarian or Serbo–Croatian than German. The Club occasionally also publishes in German and has established very good relations with the Departments of German at the Universities of Belgrade and Novi Sad. Despite its remarkable achievements, some German sources present this organisation wrongly. In some German publications (Seewann and Dippold, 1997: 1064), the Club is mentioned under the name '*Duna*' ('Danube' in Hungarian), while its real name is '*Deutscher Klub Donau*'. Although this may suggest a strong Hungarian influence, the German identity of the members of the Club is beyond any doubt.

---

13. Private information obtained during field research conducted in spring and summer 1998 in the Vojvodina and Belgrade.

There is no political organisation of Yugoslav Germans. They belong to a broad range of political parties in Yugoslavia, but they do not usually hold publicly prominent positions. At the moment a German is sitting in an informal regional shadow cabinet in the Vojvodina, holding the portfolio of Urban Planning and Civil Engineering. Also, the secretary of the regional committee for the Banat of the Serbian Radical Party (led by the prominent nationalist Vojislav Šešelj), Gertrud Wagner, is a German. Even more interesting than the fact of her German ethnicity is to learn that a female occupies a senior position in a predominantly nationalist and openly patriarchal party.

With the settlement of the situation on the territories of the previous Yugoslavia, there should arise a possibility for both Serbs and Germans to redefine their relationship. Obviously, there is a need for both sides to apologise to one another for many mistakes, and for the pain and grief mutually inflicted on each other in the past. Recently, a number of books have been published on the history of the Banat Germans from a fairly unbiased perspective. However, there is still a lack of in-depth academic studies which would look at the common history issues in a more modern and policy-orientated way. Romantic, non-fiction, history-based novels, such as *One World on the Danube* (Stefanović 1996), can certainly contribute to better mutual understanding. The Yugoslav bi-weekly '*Duga*' has recently (1997/98) published a series of articles on the history of Danubian Germans, ranging from the Seventh SS-division 'Prince Eugen' to the exodus and suffering of Germans after the Second World War. It may be that chances have been missed in the past, but certainly there are more to come, as mutual influence has never been negligible.

The German identity of Yugoslavia's Germans has varied significantly over time. Sometimes it may mean support of the 'German Cause', while at another moment it may involve the full support and understanding for the country of their current citizenship. In interviews conducted with ethnic Germans in Yugoslavia, they perceived themselves as Germans (or part-Germans) when speaking about the relationship with the most numerous nation in the country (Serbs). However, when putting the Serbs (or the Yugoslavians in more generic terms) against other nations of the previous Socialist Federative Republic of Yugoslavia, they identified themselves with the Serbs (using the pronoun 'we').

Conclusion

Ethnic Germans played an important part in the history of the Vojvodina from the early eighteenth century to the end of the Second World War. In the nineteenth century, the German population faced many similar, if not identical, problems to the local Serbs, who had been living there for centuries, as both of them were subjected to Magyarisation. After the First World War Germans in Vojvodina had a more advantageous position compared to other minority groups. They had their primary and secondary schools, cultural and economic organisations, and newspapers. However, during the Nazi occupation between 1941 and 1945, mutual trust failed, as large numbers of Germans opted to become members of the SS. The Seventh SS-division 'Prince Eugen', which committed unimaginable atrocities in Bosnia during the *Schwarz* and *Weiss* operations in 1943, had been recruited predominantly from the Banat Germans. As a response to these actions, retaliation was common in 1944/45, and detention camps were in operation until 1948. After 1948 (Tito's break with Stalin) the situation slowly began to normalise. During and after the Trieste crisis in 1953, when some Germans objected to being sent to posts along the Yugoslav–Italian border, the situation reversed again. All the 'privileges' were revoked and, for a couple of years, ethnic Germans in Yugoslavia were deprived of their schools and organisations and of the right to use their mother tongue in public. Therefore, many of them fled the country in the mid-1950s. A later wave of emigration in the 1960s had mainly economic reasons.

Never officially deprived of their citizenship rights after 1946, Yugoslavia's Germans from time to time faced some social obstacles without an obvious reason. The government attitude towards them fluctuated directly with the political situation and the accompanying policy agendas. After the last large migration wave in the 1960s, a very small German group remained in Yugoslavia. Less than 4,000 people now declare themselves as Germans. However, if the criteria of Article 116 of the German Constitution were to be applied, the number of people who can claim to be Germans might rise to some ten to twelve thousand. A majority of them have declared themselves as Hungarians or Slovaks, and usually come from first- or second-generation mixed marriages (often a grandmother was German).

German culture also undoubtedly influenced to a great extent the organisation of social life in Yugoslavia. Modern social institutions in Serbia and later Yugoslavia are to a great extent fairly successful copies of their German counterparts. By and large, the Serbian Civil Service has historically been based on German values, and the concept of state is German-initiated as well (Sevic, 1998). This certainly contributes to the better overall understanding between the two nations.

Today, the German national community in Yugoslavia is small and dispersed. Since 1992, a German Club 'Danube' has been operating in Novi Sad. The Club is not only the main, but also a unique German organisation, which supports the preservation of the German language and culture and the mutual understanding amongst the different nationalities living in Vojvodina. The Club should also be commended for the revitalisation of German cultural events and organising the German ethnic community in Yugoslavia. It has also contributed to the fact that many of the people who had German ancestors are now returning to their roots and appreciating their family history.

After almost three centuries in Vojvodina, Yugoslavia's ethnic Germans preserved much of their German identity and national pride, probably even more than anyone in Germany might expect (cf. Seewann and Dippold, 1997). They mixed with many other nations, but they will proudly demonstrate their German heritage and ethnic origin, even if they have only a very small drop of German blood in their veins.

References

Biber, D., *Nacisem in Nemci v Jugoslaviji 1933–1941*, Ljubljana, 1966.

Dokumentation der Vertreibung der Deutschen aus Ost-Mitteleuropa – Das Schicksal der Deutschen in Jugoslawien, Düsseldorf, 1961.

Janko, S., *Reden und Aufsätze*, Bečkerek, 1944.

Jankulov, B., *Pregled kolonizacije Vojvodine u XVII i XIX veku*, Novi Sad, 1961.

Jireček, K., 'Trgovački puteri i rudnici Srbije i Bosne u srednjem vijeku', in *Zbprnik konstantina jirečeka*, Belgrade, 1953, pp. 205–301.

'A vajdasági németek második világháború utáni sorsa', in *Magyar Szó*, 15–21 March 1998.

Mitrović, M., 'Naseljavanje i kolonizacija Vojvodine 1690–1945', in *Godišnjak Društva istoričara Vojvodine za 1982. godinu*, 1982, pp. 195–97.

Popovic, D., *Srbi u Vojvodini*, 3 vol., Novi Sad, 1957–63.

Seewann, G., and Dippold, P., eds., *Bibliographisches Handbuch der ethnischen Gruppen Sudosteuropas*, 2 vol., München, 1997.

Šević, Ž., *Experts and Nation-State Building on the Balkans: Historical and Contemporary Perspectives*, Paper for the Schloßmann Seminar, Max Planck Institute, Berlin, 26–28 November 1998.

Šević, Ž., and Rabrenović, A., 'Yugoslav Civil Service: Tradition vs. Transition', in *Comparative Civil Service Systems*, ed. T. Verheijen, Aldershot, 1999.

Stefanović, N., *Jedan svet na Dunavu*, Belgrade, 1996.

Weber, K., *Leidensweg der Deutschen im kommunistischen Jugoslawien*, 4 vol., München, 1994.

Wüscht, J., *Beitrag zur Geschichte der Deutschen in Jugoslawien für den Zeitraum von 1934 bis 1944*, Kehla. Rh., 1966.

CHAPTER 11

Ethnic Germans in Russia and the Former Soviet Union

Gerd Stricker

German migration to Russia happened in several stages. As early as the sixteenth century, thousands of German craftsmen were invited to Russia, settling in Moscow's 'German suburb' and building their first Lutheran church here in 1576. Mass migration, however, only began 200 years later. Invitation manifestos by Katharina II in 1763 and Alexander I in 1804 guaranteed significant privileges – settlement as free farmers, free-of-charge land allocations, several tax-free years, no military service, German as the administrative language up to and including county level, German schools, and religious freedom. By 1769, about 23,000 colonists lived on the bank of the river Volga in an area of the size of today's Armenia; in the years between 1804 and 1856, some 100,000 settled on the coast of the Black Sea, while several thousand others moved on to the Caucasus. Among these 'Black Sea Germans', Mennonites accounted for about one-tenth. In the period between 1860 and 1880, about 170,000 Germans from the Russian and Prussian areas of Poland settled in Volynya. Between the turn of the century and the beginning of the First World War, the overpopulation of ethnic German villages triggered an emigration wave of about 100,000 German colonists to Siberia from the German settlements in the Volga and Black Sea regions. According to the 1897 census, the ethnic German minority with its 1.8 million members was the eighth strongest among Russia's one hundred nationalities.

Initially, German colonists were engaged in agricultural activities only, yet towards the end of the nineteenth century, when no more new land was available and when the existing farm land had been split too many times down the generations, they became leading in agricultural engineering and mill factories, but also turned successfully to textiles manufacturing and tobacco production.

German colonists had been allocated settlement areas according to religious criteria. Lutherans made up for 67 percent of all colonists in 1897, 4.7 percent were members of the Reformed Church, 18 percent were Catholic, and 8.3 percent Mennonites. There were only very few Baptists and Adventists. Together with Estonians and Latvians, the Lutherans formed the *Evangelisch-Lutherische Kirche in Russland* in 1832. In 1917, this church had about 3.2 million members, among them 1.1 million Germans including members of the Reformed Church. Its ministers were trained at the Faculty of Theology of the German University of Dorpat (Tartu), which had been founded in 1802. German Catholics (350,000 in 1897) had had their own diocese in Saratov since 1847, including a German bishop and a seminar for priests. Both the German Protestant and Catholic churches suffered from a permanent shortage of clerics, each of whom had to serve a number of villages simultaneously. Many Lutheran ministers could visit their villages only once a year. Although they were substituted by the school master during the rest of the time, laic movements developed that had a tense relationship with the official church (Stricker 1997: 324–78).

Every German village had its own school. Even though their level was not extremely high, it was well above that of neighbouring Russian and Ukrainian villages and had managed an 80 percent degree of literacy in German in the settlement area along the river Volga in 1914, the second highest in the Russian empire after St Petersburg, while the comparable degree of literacy among Russians was only 28.4 percent (German 1994: 74). For a long time, Russian officials had resisted the opening of German teacher-training institutions so that it was only around 1850 when a greater number of them were founded. The revoking of the German privileges in 1871 initiated a first wave of Russification, including attempts at introducing Russian as the teaching language in German villages. Because of a protests and lack of success, these attempts were stopped in 1907, and the years before the First World War saw a flourishing of educational facilities in the areas where ethnic Germans settled (Stricker 1997: 420–64).

Communism: From Revolution to Deportation

The Russian revolution of 1917 hit German colonists probably harder than their Russian neighbours – they were considered to be rich and consequently persecuted as Kulaks, their property being looted. According to Lenin's nationalities policy ('National in its form – bolshevist in its content'), the Autonomous Socialist Soviet Republic of the Volga Germans was founded 1924, along with a number of German rayons in Russia (6), Ukraine (11), Georgia (1), and Azerbaijan (1). However, with the beginning of forced collectivisation in 1928/9, these areas were systematically undermined in their national character, as Stalin equated nationalities policy with Russification (Brandes 1997: 152–61).

From the beginning of the Soviet Union, the German areas had lacked native German party members so that native Russian party functionaries and civil servants came to play an ever-increasing role. The Great Terror began there as early as 1934 – ethnic German party officials, civil servants, professors and teachers, although some of them at least nominally being communists, were purged; many of them were executed or died in forced labour camps. In 1939, the German rayons were abolished, i.e., Russian (even in the Ukraine) replaced German as the teaching and administrative language. Eventually, the German Volga Republic was officially dissolved on 28 August 1941.

The prior decline of the German settlement areas can be exemplified with developments in the educational system. The 'clerical-bourgeois school system' was destroyed, yet the reconstruction of an alternative was not successful in the Volga Republic, the degree of literacy sank to 38.6 percent in 1928 (German 1994: 74). Even though a new school system was being built in the 1930s, there was little success in German due to the mass arrests of German teachers (Stricker 1997: 465–81).

The German churches did not suffer as much from persecution as their Russian Orthodox counterparts in the 1920s.

However, with the Law on Religion of 1938, a systematic persecution of everything religious began, resulting in all of the 94 Catholic priests being arrested by 1928 and all of the 92 Lutheran ministers sharing this fate by 1937. All German churches were closed by 1938, thus forcing believers to go underground (Stricker 1997: 379-91).

Second-Class Citizens – Ethnic Germans during the Deportation Era

The German attack on the Soviet Union on 22 June 1941 provided Stalin with a reason to dissolve the Volga Republic and deport the entire German population of about one million people from the European to the Asian part of the Soviet Union by the end of 1941. Women between 16 and 45 and men between 15 and 55 were assigned to the 'Trudarmya' in forced labour camps (dissolved only in 1945/6), while the remaining elderly and children were confined for fifteen years to those areas in Siberia or Central Asia where they had been deported. The human casualties of deportation and forced labour camps by 1946 are generally estimated at 300,000 ethnic Germans (Hilkes/Stricker 1997: 221–31). From the beginning of the deportation, ethnic Germans were deprived of all their rights, most aspects of their lives from then on being determined by the local KGB office. In this situation, German schools and any form of religious life were impossible, as was attending institutions of higher education. Only after the situation had become a little more stable did ethnic Germans have access at least to Soviet/Russian schools and began secretly to organise an underground religious life.

In 1955, the Special Regime to which the ethnic Germans had been subjected was abandoned; in 1964 deportation was characterised as one of the terror acts committed by Stalin, and ethnic Germans were formally rehabilitated. Although these two steps brought certain minor improvements, such as free choice of occupation and area of residence, and access to higher education, ethnic Germans were continuously denied a return to their traditional areas of settlement in the European parts of the Soviet Union and the foundation of German schools. Legal provisions were made in 1957 for the institutionalisation of special German classes for ethnic Germans, three German newspapers were printed, and small-scale literary publication began. Yet all this resulted in anything but a tactical improvement, as headteachers prevented special German classes, newspapers were organs of communist propaganda, and literature was only printed in extremely small amounts (Hilkes/Stricker 1997: 221–49). Only since 1972 were ethnic Germans allowed to leave Soviet Asia and settle in the European parts of the USSR. Yet, thirty to thirty-five years after their deportation they found their villages ruined or occupied by Russians or Ukrainians. Only some 50,000 dared to return, most of them hiding the fact that they were ethnic Germans as their defamation as 'fascist' and 'traitors' continued.

The living conditions of ethnic Germans in Central Asia stabilised. In the 1980s, their economic situation was comparable to that of their Russian neighbours, and the deficits in education had been partly overcome by then as well. However, without some sort of autonomy status for ethnic Germans in the most important settlement areas in Western Siberia and Kazakhstan, developments of their ethnic German identity and linguistic capabilities were predictably bleak. At the latest, the third generation of those ethnic Germans who had never been exposed to German schooling or a German cultural environment, would become completely Russified in their language and mentality. As consecutive Soviet governments after 1964 refused to concede any form of territorial autonomy, these fears had become reality by the end of the 1980s – hardly anyone of the younger generation of ethnic Germans is now able to speak German (Hilkes/Stricker 1997: 239–48).

For a long time, (underground) Lutheran, Catholic, and Mennonite communities had provided facilities to speak German, especially after 1965 when religious persecution was eased, in particular for the Lutheran Church, of whose 500 communities about half had been legalised by 1986. This was in stark contrast to Roman Catholics, who had always been viewed with suspicion throughout the pre-perestroika period, resulting in only 16 communities having legal status in Soviet Asia in 1986. Yet even Lutherans were not allowed to have an umbrella organisation for its many communities before 1988. Eventually, the churches not only suffered from administrative and political pressures but also from linguistic problems. The more the younger generation stayed away from religious services because they could no longer follow linguistically, the clearer it became that there were only two alternatives – the introduction of Russian as church language or the isolation of the communities and their consequential decline (Stricker 1997: 408–16).

After the End of Communism

Similar to the ethnic Germans in Romania, the collapse of communism in Eastern Europe was welcomed by many Germans in Russia not so much as a departure point into a better future within their host-country, but rather as the long awaited opportunity to leave for their ancestral home – Germany. In the past hundred or so years, the wish to leave Russia has become more and more urgent as a consequence of the fundamental repressions the ethnic German community has lived through – the first wave of Russification between 1875 and 1906, the Russian Revolution of 1917 and the subsequent forced collectivisation, and eventually the deportation of the ethnic German minority from their traditional settlement areas, all of them apparently aimed at their annihilation as a minority through assimilation. All this resulted in the wish to (re)migrate to Germany becoming an integral part of the identity of the older and middle generation of ethnic Germans. After all attempts at reconstituting the Volga Republic had failed in the 1960s, the 1970s already saw a significant move of ethnic Germans from the Soviet Union to the Federal Republic of Germany, while in the 1980s ethnic Germans publicly expressed their wish to leave in (illegal) demonstrations at the Red Square in Moscow, which led to their immediate arrest.

Gorbachev's efforts to be seen by the West as a reformer and democrat were directed at all spheres of Soviet life, among them, of course, the nationalities problem. In order to secure the goodwill of the German government and massive foreign investment from German banks, Gorbachev initiated a reform of the emigration laws in 1989, which became the legal basis for the mass exodus of Russian Jews to Israel and of ethnic Germans to the Federal Republic.

While in the years between 1955 and 1986 only 104,000 ethnic Germans left the Soviet Union, between 1986 and 2000, 2.3 million people with an ethnic German background migrated to Germany, and it is estimated that one to two million others are still awaiting their immigration permit. These numbers may seem surprising if seen in connection with the 1989 census, in which only 2.04 million people identified themselves as ethnic Germans. The explanation, however, is rather simple. First, a great number of ethnic Germans registered as Russians fearing otherwise reprisals for themselves and their children because of their ethnicity. Second, children from German–Russian and German–Kazakh mixed marriages were almost exclusively counted for the 'other' nationality, whereas today this practice has been reversed to guarantee them a rightful claim to immigration to Germany. Third, non-German partners of ethnic Germans also have a claim to migrate as part of the family to Germany (Hilkes/Stricker 1997: 251). For these three reasons, the number of those who are able to emigrate to Germany has increased drastically. This migration psychosis is based upon the mistrust harboured by ethnic Germans against Russians and Russia because of the traumatic experiences they have had in recent history. This is expressed in statements like these – 'Whoever wants to see their children grow up as Germans has to leave now.' or 'Today we have the opportunity to leave, but who knows what will be tomorrow' (Hilkes/Stricker 1997: 257).

The 'ethnic' losses suffered as a consequence of the mass emigration, not only deprived the German minority of its cultural, clerical, and technical elites, but also contributed to the general destabilisation of the minority that had been caused by the breakup of the Soviet Union. In Central Asia, ethnic tensions and migration pressure not only affected the Russians as former colonists, but all European Christian populations, including ethnic Germans, who had been deported there in the 1940s. In Kazakhstan, the decline is estimated to be from around 960,000 ethnic Germans in 1989 to 370,000 in 1996, in Kyrgyzstan only 26,000 of the 101,000 Germans in 1989 were left in 1995 (Kyrgyzstan 1996: 19). This purely numerical decline is also obvious in the breaking-apart of the social structures that had grown since the deportation in 1941 – most of the religious facilities in Kazakhstan and Central Asia, for example, are either empty or have been sold to Muslim groups.

The ethnic Germans from Central Asia, however, have not only fled to Germany proper, but also to the German settlements in Siberia, where they fill some of the gaps left by the previous mass exodus from there. However, these migrants to Siberia do not have an automatically stabilising effect. On the contrary, many of them see Siberia merely as a stopover on their way to Germany. Furthermore, they are also significantly different in their mentality from ethnic Germans in Siberia. Ethnic Germans in Central Asia had been a small minority in comparison to the titular nations in the former Soviet republics and had been more closely affiliated with the Russians, partly even sharing their master-race mentality vis-à-vis the native population. Thus they became mentally and linguistically more assimilated than the ethnic Germans in Siberia, a fact that now creates occasional tensions between the two groups. Yet the overarching, and in the long term often unanswerable, question that remains for all ethnic Germans in the successor states of the former Soviet Union is whether they should or should not migrate to Germany.

The Denial of Autonomy

Ethnic Germans in the Soviet Union linked their hopes to Gorbachev's reform policy. Since 1987, German newspapers had been able to report on formerly banned topics such as the deportation. Supra-regional organisations were legalised, for example, the All-Union Association for Politics, Culture, and Education, 'Rebirth' (*Wiedergeburt*), which initially was the only representative of ethnic German interests, demanding political and legal rehabilitation, promotion of German language, culture, and customs, and, above all, the restoration of an autonomous German territory (Eisfeld 1990: 19ff.). The formation of competing organisations, allegedly infiltrated by the KGB to paralyse the autonomy movement, weakened the political stance and influence of the ethnic German minority. Neither the Soviet nor the Russian leadership was or is particularly interested in a German autonomous area (Hilkes/ Stricker 1997: 243f.). Eventually they succeeded, as ethnic German organisations moderated their demands to fit Russian interests, requesting only German cultural autonomy. This way Russian authorities managed to prevent ethnic Germans from successfully resisting their Russification as all such attempts were not, and cannot be, successful without territorial guarantees and protections, without German schools, a

German and German-speaking administration, and independent cultural facilities (Hilkes/Stricker 1997: 237ff., 248f.).

Earlier on, Gorbachev had raised hopes for the restoration
of autonomy by making concrete commitments. In 1989, even
the Nationalities Chamber of the Supreme Soviet supported
the restoration of the Volga Republic. Yet demonstrations of
Russian nationalists, organised by the Communist Party and
the KGB and chanting 'Fascists out!' and 'We don't want a
Fourth Reich!', had their effects on policy makers, resulting in
the nationalities chamber reversing its earlier decision. Eventually, Boris Yeltsin's winter 1992 visit to the Volga area put a
definite end to all autonomy hopes, when the Russian president promised demonstrating Russians that there would be no
autonomy for ethnic Germans (Hilkes/Stricker 1997: 248f.).
Various other resettlement projects (south Ukraine, northern
East Prussia/Kaliningrad) have been phased out as well.

German Rayons

In cooperation with the Russian and German governments
and financed mostly by Germany, two German rayons were
created in Halbstadt in the Altay Mountains in 1991 and in
Asowo near Omsk in 1992. Facing serious social and economic challenges caused by the mass migration of ethnic Germans to the Federal Republic, the German government has an
ever-increasing interest in the improvement of the living conditions of the ethnic Germans in Russia and Kazakhstan.
Within the framework of the 1990 German–Russian Treaty on
Good Neighbourly Relations, Partnership and Cooperation,
the German and Russian governments promote a wide variety
of economic, administrative, educational, linguistic, and cultural projects, all of which are aimed at opening new perspectives for ethnic Germans in Russia and Kazakhstan and
stabilising their overall situation. This way, the German government hopes that the number of ethnic Germans wishing to
leave for Germany will decrease, provided the living conditions in their present settlement areas improve visibly.

While German aid to ethnic Germans these days is almost
entirely focussed on the two German rayons and is the maximum of what is possible under the present conditions, it is,
however, a far cry away from the opportunities that would

have been available had a German autonomous area been restored. The German rayons are small counties with about 30,000 not exclusively German inhabitants and with an ethnic German, but Russian-speaking, administration. All improvement projects incorporate the entire population of these areas in order to make sure that no ethnic tensions arise between the German communities and their neighbours.

One major project, not only in the two German rayons, is the creation of so-called *Begegnungszentren*, centres of cross-cultural encounters, that offer German language courses and literature classes, German libraries, newspapers, audio–visual aids, music, and information about contemporary Germany. The language courses are provided not only to enable ethnic Germans to learn their ancestral language, but also to provide them with an essential prerequisite for successful integration in Germany, should they decide to leave. The highly successful language offensive in many *Begegnungszentren* throughout the successor states of the former Soviet Union, however, must also be seen in the context of a new German government policy, introduced in 1995, which requires a minimum knowledge of German as a precondition for immigration to Germany.

Occasionally, *Begegnungszentren* are combined with religious institutions to the mutual benefit of churches and the German government – the churches receive generous financial aid, while the German government can use the already existing infrastructure of the Lutheran and Roman Catholic churches.

What is still missing in the German rayons, however, are German schools. While German kindergartens have been set up, the Russian authorities have continued to deny permits for the creation of German schools, a manifestation of the still-existing deep mistrust towards the ethnic German minority. Within the existing educational system, the earlier practice of special German classes for ethnic German students has been abandoned, as fewer and fewer pupils participated in these optional classes. Efforts now concentrate on the promotion of classes teaching German as a foreign language, arguing that young ethnic Germans these days speak almost exclusively Russian at home and have no prior knowledge of German, just like their native Russian class mates.

In the final analysis, the creation of the two German rayons has not prevented ethnic Germans from emigrating. Many of those who fulfil the cultural and linguistic conditions for immigration have left for Germany. Thus, there is a fear that those who remain will have little interest in German culture and language, a trend that will be accelerated by the migration to these areas of ethnic Germans from Kazakhstan, who are already significantly assimilated to Russian culture. This way, the ethnic German character of the two rayons will be lost sooner or later, making them less attractive as a home for those who had seen them as 'islands of hope' for ethnic Germans in Russia (Klaube 1994: 81–87).

The Churches

The assumption made in religious circles that ethnic Germans had been more faithful to the religion of their forefathers than their Russian neighbours has proven to be wrong. Among all confessions, about 15 percent of ethnic Germans remained active members of religious communities during the Soviet period, a figure that is not significantly above that for ethnic Russians.

Since 1988, the Lutheran Church was able to build a USSR-wide organisation. Today it is estimated that there are about 650 communities (Stricker 1997: 406), primarily in Siberia, Kazakhstan, and Central Asia. Prior to the perestroika period, there had been very few urban religious communities in the European parts of the Soviet Union, but since 1988 their number has grown considerably. Since the collapse of the Soviet Union, the 'Lutheran Church of Russian and Other States' forms a confederate union of (national) churches. Even though the church seems well structured and organised from the outside, it faces tremendous challenges on the inside. The most severe of them is the constant lack of personnel. Most staff now come from Germany, remaining on the payroll of their home churches. Despite the fact that there has been, since 1997, a theological seminar near St Petersburg and that some of the constituent churches, for example the Lutheran Churches of Ukraine and Kazakhstan, offer training courses for lay ministers, the lack of applicants persists. The reason for this is primarily that most of the communities have not seen any theologically trained ministers since 1937/8 (Stricker 1997: 397–402). After decades of lay preachers and lay leadership, the communities now resent the fact that they should pay for a minister in these economically difficult times.

Continued emigration has only added to this personnel problem. Ever more frequently church elders and preachers leave their communities for Germany, successors are hard to find, and if found, they cannot normally measure up to the qualities of their predecessors. Ironically, now that the Lutheran Church has all possibilities to develop, the mass emigration poses a threat to its survival (Stricker 1997: 402–6). Another problem is linguistic in nature. While in the Siberian communities German still dominates as the language of church services, many communities in the big cities, in the European part of Russia, and in Ukraine now offer parallel German and Russian services, as this is the only way to reach out to the younger generation.

The Roman Catholic Church has been hit even worse. A German diocese, like the one of Saratov, which survived well into the Soviet era, does not exist any more. During the period of deportation and persecution, Catholics were served by travelling underground priests. The few (16) Catholic communities registered in Soviet Asia before 1987 were multinational congregations, rather than a place where ethnic Germans could cultivate their cultural identity. In the Russian Federation and Central Asia, the Vatican does not have dioceses now, but instead five Apostolic Administrations (with about 215 parishes in the European part of Russia and in Siberia, and about 50 in Kazakhstan), over three of which Polish bishops preside. The ethnic German bishop Joseph Werth heads the 151 communities of the Apostolic Administration of Western Siberia in Novosibirsk, and the German bishop Klemens Pickel serves 55 newly created ethnic German communities in the Volga area. Almost all of the 250 priests working in the European parts of Russia, in Siberia, in Kazakhstan, and in Central Asia come from abroad – mostly from Poland, Italy, Slovakia, and Germany. The central training seminar for priests, which had to be relocated from Moscow to St Petersburg in 1996 because of anti-Catholic activities of the Russian Orthodox Church and the state authorities, is a long way from satisfying the demand for priests, not least because among Catholics there is a lack of applicants for priesthood as well.

The numbers mentioned above refer to pastoral centres, i.e., the permanent residences of priests, from where they serve a number of so-called affiliated communities, some of them hundreds of miles away (Becker 1995: 28f.). The members of these communities are mostly German, Polish, and sometimes Lithuanian. The language during the service is now, for the most part, Russian, while during mass prayers, songs, and hymns are included in the native language of each of the communities (Börsch 1995: 33f.).

Similar to the Lutheran communities, the Catholic ones in former Soviet Asia are characterised by a very conservative spirituality that grew during the years of illegality. Neither deportation and persecution nor isolation and the lack of priests were a suitable basis for theological reflection, when the very survival of the community and its members was at stake.

As there were only a few Lutheran communities in the deportation areas until the 1970s, many Protestant ethnic Germans turned to Russian Baptists, whose communities enjoyed legal status. Similarly, many young ethnic Germans who were unable to follow church services in German began to attend Baptist services. Thus, while the number of Baptists was hardly measurable before the First World War, they made up for a significant percentage of those ethnic Germans who actively maintained their belief during the Soviet period (Dietz/Hilkes 1992: 90). However, the high proportion of Baptists among active ethnic German Christians has also to do with the fact that in 1963 the Soviet religious authorities managed to convince a significant part of the Mennonites to join the All-Union Council of Evangelical Christians – Baptists (Stricker 1984: 57–98). Therefore, most of the émigrés with Mennonite names today are Baptists. Because of their family connections to Germany, Canada, and the United States, the major part of the Mennonite community has left the former Soviet Union (Hildebrandt 1997: 321f., Stricker 1997: 416–9).

Outlook

The editor-in-chief of the German *Rundschau* in Uljanovsk in the Ural Mountains, Professor Eugen Müller (1998), is very pessimistic with regards to the future of the ethnic German community in Russia. In an article entitled 'We are no longer a people', he claims that the history of ethnic Germans in Russia is obviously coming to an end:

... half of the ethnic Germans has already migrated to Germany. The rest is dispersed all over the former Soviet Union. Are we still a people? ... It seems that the ethnic Germans did not manage to maintain their identity in the Soviet period and to overcome the severe consequences of years of deportation and ban of the German language. That the ethnic Germans can and do only speak Russian in meetings and at conferences is well known. But that there is to date not a single German school in Russia nobody wants to acknowledge. As decent citizens of Russia we pay our taxes and fulfil all responsibilities. But different from the Tatars, Kalmyks, Tshuwashs and other minorities in Russia, we don't get our territory back. ... We have ceased to exist as a people fused together by a common culture, history, and language. There are no ethnic Germans left in Russia anymore. What is left are assimilated Germans, who no longer maintain any kind of Germanness.

Thus, we do not have a future in Russia. ... Those who remain there sing Russian songs on holidays, because they don't know German ones. The older generation is content with remembering the past. The middle generation, however, is in a more tricky situation: according to their name and their relationship to their Russian environment they should feel like Germans, but they don't. Therefore, they either migrate to the German fatherland where they don't feel at home and are being called Russians, and hope for a better future for their children. Or, they stay in Russia without caring any longer about their German name, origin, and language.

And their children? In Germany they will be Germans, in Russia – Russians.

References

Becker, G.P. and Gawol, L., 'Zur Seelsorgsituation katholischer Gemeinden. Traditionsverlust und Ausreise', in *Glaube in der 2. Welt* 7–8 (1995), pp. 36–40.

Börsch, P.J., 'Katholische Diaspora in Zentralasien' 1995, in *Glaube in der 2. Welt* 7–8 (1995), pp. 32–35.

Brandes, D., 'Einwanderung und Entwicklung der Kolonien', in *Rußland*, ed. G. Stricker, Berlin, 1997, pp. 131–213.

Dietz, B. and Hilkes, P., *Rußlanddeutsche – Unbekannte im Osten. Geschichte, Situation, Zukunftsperspektiven*, Munich, 1992.

Eisfeld, A., 'Zur jüngsten Entwicklung der Autonomiebewegung der Sowjetdeutschen', in *Osteuropa* 40 (1990), pp. 11–32.

German, A., *Nemetskaya Avtonomiya na Volge 1918-1941*, Saratov, 1994.

Hildebrandt, G., 'Die Kolonisten am Beispiel der Mennoniten', in *Rußland*, ed. G. Stricker, Berlin, 1997, pp. 262–323.

Hilkes, P. and Stricker, G., 'Die Jahre nach dem Zweiten Weltkrieg', in *Rußland*, ed. G. Stricker, Berlin, 1997, pp. 221–61.

Klaube, M., 'Emigration und Migration in den beiden deutschen Landkreisen in Westsibirien', in *Osteuropa* 44 (1994), pp. 74–89.

Kyrgyzstan v tsifrach 1995. Kratkiy statisticheskiy sbornik, Bishkek, 1996.

Müller, E., 'Wir sind kein Volk mehr', in *Frankfurter Allgemeine Zeitung,* 1 August 1998, p. 10.

Stricker, G., 'Mennoniten in der Sowjetunion. Eine Facette rußlanddeutscher Kirchengeschichte', in *Kirche im Osten* 27 (1984), pp. 57-98.

Stricker, G., ed., *Rußland* (=Deutsche Geschichte im Osten Europas, Bd. 10), Berlin, 1997.

Germany and her Minorities

CHAPTER 12

Changing Priorities or Changing Opportunities? German External Minority Policy, 1919–1998

Stefan Wolff

G iven the numerous incompatibilities of political and ethnic boundaries in Europe, it is hardly surprising that,
since the emergence of the nation-states, external minorities
have played a role in the foreign policy considerations of their
host and kin-states. For Germany, this began as early as
1870–1 in relation to Alsace–Lorraine. It was an important
issue on the German foreign policy agenda in the inter-war
period with respect to the territories ceded to France, Belgium,
Poland, and the (formerly Austro–Hungarian) *Sudetenland* that
became part of the newly established Czechoslovak Republic.
After, and as a consequence of, the Second World War, the
Federal Republic of Germany also concerned itself with the
fate of the German minorities in countries with which Germany had never had common borders, but which, as a result
of migration, nevertheless hosted substantial populations of
ethnic Germans. Eventually, a qualitatively new stage of the
relationship between Germany and its neighbours in Central
and Eastern Europe began after the collapse of communism in
the late 1980s, early 1990s.

In all three periods, policy-makers operated on different
premises, with distinct goals, and in diverse international environments. It is difficult to give an overall assessment of the
success or failure of German external minority policy or even
to outline its major developments in any substance in the
scope of a single essay. I will, therefore, focus my analysis on
the post-Cold War period by giving an overview of the relevant policy issues and countries concerned. For reasons of

contextuality, this will be proceeded by two short sections on policy developments between the two World Wars and after 1945.

First and Second-Class Borders – External Minorities and the Policy of Border Revisions, 1919–1939

The Versailles Peace Treaty of 1919 altered the borders of Germany to a significant degree and left millions of ethnic Germans under the sovereignty of other states. In the east, Germany lost parts of East Prussia, Upper Silesia, and the territories assigned to the so-called Polish Corridor. In the west, France regained Alsace and Lorraine, Belgium acquired the areas of Prussian Moresnet, Eupen and Malmedy, and the Saar territory was put under an international protectorate with considerable economic rights accorded to France. In the north, a referendum in 1920 determined the German–Danish border in Schleswig. Furthermore, the dissolution of the Austro–Hungarian Empire and the creation of the Czechoslovak Republic placed the ethnic German population of the *Sudetenland* in another state as well.

The substantial loss of territory and population and the enormous amount of reparations Germany had to pay to the allied and associated powers formed a considerable part of the background against which German foreign policy was formulated throughout the 1920s. The two major policy goals Germany pursued throughout the inter-war period were the revision of the borders in the east and relief from reparations payments. As both issues depended essentially on the goodwill of the western powers, they were closely interlinked with one another and related to the question of Germany's western borders, which, in turn, assigned an instrumental role in particular to the German-speaking populations of Alsace and Lorraine and South Tyrol.

Between 1919 and 1922, Germany had tried to turn the question of Alsace and Lorraine into a precedent for the right to self-determination to which not only defeated states, but also the victorious powers, had to bow. However, the German Foreign Office soon had to realise that the difficulties which existed in Alsace and Lorraine were an internal affair of the French Republic. Consequently, a 1922 analysis of the situation acknowledged that Alsace and Lorraine did not qualify as a minority problem in the strict sense of the concept since the population did not insist on its different ethnicity (*Fremdständigkeit*), let alone on their German origin.[1] Although this assessment was accurate for the early 1920s, it had to be changed later, when Alsatians began to see themselves as a minority, in the way the League of Nations[2] defined the term, and increasingly insisted on their distinctiveness, if not in terms of ethnicity, then certainly in terms of culture, language, and tradition. The rediscovery of their German roots and the recognition of the German element in Alsatian culture, in turn, led the Foreign Office to support cultural efforts in Alsace in addition to more serious political considerations and a policy of funding political parties there. While realising that regaining the former *Reichsland* was impossible, a formal abandoning of all territorial claims could assure the French government of the security of its eastern borders with Germany. At the same time, continuing problems in Alsace and Lorraine would weaken French resistance against desired border changes in the 'German East'. While the former was achieved with the Treaty of Locarno in 1925,[3] the latter policy was pursued from the second half of the 1920s onwards, mostly through the funding of cultural activities, but also by supporting, especially between 1927 and 1929, Alsatian particularist political propaganda,[4] which, initially channelled through the private

1. Internal policy document of the German Foreign Office, 1922. Cited in Rothenberger (1975: 74).
2. A resolution adopted by the League of Nations in September 1922 obliged all states to protect minorities under their jurisdiction regardless of whether the post-1919 peace treaties had made specific demands vis-à-vis these states. Thus, the victorious states were as obliged to protect minorities in their boundaries as were defeated ones.
3. Article one of the treaty reads: 'The High contracting parties collectively and severally guarantee, in the manner provided in the following articles, the maintenance of the territorial *status quo* resulting from the frontiers between Germany and France and the inviolability of the said frontiers as fixed by or in pursuance of the Treaty of Peace signed at Versailles on the 28th June, 1919, and also the observance of the stipulations of articles 42 and 43 of the said treaty concerning the demilitarised zone.'
4. Rothenberger gives the following figures of financial support: 141,247 *Reichsmark* in 1925/26; 548,331 *Reichsmark* in 1926/27; and 840,000 *Reichsmark* between 1927 and 1929. Cf. Rothenberger (1975: 138–51).

organisations of the Alsatian émigrés[5] was abandoned soon after Stresemann's death in 1929. The reason for this was not only a lack of success, but also the fact that French suspicions about the true source of the funds grew, and alienating France was considered counter-productive. In 1930/31 cultural funding continued at a reduced level, and even after Hitler's takeover in 1933 it was not immediately abandoned. In all this time, the objective of support was not to encourage Alsatian separatism, but rather to make France more willing to concede border revisions in the east.

The situation in South Tyrol, which had been annexed to Italy in 1919, was somewhat different, yet the area played a similarly important part in German foreign policy. While Austria had never accepted the loss of South Tyrol, international developments forced successive Austrian chancellors to recognise the importance of an alliance with Italy against German annexation plans. In 1928 chancellor Seipel declared that South Tyrol was an internal Italian affair, and in 1930 a friendship treaty was signed between Italy and Austria. Thus left with little support from Austria, many South Tyrolese vested their hopes in Hitler and his pan-German aspirations to remedy their situation.

After Hitler's seizure of power in 1933, the institutions of external minority policy were gradually turned into instruments

---

5. The two organisations were the *Alt-Elsaß-Lothringische Vereinigung* and the *Hilfsbund*. While the organisations of the *Reichsland* émigrés were generally less willing to accept that there would be no border revision, the two émigré organisations' and the Foreign Office's aims met in one crucial point – the attempt to minimise the impact of French assimilation policies in Alsace. However, the aims of the two émigré organisations were not identical. The *Hilfsbund* was primarily concerned with the integration of émigrés in German society and their compensation for the losses they had suffered. In the course of time, its importance diminished simply because of its success in facilitating the integration process. This is obvious in terms of the membership figures: in 1920, there were 33,000 members, in 1925 20,000, and in 1933 only 7,000. The *Alt-Elsaß-Lothringische Vereinigung*, by contrast was primarily a cultural and scholarly organisation with its own institute at the University of Frankfurt/Main. By supporting the particularist movement in Alsace with the help of the Foreign Office, the *Alt-Elsaß-Lothringische Vereinigung* contributed significantly to the rise of Alsatian particularism despite the fact that its aim (self-determination) was not identical to that of most particularists (some degree of autonomy within the French polity) (Grünewald 1984: 185–90). With financial support from the Foreign Office decreasing after 1930, the collapse of the two organisations could only be prevented by their fusion in 1933.

of aggressive national socialist foreign policy.[6] The *Volksdeutsche Mittelstelle* (a department in the ministry of foreign affairs to co-ordinate ethnic German policy issues) and the *Verband für das Deutschtum im Ausland* (the Association for German Culture Abroad) were taken over by committed followers of Hitler who replaced the foreign policy bureaucrats of the Weimar period. However, the basic premises of foreign policy were left unchanged, even though emphasis and rationales shifted. Hitler, too, saw the abandoning of territorial claims primarily from a tactical point of view, yet he also had ideological concerns. He considered the status of Alsatians as 'racially questionable', but this did not make him lose sight of the strategic value of the territory of the former *Reichsland* in terms of the cohesion of the 'German heartland' (Kettenacker 1973). In the light of political developments in Italy in the early 1920s and the importance of the country as an ally for Germany, Hitler had made it very clear as early as 1922 that he was not willing to sacrifice his global interests, for whose realisation he needed an alliance with Italy, for the fate of 300,000 German-speaking South Tyrolese.[7]

With respect to the former German territories in the east, the long-term policy objectives of the Weimar Republic aimed at a 'recovery' of the lost territories in Poland were complemented, from the early 1930s onwards, by a policy seeking the annexation of the German-populated areas in the

---

6. Increasingly, the *Auslandsorganisation* (the 'foreign organisation') of the NSDAP became active among ethnic Germans in Eastern and Western Europe alike. Although its popularity and success in recruitment varied – it was more effective in South Tyrol than in Alsace and Lorraine and had a stronger following in the *Sudetenland* than in Poland – local branches of the party were built up in all the diaspora groups (e.g., Romania, Hungary, Yugoslavia) except the one in the Soviet Union.

7. Gruber (1974: 171) gives the following 1922 (!) quotation from Hitler: 'Germany has to join forces with Italy which experiences a time of national rebirth and has a great future ahead of itself. In order to accomplish this, a clear and final renunciation of all claims to South Tyrol is necessary.'

   In an attempt to solve the South Tyrol question once and for all, the so-called *Option* was designed. The German-speaking population in South Tyrol was asked in 1939 to choose between remaining in Italy and being subjected to further Italianisation or to opt for relocation to the German Reich. Of the 267,265 German-speaking South Tyrolese eligible for participation 43,626 abstained. Of the 223,639 participants in the plebiscite, 183,365 voted to leave and 38,274 to stay (Figures according Cole and Wolf 1974: 57. Slightly different figures in Alcock 1970: 45ff.).

Czechoslovak Republic, especially the *Sudetenland*. Even though the popularity of national socialist ideology increased in both areas and provided Nazi foreign policy with a very effective 'fifth column' in both Czechoslovakia and Poland, only the *Sudetenland* was regained by Germany without going to war when the Munich Agreement of 1938 obliged the Czechoslovak Republic to cede significant parts of its territory to the German *Reich*.

From Westintegration to Ostpolitik – the Limits of External Minority Policy, 1949–1989

Had the major problem facing German policy makers after World War One been the territorial truncation of German territory and the reparations to be paid to the Allied powers, a new challenge presented itself after 1945. Ethnic Germans, in particular from Central and East European countries, were either expelled from their traditional settlement areas, as, for example, in Poland and Czechoslovakia, or were deported to forced labour camps in the Soviet Union, as in Romania and Yugoslavia. In any event, ethnic Germans were subjected to systematic popular and state discrimination as a result of the atrocious occupation policies of the Nazis during the war.[8] Even though this wave of repression and expulsion had ended by the early 1950s and ethnic Germans had their citizenship rights gradually reinstated, their situation was still not considered satisfactory by the West German government, partly because they suffered all the 'usual' disadvantages of life under communism, and partly because the experience of German occupation by the titular nation of their host-state made them vulnerable to continued discrimination.[9]

However, in the early years of its existence, the Federal Republic was preoccupied with other issues both domestically and in its international relations. Domestically, the rebuilding of society and the economy, including the integration of millions of refugees and expellees, took priority. On the

8. Ethnic Germans in the Soviet Union had been deported to the Central Asian Republics from their settlements in the European parts of the country after Hitler Germany's attack in 1941.

9. As the previous case studies have indicated, the levels of discrimination differed over time and from country to country.

international stage, the German Chancellor Adenauer had set a foreign policy agenda whose foremost aim was to ensure the integration of the country into the Western Alliance.

This process of integration into the West, which provided a path to political security, economic recovery, and gradually also to social prosperity, was the preferred option of the overwhelming majority of the population and politicians. Yet, at the same time, the Western alliance as a symbol of post-war developments signalled, at least temporarily, an acceptance of the *status quo*, which, given the German borders in 1949, found significantly less support. While it was generally accepted that neither Alsace and Lorraine nor the *Sudetenland* could rightfully be claimed by Germany, the fixing of the German–Polish border along the Oder–Neiße line was renounced in public by West German politicians of nearly all political colours, including the Chancellor and his cabinet ministers. Simultaneously, however, it was equally clear that the federal government was in no position to offer a credible political approach as to how to revise the German–Polish border. Not only was this contrary to the interests of all four allied powers of the Second World War, but West Germany itself no longer had a common border with Poland. Despite the claim of the Federal Republic to be the sole representative of the German people (*Alleinvertretungsanspruch*),[10] it was a matter of political reality that the East German state had officially recognised the new border in a treaty with Poland in July 1950.

When integration into the western world had sufficiently progressed by the mid-1950s through membership in NATO and the precursor institutions of today's European Union, Germany could, more confidently, turn eastwards again. As a result of public pressure and political lobbying by the various expellee organisations, but also as a consequence of the *Alleinvertretungsanspruch*, the Federal Republic committed itself to a foreign policy vis-à-vis the communist countries in Central and Eastern Europe that included humanitarian efforts to improve the situation of ethnic Germans in these countries. The possibilities of direct involvement, however, were extremely limited throughout this period until 1989, so that the major instrument of German external minority policy was

10. In a speech before the German *Bundestag* on 21 October 1949, Adenauer declared that 'pending German reunification, the Federal Republic of Germany is the only legitimate state organisation of the German people.'

to negotiate conditions with the host-states that would allow ethnic Germans to migrate to Germany. A precondition for this was the establishing of diplomatic relations with the relevant states in the east bloc.

A first step in this direction was the Soviet–German treaty of 1955, followed by a verbal agreement in 1958 according to which all those persons of ethnic German origin who had been German citizens before 21 June 1941 were entitled to repatriation.[11] This policy was continued by all successive governments, and after 1970 it began to include a variety of other states in the Soviet zone of influence. Treaties with Poland (1970) and Czechoslovakia (1973) specifically addressed the sensitive issues of borders, confirming that the German government of the day respected the territorial *status quo*. Although both treaties thus included provisions to the effect that the signatory states assured each other of respect for each other's territorial integrity and of the fact that neither had territorial claims against the other (cf. *Bulletin* 1970: 1815 and *Bulletin* 1973: 1631), two rulings of the German Constitutional Court in 1973 and 1987 confirmed that Germany continued to exist in the borders of 1937.

The priority of promoting coexistence between East and West against the background of the political realities of the Cold War did not leave the West German government any other option apart from facilitating the emigration of ethnic Germans from Central and Eastern Europe to the Federal Republic, which included primarily ethnic Germans from the Soviet Union, Romania, and Poland.[12] German external minority policy was thus not very active between 1945 and 1989, partly because it had always been suspected of a hidden

11. This, however, solved only a part of the problem as it included only the Germans of the northern territories of former East Prussia, the so-called Memel Germans, and those ethnic Germans who, in the aftermath of the German–Soviet treaty of 1939, had been resettled to the then German territories from the Baltic states, Galicia, Volhynia, Bessarabia, and the Northern Bukovina, but found themselves again on Soviet territory at the end of the war. Thus, it did not cover the by far largest group of ethnic Germans who had migrated there, mostly between the middle of the eighteenth and nineteenth centuries.

12. The agreements between West Germany and some of the host-states on the repatriation of ethnic Germans included financial arrangements setting 'per capita fees' to be paid by the federal government. Average figures of annual emigration of ethnic Germans after 1950 are as follows: 1955–59: 64,000; 1960–64: 18,000; 1965–69: 26,000; 1970–74: 25,000; 1975–79: 46,000; 1980–84: 49,000, 1985–86: 41,000; 1987: 78,000 (*Infodienst* 1996: p. 2–5).

revisionist agenda not only by the host-states, but also within Germany itself, and partly because to remain in their host-countries was not the preferred option of most ethnic Germans in Central and Eastern Europe,[13] nor was it seen as an acceptable or achievable alternative by the federal government.

Promoting Democracy, Prosperity, and Ethnic Harmony – The New Policy Agenda after 1990

The General Context of External Minority Policy after 1990

The transition to democracy in Central and Eastern Europe, which began in 1989-90, provided an entirely different framework of new and enlarged opportunities for Germany's external minority policy. On the one hand, democratisation meant the granting of such basic rights and liberties as the freedoms of speech, association, and political participation, allowing ethnic Germans in their host-countries to form their own parties, stand for election, and actively advocate the interests of their group. On the other hand, it also meant that there were no longer any restrictions on emigration, and given the experience of at least the past forty years, many ethnic Germans, particularly in Poland, Romania, and the Soviet Union and its successor states, seized this opportunity and emigrated to Germany. Both developments required a measured and responsible policy response from Germany – domestically to cope with the enormous influx of resettlers, internationally to assure the neighbouring states in Central and Eastern Europe of the inviolability of the post-war borders, while simultaneously continuing the support for the German minorities at qualitatively and quantitatively new levels, and ensuring their protection as national minorities. All this had to happen within the framework of general German foreign policy premises, such as the support for the transition process to democracy and a market economy, the creation of a new collective security order embracing all states in Europe, and respect for international law and human rights.

13. Ethnic Germans in Hungary are somewhat of an exception here.

The Domestic Response – Restriction of Immigration

The most important legal act passed in response to the vast increase of ethnic Germans[14] leaving their host-states to migrate to Germany was the 1993 War Consequences Conciliation Act.[15] Entitlement to German citizenship, formerly automatic, was revoked – ethnic Germans now had to prove ethnic discrimination in their host-states and a long-standing affinity to German culture, language and traditions in order to qualify. Furthermore, the annual intake of ethnic Germans was limited to the average of the years 1991 and 1992 within a 10 percent margin, i.e., a maximum of about 250,000 people. Since, prior to this in 1990, a bill had been passed that required ethnic Germans to apply for admission to Germany from their host-states, the annual intake could effectively be restricted to these quotas. In 1996, a language test was introduced that has to be passed by ethnic German applicants for citizenship as a way of testing their affinity to German language and culture. Together, these changed regulations have considerably reduced the influx of ethnic Germans to the Federal Republic – from around 220,000 each year between 1993 and 1995, the immigration figures dropped to 178,000 in 1996 and 134,000 in 1997. For the first half year of 2000, only some 44,000 ethnic Germans had entered the country under the new regulations.[16]

The International Response – Creating an Alternative to 'Repatriation'

Realising that the changed conditions after 1990 required a fundamentally different foreign policy approach, the German

14. In 1988, over 200,000 ethnic Germans 'returned' to Germany, in 1989 it was already 377,000, and in 1990 a figure of 397,000 was recorded.

15. A further change had been suggested by the *Bundesrat* on an initiative of Rhineland Palatine in early 1997 (*Bundestagsdrucksache* 13/6915). In essence, the proposed new version of the *Bundesvertriebenengesetz*, the law on expellees, would have removed the still-existing automatic recognition of ethnic Germans from the former Soviet Union as suffering ethnic discrimination as a consequence of the Second World War, which was still in existence. After a first reading in the *Bundestag*, the bill was sent to the Interior Affairs committee of the parliament. By the end of the last parliament, there had not been a second reading.

16. This drop has two further reasons apart from legal restrictions – many ethnic Germans who have successfully applied for citizenship have not yet exercised their option to migrate to Germany, but keep it as a fall-back position. In addition, the majority of people from Romania and Poland who had wanted to leave had already done so in the late 1980s and early 1990s so that the demand from there is now greatly reduced.

government embedded its external minority policy into the wider framework of its efforts to promote democracy, prosperity, and security in Central and Eastern Europe. Given the ethno–political demography of the region with its many national minorities, latent border disputes, and inter-ethnic tensions, it was obvious that the role of minorities would be a crucial one in two ways. The ultimate test of successful democratisation would have to include an assessment of whether or not members of national minorities, individually and collectively, were entitled to full equality and the right to preserve, express, and develop their distinct identities in their host-states. Furthermore, it would not be possible to operate a viable collective security system without settling existing ethnic and territorial conflicts and establishing frameworks within which future disputes could be resolved peacefully. Taking these assumptions as a starting point, the German government concluded that national minorities could play a crucial part in bringing about results in these two interrelated processes as they could bridge existing cultural gaps.[17] The federal government sought to create partnerships with the Central and East European host-states and the German minorities living there that, on the basis of international treaties and bilateral agreements,[18] would promote the government's 'overall foreign policy concept of a European peace policy of reconciliation, understanding, and cooperation' (*Bundestagsdrucksache* 13/3195). Cultural, social, and economic measures to support German minorities, although primarily 'aimed at an improvement of the living conditions of ethnic Germans in their host-countries', would naturally benefit whole regions and their populations independent of their ethnic origin, and thus promote inter-ethnic harmony and economic prosperity while strengthening the emerging democratic political structures (*Bundestagsdrucksache* 13/3428 and *Bundestagsdrucksache* 13/1116). Thus, by creating favourable conditions for the integration of ethnic Germans in

17. Cf., for example, 'Vertriebene, Aussiedler und deutsche Minderheiten sind eine Brücke zwischen den Deutschen und ihren östlichen Nachbarn' (*Bundestagsdrucksache* 13/10845).

18. The key international agreements in this context are the 1990 Copenhagen document of the CSCE and the Council of Europe's Framework Declaration on minority rights. Bilateral treaties exist between Germany and Poland, the Czech and Slovak Republics, Hungary, Romania, and Russia. Major bilateral agreements were concluded with Ukraine and Kazakhstan. Cf. Heintze in this book.

the societies of their host-states as citizens with equal rights, the German government hoped to provide an alternative to emigration (*Bundestagsdrucksache* 13/3428).

Case Study I: Poland

The relations between Germany and Poland have their legal basis in the 1990 border recognition treaty, in which the Federal Republic explicitly guaranteed the Oder-Neiße line as the common border, and in the 1991 treaty on good neighbourly relations and cooperation. Prior to that, in 1989, a joint declaration by the German Chancellor and the Polish Prime Minister acknowledged the existence of a population of German descent in Poland and of the need to protect its cultural identity.

To secure a legal framework for the development of the German minority in Poland was only one part of German foreign policy and has been complemented by substantive material aid in the areas of culture and education (the responsibility of the Foreign Office), economic reconstruction (the responsibility of the Ministry of the Interior), and social and community work (the responsibility of the German Red Cross, before 1990 also through the Ministry of Inner-German Affairs). Material aid had been committed to the German minority before 1989, but in comparatively smaller proportions. The changes in Poland in 1989/90 allowed the allocation of larger funds, through different channels, and for new purposes.

Table 5: German Financial Support for ethnic Germans in Poland, 1987–94

	AA	BMI	DRK	BmfiB
1987	–	–	2.5	2.6
1988	–	–	2.4	3.7
1989		–	2.8	5.5
1990	5.5	6.8	3.3	5.3
1991		24.2	3.1	–
1992	3.5	26.5	1.4	–
1993	6.5	25.7	1.1	–
1994	6.5	25.3	1.4	–

All figures in millions of Deutschmarks. AA – Foreign Office, BMI – Ministry of Internal Affairs, DRK – German Red Cross, BMfiB – Ministry of Inner-German Affairs.
Source: Bundestagsdrucksache 13/1036

Geographically, material support has always been concentrated on the Upper Silesian region.

Funding in the education and cultural sector has included a variety of activities. The German government has provided staff support to improve the quality of German language teaching in Poland. The number of teachers sent to Poland has increased from just one in 1989 to 111 in 1994. In addition, four federal government-sponsored experts on German language teaching have been working in Poland since 1994; the German Academic Exchange Service is funding twenty-six lecturers at Polish universities, and the Goethe Institute has supplied eight lecturers for the further training of Polish teachers of German. Since 1993, members of the German minority in Poland have had access to a special grant programme to study in Germany for a period of up to twelve months. The federal government also provides partial funding for TV and radio broadcasts and print media of the German minority and supplies German newspapers and magazines to the friendship circles of the minority.

Financial aid channelled through the Ministry of the Interior was given to various associations of the minority. The annual amounts increased from 4.7 million Deutschmarks in 1991 to 5.8 in 1992, and then dropped to 5.7 and 5.4 million Deutschmarks in 1993 and 1994, respectively. A far larger amount of money, however, has been spent on projects to support the economic recovery of the areas in which members of the German minority live, thus benefiting not only the minorities, but also these regions and their (other) population as a whole. Efforts here were concentrated on infrastructural improvements, e.g., water supply systems, and on promoting small businesses and private farms. Funding of such projects increased from 700,000 Deutschmarks in 1991 to 8.7 million Deutschmarks in 1994 and again to 14.8 million Deutschmarks in 1996. For the distribution of these funds, the federal government uses the Foundation for the Development of Silesia, a private body registered in Opole, and partly funds three staff positions there.[19]

In the social area, the German government has provided funds for the improvement of medical services in Upper Silesia and for the setting-up of a network of *Caritas*-operated centres to care for the elderly (*Bundestagsdrucksache* 13/1116).

19. Similar foundations exist in Romania, Russia, and the Czech and Slovak Republics.

Case Study II: Russia

As with the German minority in Poland, the legal framework of German external minority policy vis-à-vis Russia is provided by a bilateral treaty between the two states. Unlike the Polish case, however, the German minority is far larger and more dispersed. Although German efforts, again, encompass cultural, economic, and social projects, they can only target specific regions and not yet cater for all members of the minority in the same way. The grounds the German government gives for focussing its efforts on three specific areas are based on the assumption that a significant section of ethnic Germans does not necessarily want to migrate to Germany, but seeks to live in areas together with other ethnic Germans. Therefore, the federal government sees it as essential to stabilise particular settlement areas, by providing housing for ethnic Germans coming to these areas from other parts of the Russian federation and from the Central Asian successor states of the former Soviet Union, and by improving the general living conditions in these areas in order to turn them into an acceptable alternative to 'repatriation' and ensure peaceful inter-ethnic relations between ethnic Germans, Russians, and other ethnic groups.[20]

The three areas on which material aid has been focussed since 1990 are the two German rayons Halbstadt and Asowo in Western Siberia, the Volga area, and the St Petersburg region. Projects supported by the German government include the construction of residential areas, aid for farm businesses (e.g., management and agricultural consulting, provision of machinery), loans and consulting for small-business start-ups, and occupational training to improve qualifications. In order to achieve a general improvement in living conditions, the federal government has directly funded, or backed by guaranteed loans, measures to improve the infrastructure in some of the regions where ethnic Germans live. This has included projects in the health care sector (e.g., the Ambulance Centre in Burni, Saratov area), the improvement of the local infrastructure (e.g., telecommunications network and petrol station in the Halbstadt rayon), and the expansion of retail and food production facilities (e.g., the dairy farm in

---

20. On a smaller scale, similar efforts are also made in the Central Asian republics and in Ukraine.

Baskatowka, Marx area). Most of these projects are co-funded by the Russian government, but the majority of the financial support is provided by Germany (1996 almost 90 million Deutschmarks, i.e., 60 percent of the overall financial resources made available for German minorities in Central and Eastern Europe).

Given the decades of communist rule during which ethnic Germans were denied the right to express and develop their cultural identity, a considerable amount of effort and funding is spent on projects in relation to education and culture. Since 1990, almost ninety cultural centres have been set up throughout the Russian Federation to give ethnic Germans an opportunity to become familiar with present-day Germany and, above all, to learn the language of their ancestors. Using existing infrastructure the German government has supplied these centres with technical equipment, books, and newspaper and magazine subscriptions. Most of the projects in the cultural sector happen in cooperation with the Russian government, which normally commits funds to the maintenance of buildings and the payment of staff.

The particular emphasis on educational efforts in the areas of language teaching and information about Germany is derived from the need to prepare ethnic Germans better for their potential migration to Germany in order to make integration into German society easier. In the medium term, the German government has planned to provide up to 100,000 places on language courses and to increase the number of cultural centres to 250. Language courses are offered at varying levels and lengths (from 32 to 200 hours). Special programmes for young ethnic Germans include language classes and summer camps, both aimed at securing knowledge about, and awareness of, their German roots among the coming generations. Despite good intentions, however, the decreasing availability of funds over the past years has limited the success of this policy, if only in terms of the number of people that could be reached.

Case Study III: Romania

Based on the German–Romanian treaty of April 1992, the aim of German external minority policy vis-à-vis Romania is to secure and improve the living conditions of the German minority in the country in order to provide its members with a viable future in their host-state. In contrast to Poland, but similar to Russia, there have never been border or territorial disputes between Germany and Romania, so that German foreign policy has a primarily humanitarian dimension.

Because the Romanian constitution does not allow for positive discrimination as a means to remedy the situation of historically disadvantaged minority groups, the German–Romanian treaty, in its article sixteen, states specifically that all concrete measures, taken jointly by the two governments to secure the continued existence of the German minority and to support it in the reconstruction of its social, cultural, and economic life, must not disadvantage other Romanian citizens. As this coincides with one of the objectives of Germany's external minority policy – contributing to an environment of inter-ethnic harmony – this has not limited the humanitarian aid efforts.

As in Russia and Poland, the aid projects can be grouped into three main areas – social, economic, and cultural. About seventy cultural centres have been set up since 1990, enabling the German minority to preserve, develop, and express its cultural identity. Language teaching, again, plays an important role in the cultural sector, but it is primarily aimed at preserving the already existing relatively high level of knowledge. Part of the aid package, therefore, is infrastructural support, such as the reconstruction of the main building of the Honterus secondary school in Kronstadt. A special youth programme has been operated since 1995.

Social projects have included the provision of medical equipment to hospitals in areas where ethnic Germans live, yet because of the general situation in Romania, these projects have great importance well beyond the regions at which they were originally aimed. Medical support has also encompassed the supply of spare parts, medication, and first aid equipment.

The economic aid programme has focussed on small businesses and the agricultural sector. Loans for start-up companies on preferential conditions, and the supply of technology and machinery, support around seventy companies founded or run by ethnic Germans in Romania every year. The initial emphasis on providing farms with modern equipment was replaced a couple of years ago by a programme of support for the creation of networks that enable ethnic Germans (and their

Romanian neighbours) to achieve greater cost efficiency. In this context, a project to form a regional community of agricultural producers and an initiative to set up an organisation for the wholesale distribution of fuel have been funded by the German government. Another source of support have been training programmes for agricultural engineers and managers in, and funded by, the Federal Republic of Germany. The agricultural support programme as a whole has been co-ordinated and administered by two German experts.

The total of financial support committed to the support of the German minority in Romania between 1990 and 1997 amounted to 138 million Deutschmark. For 1998, seven million Deutschmark were made available, a significant decline compared to earlier years which was caused by the generally more difficult economic situation in Germany.

Case Study IV: The German–Czech Declaration

Humanitarian aid to support ethnic Germans in their host-states has not been the only aspect of Germany's external minority policy after 1990. Reconciliation with its immediate neighbouring states in Central Europe, i.e., Poland and Czechoslovakia/the Czech Republic, has been of no lesser importance. In particular because of the role of the German minorities in the inter-war period and their expulsion from western Poland and the *Sudetenland*, bilateral relations between the countries have never been completely free from certain strains. These issues have been resolved relatively smoothly with Poland and have not caused major problems recently.[21] In contrast to this, the German–Czech relationship after 1990 has several times been affected negatively by the problems associated with the German minority in the country.

In Germany's relationship with Czechoslovakia and after 1993 with the Czech Republic, territorial issues never played a part, because all West German governments after 1949 and after German reunification had accepted the formula of 'Germany in the borders of 1937' as the Allied Powers had

21. Historically the problems with Poland have been much more complex – German oppression of Poles has been more fierce and lasted longer than that of the Czechs, and the number of expellees from Poland (9 million) exceeded those from the Czech Republic several times. Their resolution was therefore given higher priority in Germany's foreign policy.

determined it in the London Protocol of September 1944 (Kimminich 1996: 33). After years of negotiations and crises, the German–Czech Declaration of 21 January 1997 (*Bundestagsdrucksache* 13/6787) was the smallest common denominator the two governments could find on the two most critical issues – the role of the Sudeten Germans in the breakup of Czechoslovakia in 1938 and their collective victimisation and expulsion after the end of the Second World War. The German government accepted the responsibility of Germany in the developments leading up to the Munich Agreement and the destruction of Czechoslovakia, expressed its deep sorrow over the suffering of Czechs during the Nazi occupation of their country, and acknowledged that it was these two issues that prepared the ground for the post-war treatment and expulsion of members of the German minority in the country. The Czech government, on the other side, regretted the post-war policy vis-à-vis ethnic Germans, which resulted in the expulsion and expropriation of a large section of the German minority, including many innocent people. Both governments agreed that the remaining members of the German minority in the Czech Republic and the expellees and their descendants will play an important role in the future relationship of the two countries and that the support of the German minority in the Czech Republic was a matter of mutual interest. In order to fulfil this interest, a joint German–Czech Future Fund, to which Germany contributed about 140 million Deutschmarks and the Czech Republic about 25 million Deutschmark, was set up, part of which is to be spent on projects related to the support of the German minority in the Czech Republic.

Conclusion

Germany's external minority policy has undergone significant changes since it became part of the country's foreign policy agenda after the First World War. Although there were 'geographic' differences between the approach to minorities in the east and the west, the inter-war period was primarily characterised by an instrumentalisation of the minorities question to change the borders established in the Treaty of Versailles in 1919. Border alterations in the east, facilitated by border guarantees in the west, were the foreign policy goal of the Weimar Republic as well as of Nazi Germany, distinguished only by the intensity and means with which this aim was pursued.

The east–west difference remained after 1945, but was, to some extent at least, externally determined. Collective victimisation of ethnic Germans, coupled with expulsions (in Poland and Czechoslovakia) and deportations (in Romania and the Soviet Union) as a result of the Second World War, affected members of the German minorities in Central and Eastern Europe much more than in their settlement areas in the west. Simultaneously, the foundation of the West German state and the importance of its integration into the emerging western alliance set different priorities for foreign policy makers in post-war Germany. Part of the acceptance of responsibility for the consequences of the Second World War was the tacit recognition of the geopolitical and territorial realities of Europe by successive German governments, while the political engagement for German minorities in Central and Eastern Europe, even if was not put aside completely, was at least scaled down. In particular after 1969, when *Ostpolitik* was elevated to qualitatively new levels of reconciliation, the Federal Republic tried to facilitate the emigration of ethnic Germans from their host-countries and their smooth integration into German society, rather than to demand their recognition and protection as minorities.

From the end of the 1980s onwards, this began to change gradually. The democratisation of the formerly communist societies in Central and Eastern Europe opened new opportunities for Germany's external minority policy. Greater possibilities to support the German minorities in their host-states, the need to do so in order to halt, and eventually reverse, the mass exodus of ethnic Germans, and the genuine interest of the former communist countries in improving their relationship with Germany, which was seen as an important stepping-stone towards accession to the European Union and NATO, complemented each other in a unique way. Germany's desire to bridge the gap between cultures and across history could only be fulfilled through reconciliation and mutual understanding. Part of this was the eventual unconditional recognition of the borders with Poland and Czechoslovakia. Yet, a common future of Germany and its eastern neighbours could not be secured without addressing the situation of the German minorities in these countries. On the basis of numerous treaties and within the framework set out by the 1990 Copenhagen Declaration of the CSCE, Germany and Poland, the Czech and Slovak Republics, Hungary, Romania, the Russian Federation, Ukraine, and Kazakhstan have developed relationships that allow both respective parties, with the participation of representatives of the German minority in each country, to tackle the issue of minority protection and external support for ethnic Germans. For historical as well as contemporary reasons, this has remained a very sensitive problem. Countries in Central and Eastern Europe have seen a resurgence of minority-related questions during the transition process to democracy. German external minority policy, therefore, has always only been one part of a more comprehensive foreign policy approach towards its eastern neighbours that aims at a stabilisation of democracy and the creation of a market economy in these countries as the wider social framework within which harmonious inter-ethnic relationships can develop that will inevitably benefit the German minorities as well.

Almost a century of external minority policy has seen different policy agendas being pursued by different German governments. These were partly determined by domestically formulated objectives, partly also by existing opportunities and the way in which they were perceived by policy makers. Gradually since the early 1970s, however, the deliberate setting of a different foreign policy agenda in the form of the new *Ostpolitik* has also contributed to changing and eventually increasing opportunities for a successful external minority policy that does not treat minorities as objects of farther-reaching policy goals, but makes them one of the beneficiaries of a cooperative rather than confrontational foreign policy.

References

Alcock, A.E., *The History of the South Tyrol Question*, London, 1970.
Bundestagsdrucksachen 13/1036, 13/1116, 13/3195, 13/3428, 13/6787, 13/6915, 13/10845.
Cole, J. and Wolf, E.R., *The Hidden Frontier*, New York and London, 1974.
Gruber, A., *Südtirol unter dem Faschismus*, Bozen, 1974.
Grünewald, I., *Die Elsass-Lothringer im Reich 1918–1933*, Frankfurt am Main, 1984.

Info-Dienst Deutsche Aussiedler, no. 82, 1996.

Kettenacker, L., *Nationalsozialistische Volkstumspolitik im Elsass*, Stuttgart, 1973.

Kimminich, O., 'Völkerrecht und Geschichte im Disput über die Beziehungen Deutschlands zu seinen östlichen Nachbarn', in *Aus Politik und Zeitgeschichte*, no. 28, 1996, pp. 28–38.

Rothenberger, K.-H., *Die elsaß-lothringische Heimat- und Autonomiebewegung zwischen den beiden Weltkriegen*, Frankfurt am Main, 1975.

CHAPTER 13

The Status of German Minorities in Bilateral Agreements of the Federal Republic

Hans-Joachim Heintze

L arge groups of ethnic Germans have traditionally been living in a number of other European states as national minorities. Although there is no universally accepted definition of the term, in East Central Europe and in Germany national minorities are commonly understood to be population groups whose ethnic kins are the titular nation of another state (Franke and Hofmann 1992: 401). In contrast with other minority groups, national minorities can count on the support of their mother country as a guaranteeing power, as the case of South Tyrol and Austria demonstrates, where Austria's role has explicitly – at least as a general obligation – been defined in an international treaty.

However, other cases – including that of German minorities in Eastern Europe after the Second World War – indicate the difficulty that mother countries face in committing themselves to protecting their kin-groups in other states. Especially during the Cold War, such initiatives were often seen as interference into another state's internal affairs and accordingly rejected or hindered. It was only in 1986 that the Vienna CSCE conference addressed the issue and accorded members of national minorities the right to have cross-border contacts with citizens of other states with whom they share common ethnicity or cultural traditions (Frasnelli 1992: 156ff.). This approach was taken up again at the 1991 CSCE expert meeting on national minorities in Geneva, when it was determined that 'issues in relation to national minorities and the fulfilment of international obligations with respect to the rights of members of national minorities are a legitimate international concern and therefore not exclusively an internal affair of the respective state' (Bundesregierung 1991: 864).

This principle was confirmed, rather than introduced, by the Charter of Paris for a New Europe and had been the German policy approach vis-à-vis host-states of German minorities for a long time. Obviously, it was only after the collapse of communism in Eastern Europe that the respective opportunities arose more widely in former socialist countries as well. Building on the successful policy towards the German minority in Denmark, a number of bilateral agreements have been concluded in which the rights of German minorities are addressed.

The German Minority in Denmark and the Bonn–Copenhagen Declarations

The Bonn–Copenhagen Declarations of 1955 was the first successful step to address the issue of German minorities after the Second World War. They managed to overcome the German–Danish national 'conflict' (Hansen 1993: 39) and contributed to a popular attitude towards minorities that sees them as a cultural enrichment rather than as a threat (Lammers 1995: 8). In view of the century-old 'border struggle' between the two countries, this has been a remarkable success, and could well provide a model for similar conflicts elsewhere.

Nevertheless, the situation of the German minority in Denmark is different in a number of ways from that of other such minorities. Both the Danish and the German minorities in the region did not come into being because of migration, but because of the alteration of borders. Furthermore, the German response to their being a minority was very different from that of the Danes. While the former insisted on the *objective* fact of (kin-) ethnicity and sought a bilateral agreement to secure their rights, the latter's approach was informed by the *subjective* declaration of their nationality, making the protection of a minority an internal affair of the respective host-state. Consequently, the two kin-states had a very different policy approach, too. Based on the concept of group rights, the state government of Schleswig-Holstein in Germany guaranteed the Danish minority certain rights in a unilateral declaration on 26 September 1949. The Danish government, for its part, was not prepared to do the same. In a statement of 27 October 1949 they merely guaranteed that all constitutionally guaranteed rights would, without any limitation, apply to the German minority as well, thus excluding any affirmative action or positive discrimination for the benefit of the minority as a whole.

This, however, was changed in the context of Germany's accession to NATO in 1955 (Johannsen 1993: 51). One of the preconditions for that was that any bilateral problems potentially straining the internal relations of the alliance be eliminated, and this included the situation of the minorities in the German–Danish border region. The Danish refusal to sign an international treaty left only the possibility for a unilateral declaration by each government. In a joint ceremony in Bonn on 29 March 1955, Chancellor Adenauer signed a 'Declaration by the Government of the Federal Republic of Germany' and the Danish Foreign Secretary Hansen signed a 'Declaration by the Danish Government'. In addition, it was agreed in a concluding document on the negotiations that both governments would present their respective declarations to parliament for approval. This way, a procedure was chosen that was similar to the ratification process of international treaties without actually being one. Instead, two single unilateral legal acts had been produced that assure members of both minorities that constitutional rights and freedoms of their respective host-states apply to them without any limitation. In each declaration's second paragraph, individuals are guaranteed the right to declare their nationality and their affinity to either German or Danish culture without the authorities being allowed to challenge this declaration in any way. Moreover, the use of the mother tongue must not be restricted. A guarantee of parliamentary representation, however, is not included in the declarations (Ipsen 1997: 336).

The principle of reciprocity, on which both declarations are based, is the key difference between the German–Danish situation and a number of other minority conflicts involving German minorities. The existence of analogous minorities, and the preparedness of each kin-state to be simultaneously a responsive and responsible host-state, made it possible that concrete regulations in the 1955 declarations could be kept down to a minimum without endangering the spirit of the project. In addition, the process of European integration superseded the German–Danish minority problem. The membership of both states in the European Communities and later on in the European Union diminished the importance of borders and increased that of the region, thus putting minority policy in a new perspective, too.

The German–Polish Treaty

According to the German Federal government, the German–Polish treaty has made a significant contribution to the calming and stabilisation of the situation of the German minority in Poland (*Infodienst* 1996: 18). In particular, the negotiations leading up to the treaty succeeded in overcoming the long-standing Polish position that there was no German minority in Poland at all. This position was maintained until the 1980s (Czaplinski 1984: 135), and most profoundly expressed in a 1979 report of the then People's Republic of Poland to the UN Human Rights Commission which made no comments on the situation of minorities at all (UN-Doc. A/35/40: 12f.).

Today the existence of a German minority in Poland is not disputed any more. This, however, was not only a success of German diplomacy and negotiation, but must also be attributed to the fact that the CSCE had taken up the topic of minority rights and minority protection during the 1980s, so that internationally accepted legal standards were already in existence. Furthermore, it was crucial for success that the German government decided not to insist on addressing the issue of German expulsion after the Second World War (Kimminich 1991: 383), even though this was not without problems domestically (EA 47 [1992]: 369). The course of negotiations leading up to the treaty confirms this as much as the Polish view that a breakthrough was eventually only achieved because of the possibility of relating the minority issue to CSCE standards (Czaplinski 1992: 171). Yet it is not only the relation to the CSCE standards that makes this treaty important, but also the fact that it was the first document to be signed between the

Federal Republic and a former eastern bloc state that included provisions in relation to German minorities.

The specific regulations in this respect are detailed in articles twenty and twenty-one. Based on the principle of reciprocity, members of the respective (German or Polish) minorities are guaranteed the right to express, maintain, and develop their identity individually or collectively and are assured protection from forced assimilation (Art. 20/1). The treaty leaves it to the individual to determine his or her membership in the minority, independent of objective criteria of descent (Blumenwitz 1992: 82). Specific rights accorded in article 20/3 include the private and public use of the minority's mother tongue, the foundation of organisations for the preservation of their identity, and the right to use their mother tongue as the language of instruction in religious classes. In addition, cross-border contacts with members of their ethnic group are permitted and members of the minorities have the right to use their names in their native language. Poland has committed itself to protecting the ethnic, cultural, linguistic, and religious identity of the minorities on its territory and to establish conditions in which the development of this identity can be promoted within the existing legal framework. Furthermore, it has been acknowledged in the treaty that constructive cooperation in this area is of particular importance as it strengthens peaceful coexistence and good neighbourly relations between the German and Polish peoples while at the same time contributing to reconciliation and mutual understanding. Instruction in German, which does not affect the requirement to learn the country's official language, and the use of German by authorities will be provided for as far as is necessary and possible within the framework of existing legal regulations in Poland. The history and culture of the German minority will be given greater prominence in education. Minority members have the right to participate actively in public life, including in decisions affecting the protection and promotion of their identity. Necessary steps in this respect will only be taken after a consultation process in accordance with the decision making procedures of the respective state (art. 21).

The German–Polish treaty is an effective instrument to solve the complicated problems that arose between the two states in the aftermath of the Second World War. It has also affected the situation of the German minority in Poland positively. The treaty demonstrates that comprehensive minority protection presupposes a democratic constitutional framework of the states involved. Aimed at German–Polish reconciliation and based on the principle of reciprocity, the treaty is fundamentally different from treaties concluded in the inter-war period under the League of Nations regime that tried to solve minority problems independent of the state of bilateral relations, thus making minorities a factor for political confrontation (Barcz: 307). A further important feature of this treaty is the fact that it does not constitute a specific bilateral arrangement, but rather that it represents the application of standards set by international organisations, thus underlying the integration of both states into the European catalogue of norms.

The German–Romanian Treaty

The German–Romanian friendship treaty of 21 April 1992 is an important document with respect to the legal position of the German minority in Romania, as it provides a solid and comprehensive basis for the future of the minority in Romania. Nevertheless, the treaty was signed too late to relieve the emigration pressure caused by decades of suppression under communism. The lost trust in the state authorities could and can be rebuilt only gradually, despite the fact that the Romanian state is obviously interested in the minority staying in the country and has had some success over the past years in encouraging members of the ethnic German community not to emigrate to Germany (Klöck 1997: 17).

The treaty has incorporated the most far-reaching minority regulations existing in international law, above all the 1990 Copenhagen Document on the Human Dimension of the CSCE. This and other relevant CSCE documents have been declared law in the bilateral relationships between Germany and Romania according to Article 15 of the treaty. Using this article as a basis, the treaty goes on to specify the rights of members of the German minority in Romania, i.e., the rights of Romanian citizens of ethnic German origin are accorded in addition to general human rights and liberties, which they can exercise without discrimination and in full legal equality with all other citizens. Thus, they are entitled, individually or collectively, to maintain, express, and develop their ethnic, cultural, linguistic, and religious identity. The Romanian state will refrain from all attempts at forceful assimilation. Members of the German minority have the right to participate actively in public affairs, including all matters relating to the protection and promotion of their identity. Membership of the German minority in Romania is a private and individual matter which must not be used to the detriment of the respective individual.

Similar to other treaties on good neighbourliness, the treaty with Romania includes a mechanism to resolve disputes arising in relation to the regulations of the treaty, which proves once more that both signatories are serious about the treaty's implementation. According to this mechanism, both states are entitled to apply the relevant CSCE dispute settlement procedures in cases of disagreement in relation to the interpretation or implementation of all articles relating to minority rights. In the interest of the German minority and in order to promote mutual understanding, trust, and respect, both parties declared that neither of them would claim the inapplicability of any of these dispute settlement procedures.

Furthermore, Article 15 compels Romania to protect and support the identity of members of the German minority by concrete measures. Favourable conditions are to be provided for the operation of German schools and cultural institutions in areas where members of the minority live. Romania is to facilitate measures taken by the German government in support of the minority group. A German–Romanian government commission on minority-related issues is to meet on an annual basis, to discuss the situation, and to consult on future steps. Moreover, the signatories agreed to back concrete programmes to secure the existence of the German minority in Romania and support its social, cultural, and economic life. These measures, however, are to be taken in such a way that they do not violate the rights of other Romanian citizens.

So far, the treaty has been implemented successfully and to mutual advantage. The German minority is organised in the Democratic Forum of Germans in Romania. The forum is an umbrella organisation with five regional branches and about 50,000 members in total. In the Romanian parliament, the German minority is represented with one, constitutionally guaranteed member. The positive relationship between minority and authorities has been further enhanced by the inclusion of ethnic Germans in Romania in the restitution programme of land and property that was collectivised under communism.

The German–Soviet Treaty of 1990

The treaty on good neighbourly relations, partnership, and cooperation concluded between the Federal Republic of Germany and the then Soviet Union defines the legal status of the German minority in Russia, where the treaty continues to be valid after the dissolution of the Soviet Union. In article fifteen the two signatories agreed to increase the opportunities for teaching and learning each other's language in institutions of secondary and higher education in both countries, including the creation, where possible, of bilingual schools. Ethnic Germans in Russia, and Russian citizens residing permanently in Germany, are guaranteed the right to develop their national, linguistic, and cultural identity.

In the course of the further implementation of the treaty, Germany and Russia signed a protocol on 10 July 1992 on 'Cooperation for the Gradual Restitution of Statehood for Ethnic Germans in Russia.' In this protocol, the Russian government committed itself to the restoration of the Volga Republic, provided that this would not impede on the interests of the local Russian population. The two important dimensions of this part of the protocol are that the injustice of the dissolution of the Volga Republic under Stalin would be corrected, and that a territorial centre for the representation of ethnic German interests in the Russian Federation would be established.

The protocol went on to declare the commitment of both governments to contribute to the preservation, expression, and development of the national and cultural identity of the German minority in Russia. The Russian government was supposed to develop a plan for the gradual implementation of the treaty and the protocol, to determine which transitional and additional arrangements would be necessary in this context, and to establish regulations that would enable ethnic Germans to enjoy the right of land property transactions. Furthermore, the status and authority of future autonomous territorial units were to be drafted in accordance with the constitution and other relevant legislation of the Russian Federation.

With respect to cultural, social, and educational institutions, both governments committed their support – Russia took on the responsibility of providing the legal and organisational framework, Germany assured the supply of funds and personnel.

Although the Russian government officially notified its German counterpart on 23 March 1993 that the protocol had been put into force, its implementation was seriously hampered by the opposition of the local Russian population, despite the international legal status of the document and the generous material support from Germany. The restoration of the Volga Republic, therefore, has been abandoned. More successful was the creation of, and further support for, the German Rayons in Siberia.

Nevertheless, despite the existing legal framework, the success of German external minority policy vis-à-vis Russia has been rather limited so far, extending only to a handful of villages and to the promotion of the German language.

The Legal Status of German Minorities in Other CIS States

Kazakhstan is host to approximately 600,000 ethnic Germans who mostly live in the northern parts of the country. Many of them are still continuing to emigrate – either to Germany or to the German Rayons in Siberia. The Kazakh government has repeatedly emphasised its regret over the emigration of members of the German minority, primarily because of the drainage of skilled labour and of economic and professional resources. Supported by the German government, Kazakhstan has taken steps to improve the living conditions of ethnic Germans in the country. An inter-governmental conference has been in operation since 1992 and is co-ordinating these efforts, which, by 1997, had resulted in a decrease in the number of emigrants. Given the territorial distribution of the minority, German support is focussed on the northern part of the country and on agricultural and humanitarian programmes.

The situation in the two other Central Asian countries with formerly strong German minorities is much worse. Of the 100,000 ethnic Germans in Kyrgyzstan in 1989, most have now left the country, as have about 30,000 members of the minority in Tajikistan. The small number of ethnic Germans who have so far resisted the nationalist emigration pressures are supported by the German government with humanitarian aid.

A slightly larger group of about 40,000 ethnic Germans lives in in Ukraine. Their legal status had been unclear for a long time, because the Ukrainian government was not prepared to come to a settlement of the citizenship issue, which affected in particular those members of the minority who moved to Ukraine after 1992, but who could not prove that they, or their ancestors, had been living there prior to the deportation of 1941. Even though the citizenship issue is still not completely resolved, a German-Ukrainian agreement, signed on 3 September 1996, regulates the status of all residents in Ukraine – citizens and non-citizens alike – who declare themselves for ethnic, cultural, linguistic, or religious reasons as members of the German national minority. Their identity is now being protected through the commitment of both signatories. Although the agreement does not explicitly state the legal validity of the accord, it reiterates the applicability of OSCE regulations in relation to minorities.

The German–Czechoslovak Treaty

Signed on 27 February 1992, the Treaty on Good Neighbourly and Friendly Relations between the Federal Republic of Germany and the Republic of Czechoslovakia regulates the status of the German minority in its article twenty. Apart from the right to choose and declare their nationality freely, the members of the minority are accorded a catalogue of rights aimed at enabling them to preserve their specific identity. Of particular importance in this context is that, going beyond earlier agreements, the signatories accept the political obligations of the CSCE process, especially those of the Copenhagen document, as legally binding.

According to the treaty, members of the German minority have the right, individually or collectively, to express, preserve, and develop their ethnic, cultural, linguistic, and religious identity. They are legally protected from forced assimilation and their membership of the German minority must not be used to their disadvantage.

After the dissolution of Czechoslovakia, the treaty continued to be a valid legal document in both successor states. In the

Czech Republic it fits in very well with the comprehensive framework of minority rights incorporated in the constitutional and other legislative frameworks. Members of minorities are generally allowed to form their own ethnic organisations and to disseminate and receive information in their native language. There is no official language in the Czech Republic, and local communities are entitled to create schools with special minority language classes, pending the approval of local education authorities. However, as the German minority is comparatively small (only 0.3 percent of the total population) and is rather dispersed throughout the country, German is only taught as a foreign language in Czech schools.

In the Slovak Republic, the continued validity of the treaty was ensured by a declaration of the two governments on 24 March 1993. Although the Slovak state is committed to permit measures to support the German minority, the political practice of minority rights protection has so far suffered from the contradiction between the internationally co-operative minority policy pursued by the Slovak government and the nationalist determinants of its domestic political process.

The German–Hungarian Treaty

Closely modelled on the German–Polish treaty, the treaty with Hungary signed on 6 February 1992 includes the most far-reaching incorporation of international standards among any agreements signed by the German government since 1990. According to Article 19, the signatory states agree on the legally binding character of the Copenhagen and other CSCE/OSCE documents – a formulation that allows the interpretation that future OSCE-instruments could be automatically incorporated as well.

Conclusion: The Contribution of the Treaties to the Further Development of Minority Protection in International Law

The foremost contribution made by the treaties discussed above is the fact that they all include, in one way or another, a reference to political agreements relevant for minority protection in the framework of the CSCE/OSCE. In this respect it is particularly interesting that these regulations are not only confirmed as legally binding for the signatory states, but rather that they are, although to varying degrees, being declared as legally effective instruments in bilateral relations. This 'upgrade' raises these political norms to norms of international law.

Although the CSCE/OSCE instruments on minority protection include a number of elements of international customary law, the specific extent of the latter is still disputed. It is therefore all the more important that the non-legal political CSCE/OSCE norms are incorporated into international contract law. The necessary legalisation of CSCE/OSCE norms in international treaties on the protection of minorities is served by the treaties Germany has concluded with a number of former socialist countries in Central and Eastern Europe. Even though there are no reports so far on the legal importance and practical impact of the incorporation of these norms in the treaties, the contribution and significance of the latter has been emphasised in the Stability Pact for Europe of 20 March 1995. Aimed at a prevention of conflicts in Central and Eastern Europe, candidates for EU accession are asked to solve their (internal and bilateral) minority problems and to work towards transparent borders. Apart from the pioneering role the German treaties have played on the bilateral level, one obvious, and in some ways even more important, political consequence of their existence is that decades-long political tensions arising from the existence of German minorities are now a matter of the past as the minorities have become bridges in the relationships between Germany and its neighbours.

References

Die Situation der Deutschen in den Staaten Ostmittel-, Ost- und Südosteuropas (= *Info-Dienst Deutsche Aussiedler*, no. 79), Bonn 1996.

Barcz, J., 'Den Minderheitenschutz betreffende Klauseln in den neuen bilateralen Verträgen Polens mit den Nachbarstaaten', in *Friedenssichernde Aspekte des Minderheitenschutzes*, ed. M. Mohr, Berlin 1996, pp. 281–314.

Blumenwitz, D., *Minderheiten- und Volksgruppenrecht. Aktuelle Entwicklungen*, Bonn 1992.

Bulletin der Bundesregierung, Nr. 109, 10 October 1991, pp. 156–7.

Czaplinski, W., 'Aktuelle Richtungen des internationalen Rechtsschutzes der nationalen Minderheiten', in *Polnische Weststudien 3*, Poznan 1984, pp. 135–52.

Czaplinski, W., 'The New Polish–German Treaties and the Changing Political Structure of Europe', in *American Journal of International Law*, no. 86, 1992, pp. 163–73.

Europa Archiv, no. 47, 1992.

Franke, D. and Hofmann, R., 'Nationale Minderheiten – ein Thema für das Grundgesetz? Verfassungs- und völkerrechtliche Aspekte des Schutzes nationaler Minderheiten', in *Europäische Grundrechte-Zeitschrift*, no. 3, 1992, pp. 401–9.

Frasnelli, H., 'Sicherung der Volksgruppenrechte', in *Vereinte Nationen*, no. 3, 1992.

Hansen, R., 'Die deutsch-dänische Grenze in historischer Perspektive', in *Minderheiten im deutsch-dänischen Grenzbereich*, ed. Landeszentrale für Politische Bildung Schleswig-Holstein, Kiel 1993, pp. 13–40.

Ipsen, K., 'Minderheitenschutz auf reziproker Basis: die deutsch-dänische Lösung', in *Selbstbestimmungsrecht der Völker – Herausforderung der Staatenwelt*, ed. H.-J. Heintze, Bonn 1997, pp. 327–41.

Johannsen, P. I., 'Die deutsche Volksgruppe in Nordschleswig', in *Minderheiten im deutsch-dänischen Grenzbereich*, ed. Landeszentrale für Politische Bildung Schleswig-Holstein, Kiel 1993, pp. 41–72.

Kimminich, O., 'Die abschließende Regelung mit Polen', in *Zeitschrift für Politik*, no. 38, 1991, pp. 361–91.

Klöck, O., 'Neue Perspektiven: bei den deutschen Minderheiten in Rußland, Rumänien und Polen', *Info-Dienst Deutsche Aussiedler*, no. 90, 1997.

Lammers, K. Ch., 'Nachbarn ohne Probleme', in *Die Zeit*, 28 July 1995, p. 8.

CONCLUSION

German Minorities in East and West. A Comparative Overview and Outlook

Stefan Wolff

Today German minority groups live in four countries in Western Europe and in sixteen countries in Central and Eastern Europe.[1] Their historical origins, size, status, and degree of integration and assimilation differ greatly, not just between east and west, but also within each of these two broadly defined geographic regions. Depending mostly on these four factors, their perspectives for the future are different as well. Despite the fact that the conditions for the protection of minorities have never been as good in Europe as they are today, the question remains whether some of these German communities will have a future at all.

Between Integration and Assimilation – Ethnic Germans in Denmark, Belgium, France, and Italy

Ethnic Germans in Western Europe share the same history regarding their origin. None of the German-speaking minorities there came to their present settlement areas as migrants, as

---

1. Until the early 1990s, there was also a small ethnic German population in Turkmenistan. In the 1989 census it accounted for a little less than 4,500 people, who had come there during the deportation. The civil war in the early 1990s triggered an almost complete exodus of the Germans from the newly independent country.

some of their ethnic kins in Central and Eastern Europe did, but they have inhabited these territories for centuries, in most cases since the end of large tribal migrations around AD 500. Their current status as national, or in the case of Alsace linguistic, minorities stems from boundary revisions carried out after the First World War and confirmed in 1945 to compensate Germany's neighbours for the losses and suffering incurred as a consequence of the two wars and in order to increase their security from possible future German attacks.[2]

The democratic environment in post-1945 Western Europe in combination with the relative economic prosperity in all four countries and their participation in the various projects of European and Western integration has facilitated the process of political integration of the minorities into the polities of their host-countries. None of the German-speaking populations of the four countries harbours any significant secessionist aspirations or feels discriminated against because of their different ethnic and/or cultural identity. Yet, the way there was different in each country, and below the surface the results of this integration process differ as well.

With respect to Denmark, the German minority has developed a trans-ethnic German and Danish ethnic identity, while retaining a German national identity. This *Zweiströmigkeit*, as Pedersen has defined it, finds its obvious expression in the self-concept of being German North Schleswigians (among the older generations) or German South Jutlanders (among the younger generations). The fact that a relatively small minority of only between ten and fifteen thousand members, or around 5 percent of the population of the administrative region in which they live, has been able to maintain such a strong sense of its German origins points to the favourable conditions that have been, and are continuing to be, provided for this minority. The framework of the Bonn–Copenhagen Declarations of 1955 secures the position of the German minority in Denmark politically by guaranteeing its members full and equal access to the rights and liberties accorded to all Danish citizens.

2. Security concerns were not addressed successfully by these border alterations after 1919. Not only did they not stop Germany from unleashing yet another world war, they also effectively created fifth columns in countries that were most vulnerable to attack. Even for the time after 1945 it is doubtful whether the confirmation of the 1919 borders would have prevented a similar development, if the policy of integration had not tied at least one part of Germany firmly to the western alliance in Cold War Europe.

Increasing cross-border cooperation, which has developed subsequently, and the material and other support provided by the Federal Republic of Germany have allowed the German minority to maintain its identity as a distinct national group in Denmark. Given the high level of tolerance for, if not to say indifference to, the German minority's insistence on its distinctiveness, the social climate in Denmark is no less favourable than the political conditions. The social and economic integration of members of the minority has certainly also been helped by a long-standing tradition in the minority education system aiming at preparing each new generation for a life in Denmark as well as Germany. In the light of ever closer integration in Europe in which the importance of historically grown rather than politically defined regions is increasing at the expense of traditional concepts of nationhood, the future for the German minority in Denmark with its trans-ethnic identity looks bright.

The total number of the German-speaking population in Belgium is estimated to be around 100,000 about ten times higher than in Denmark. About two-thirds of them fall under the jurisdiction of the German-speaking community (one of the three recognised linguistic communities in the country) and enjoy special rights and protection, as the community has autonomy in all matters related to culture, education, electronic broadcasts, health, welfare, research and technology, and the use of languages. In addition, communal authority also extends to international relations in these areas and to inter-community affairs related to matters of culture and education. Even though one-third of German-speakers in Belgium fall under the jurisdiction of either the French or the Flemish community, some of them can still make use of special linguistic facilities provided for in areas with at least 25 percent German-speakers. For administrative purposes, the German-speaking community is part of the Walloon, i.e., Francophone region. Despite these rather advantageous political conditions, the linguistic situation in which the German-speaking community finds itself is rather more difficult. In the Eupen and St Vith areas, German has official status and is also the language of instruction in schools, but with the exception of the Malmédy area, where it is taught as compulsory first 'foreign' language, it is everywhere else subject to strong competitive pressure from both Dutch and French, as the two essential languages in Belgium, and increasingly also from English. Donaldson has thus argued that, while German still exercises a certain attraction as an 'economic' language, allowing its speakers to find a job in neighbouring Germany, it is, at least as far as the Walloon region is concerned, on the decline. The different degree of stigmatisation of German (and German-ness), the geographic dispersion of German-speakers across Belgium in areas where their (linguistic) identity has different constitutional statuses, and the resulting diverse levels of assimilation do not allow a picture to be painted of a more or less homogeneous ethnic group. Here lies an imminent danger for the future of the German-speaking community of Belgium, namely that of progressive assimilation into the dominant French culture of the country.

Alsace, for centuries a disputed border country between France and Germany, today is politically firmly integrated into the French state and the cultural assimilation of its population, which is of Germanic origin, has progressed very far. This becomes obvious from the degree to which the French lan-guage has spread in Alsace and the knowledge of German and/or the Alsatian dialect have declined: while there are only very few older people left who do not speak any French at all, the interest among the younger generation in the dialect is declining steadily. European integration has advantaged Alsace not only economically, but also in terms of the confi-dence Alsatians have in their place in France and Europe. Under these conditions political integration combined with partial cultural assimilation have proved to be successful poli-cies for the management of ethno-cultural differences that had escalated in the inter-war period. Nevertheless, there still exists a distinct regional identity based on the cultural and linguistic traditions of the historical Alsace, but also on the development the region has taken after 1945. Franco–German reconcilia-tion and the process of European integration have had a sig-nificant impact on the development in Alsace. With Germany no longer perceived as a threat, the perspective of a local Alsa-tian culture based on Alemannic traditions was no longer interpreted as a threat to French territorial sovereignty either. Nevertheless, there is only minimal institutional support for German, and the decline in the number of German-speakers after the Second World War simultaneously suggests little demand for such support. The local dialect, however, enjoys a significantly higher economic, social, and language status. Given that it is one of the primary focal points of an Alsatian identity that is distinct from both Germany and France, Broadbridge has concluded that the future of the Alsatians as a distinct ethno-cultural/ethno-linguistic group looks more promising. Their prospects of preserving and developing their identity seem better than that of German-speakers in Belgium, and in this the situation in Alsace resembles in some aspects that of the German minority in Denmark.

Although historically it has suffered the most of all ethnic German populations in Western Europe, the German-speaking minority in South Tyrol is today the best-protected and most empowered of all of them. As a result of complex internal and external developments after 1945, Italy's German minority enjoys an extensive set of rights and liberties within a specially crafted regional and provincial framework of autonomy that grants the minority full self-government. While this rather ideal political situation permits the comprehensive protection and development of the minority's ethno-cultural identity, it is not without problems for the future of the minority. Since the early 1970s, cultural policy, including schools and education, has been the responsibility of each language group. Since then, the SVP has pursued a course of strict segregation which has manifested itself in policy guidelines (cf. Alcock 1982: 63–64), which attempt to preserve German cultural hegemony. This policy has not only had a certain alienating effect on the Italian (and Ladin) population in the province, but has also led to the increasing cultural isolation of the German-speaking population itself. Clearly, among the younger generation of German-speaking South Tyrolese, who lack the personal experience of fascism and the early post-war period, the need for ethnic segregation is felt less strongly and traditional South Tyrolese identification patterns are increasingly being rejected. Many of the older generation, in contrast, have rightly or wrongly preserved their 'victim identity', insisting on the 1972 autonomy statute and its regulations as some form of compensation for the injustices that were inflicted on them. The particular fear of the older South Tyrolese generation in terms of the emergence of a new South Tyrolese identity, equally shared by all ethnic groups, can only be understood by imagining the consequences of such a process, namely the disappearance of ethnic borderlines in politics and society and the feared decline of the ancient South Tyrolese system of traditions, norms, and values which they had fought to preserve over the decades. It is in this context of a continued power struggle, as Schweigkofler has explained, that the success of ethnocentric German parties at recent elections becomes more understandable. Their importance could grow and they might attract a larger share of the vote, even among the younger generation, if the Italian population continues its present trend towards nationalist politics, and if political and economic difficulties occur in the future and are interpreted along ethnopolitical lines. From this point of view, the failure to establish an ethnically neutral civic identity in South Tyrol might prove to have severe repercussions for the future, simply because the German minority in Italy has not yet been able to take a similar step towards an identity that incorporates more than just one particular ethno-cultural dimension, thereby becoming less exclusive, similar to post-war developments in Denmark and France.

The essence of the problem of integration is expressed in the continuous difficulty of maintaining a careful balance between what Bergem has initially described as the dichotomy between assimilation and segregation. At least for Western Europe, the resolution of the dilemma may be to adopt an approach that contains a little bit of both.

Between Fear and Hope – Ethnic Germans in Central and Eastern Europe

For more than four decades after the end of the Second World War, the situation of German minorities in the countries of Central and Eastern Europe has been fundamentally different from that of the ethnic German communities in Western Europe. Subjected to deportation, forced labour, detention, and expulsion in the immediate aftermath of the war, their ability to preserve, let alone express or develop, their ethno-cultural identity was severely limited under the communist regimes of their host-countries. With the partial exception of Romania, members of all these minorities were subjected to various assimilation pressures ranging from the simple denial of their existence as a distinct minority group (in Poland) to the repression of their cultural, linguistic, and religious identities.

Apart from the intentional neglect of the conditions necessary for minorities in general to preserve their identities, ethnic Germans suffered additionally from the fact that it was their kin-state that had, very often with their active support, inflicted enormous suffering on the populations of their host-states. Being German in Central and Eastern Europe was thus not only unpopular, but almost invited discrimination and persecution. Added to this internal pressure, the increasing opportunities over the years to use the provisions of Article 116 of the Federal Republic's Basic Law accelerated the degree of assimilation, as the most consciously German members of the minority normally emigrated.

The democratisation process that began in Central and Eastern Europe in the late 1980s opened up not only opportunities for the consolidation of German minorities in their host-countries, but also took away all barriers to emigration previously imposed by the communist systems in these countries. Thus, until the changes in German immigration legislation in the early 1990s, a mass exodus of ethnic Germans, particularly from Romania, Poland, and the former Soviet Union, continued to weaken, if not partially destroy, the community structures of German minorities in Central and Eastern Europe. Parallel to raising the obstacles to immigration to Germany, the federal government has, since the late 1980s and particularly after 1990, taken many steps to support ethnic Germans in their host countries. This has encompassed the conclusion of bilateral treaties with most of the Central and East European states in which significant German minorities live. These treaties and similar agreements now provide the basis upon which substantial material and financial aid is channelled to German minority communities all across Central and Eastern Europe. Even though this has not necessarily stopped, let alone reversed, the assimilation process, it has at least made a contribution to slowing it down. Whether this change in the situation will only be a temporary interlude on the way to the ultimate decline of German culture in the region, or whether it will be turned into an opportunity for a fresh start, does not only depend on the continuation of German government support for the minorities or on the persistently democratic and tolerant environment in the host-states. It also depends on the minorities themselves – whether they want to, and can, seize this opportunity or whether they will perceive their only choice to be between emigration and assimilation.

Even though it is not possible to predict the outcome of the current developments conclusively, a more detailed examination of the contextual situation in which each of the German minorities in Central and Eastern Europe lives today will permit some cautious remarks about the future of 'German culture in the East'.[3]

Apart from the minorities explicitly discussed in the previous chapters, ethnic Germans also live in the three Baltic republics, in Ukraine, in the four Central Asian successor states of the former Soviet Union, and in Georgia.[4] The numerically smallest groups live in Estonia, Latvia, and Lithuania. In terms of their origin, they come from diverse backgrounds, comprising remaining members of the historic German population in the Baltics, some several thousand Memel Germans, and ethnic Germans from Russia who migrated to the Baltic republics in the Soviet era. The latter group faces severe difficulties to obtain citizenship rights in Estonia and Latvia. This, however, is not a specifically anti-German policy by the governments of these two countries, but a consequence of the discriminatory citizenship policy, which is primarily aimed at the sizeable non-indigenous Russian population. In Georgia, a similarly small group of only some two thousand ethnic Germans is still resident. Apart from their larger size, the single most significant difference between the German minorities in the Baltics and in Georgia, on the one hand, and those in Central Asia, on the other, is the fact that most ethnic Germans from Kazakhstan (almost 700,000), Kyrgyzstan (about 60,000), Tajikistan (around 30,000), and Uzbekistan (approximately 40,000)[4] have resolved to leave their host-states, because they are denied the essential conditions to preserve their identity or feel discriminated against because of their previously close affiliation with ethnic Russians or because of their Christian rather than Muslim religion. Another reason, particularly in Tajikistan, is the ongoing civil war. Their existence in these newly independent states resulted mostly from deportation from the European parts of the Soviet Union after the beginning of the war with

---

3. I have borrowed this phrase from a German government programme started in the mid eighties that uses the term *deutsche Kultur des Ostens*.

4. All figures are 1993 estimates of the German government. Cf. *Bundestagsdrucksache* 12/6162, pp. 36f.

Germany in 1941. Only in Kyrgyzstan and Kazakhstan had there been settlements since the nineteenth century. Even though the favoured destination of most émigrés remains Germany, a growing number of them settle temporarily or permanently in ethnic German settlements in Russia, especially in the two German rayons in Western Siberia. A survey among ethnic Germans in Kyrgyzstan in 1993 found 85 percent of them determined to emigrate, their preferred destinations being Germany (80 percent), Russia (6 percent), and Ukraine and other CIS states (1 percent) (Eisfeld 1993: 49).

In all these countries on the territory of the former Soviet Union, with the notable exception of Ukraine, where, supported by the German federal government and within the framework of a 1996 agreement between the two countries, the 40,000 strong German minority in Ukraine is seeking to restore its traditional settlement areas, the future for the continued existence of a German minority is rather bleak. Either the degree of assimilation has already progressed irreversibly or the conditions for a sustained recovery of the minority, including the rebuilding of viable community structures, are simply not there because of a lack of government commitment to promote minority rights, insufficient support from Germany, popular resentment against ethnic Germans, or the small number of the remaining members of the minority group. There is, however, a slim chance that the situation in Kazakhstan will change for the better. For a start, the minority there is much bigger and makes up about 6 percent of the total population of the country. Its age structure is intact and community structures are generally functioning. Even more importantly, there is an effort on the part of the Kazakh government to provide for conditions that would make it possible for members of the minority to remain in the country and be able to express, preserve, and develop their distinct ethno-cultural identity. The Kazakh Decree on Independence declared equal rights of all citizens regardless of their ethnic and/or linguistic origin to be one of the basic principles by which the country's future policy would be guided. Since the German minority as a whole is valued for its professional and labour skills, and the mass emigration of the early 1990s has left its negative mark on the economy, ethnic Germans are encouraged to stay in the country. Support from Germany has been forthcoming, and an inter-governmental conference, including minority representatives, has been in operation since 1992. By 1997, some moderate success in slowing down emigration had been achieved. Nevertheless, severe problems remain. One is the degree of Russification of the minority that had already progressed very far before the collapse of the Soviet Union. This is unlikely to be changed in the near future as part of the internal migration pattern of ethnic Germans is their increasing urbanisation, i.e., a move away from the relatively secluded rural environment in which the development of functioning community structures would have been somewhat easier. Another is that the economic situation in the country as a whole has been consistently bad since the early 1990s, resulting in an overall double-figure decline in industrial and agricultural output (Eisfeld 1993: 47).

The future prospects of the minorities in the Central European countries that have been discussed in greater detail above, i.e., the Czech Republic, Hungary, Romania, and Yugoslavia, are again diverse. Leaving aside the political uncertainties of the Yugoslav case, where the minority numbers only a few thousand, the external and internal conditions for the minorities in the other three countries are very different. They are probably best in Hungary, where more than 200,000 ethnic Germans find advantageous political conditions within a model framework of minority legislation. They are fairly well integrated into Hungarian society and have widely preserved or recently revitalised their ethno-cultural identity, even though to differing degrees, depending on the precise circumstances of each section of the German community. The political stability of Hungary and the country's success in the transformation of the economy certainly contributed to this process. Nelde has shown that, from a linguistic point of view, a number of problems remain unresolved. Yet, as Stevenson has demonstrated, the prospects for the German community to address these issues successfully in the future are relatively good, simply because of the favourable overall situation in which the German minority in Hungary finds itself today.

While it is linguistically probably the best developed of all Eastern and Central European German minorities, the future of the German-speaking population in Romania is far from certain. This is all the more astonishing given the external conditions in which ethnic Germans in Romania live. Supported by the German government and the *Landsmannschaften*, the minority is no longer subjected to any significant level of discrimination. Rather, the Romanian government has long recognised the 'value' of its German population in order to attract foreign investment and to establish mutually beneficial bilateral relationships with Germany, and through it with NATO and the European Union. Also, the German minority in Romania was the only one of its kind in Central and Eastern Europe that had not been subjected to aggressive assimilation. Exclusive German settlements in which German was the everyday language of conversation existed throughout the post-war period. Thus, the reason for the limited prospects for the future must be sought within the minority. Wagner has explained that the mass exodus of the late 1980s and early 1990s has not only considerably diminished the size of the minority, it has also rendered vital community structures dysfunctional and disrupted the formerly compact settlement pattern. In addition, the fact that primarily the young and well-educated members of the community emigrated left an over-aged population behind that is no longer represented in all strata of society. It is doubtful whether this process can be reversed and the community, even on a smaller scale, be reconstructed.

Stevenson has also concluded that, for different reasons, the situation of ethnic Germans in the Czech Republic is similarly difficult and their future even more in question than that of the German minorities elsewhere. Despite wide-ranging constitutional guarantees for the protection of national minorities, historical developments have complicated the relationship between the Czechs and their German minority. The part the minority played in the dismemberment and subsequent destruction of Czechoslovakia poisoned the relationships with the host-nation for decades to come and prepared the ground for the post-war persecution and partial expulsion of the minority. This in turn has created a resentful diaspora community in Germany that has tried over the years to exert influence on the bilateral relationships between Germany and Czechoslovakia/the Czech Republic. Successive governments of the country, therefore, have been very reluctant to make concessions on issues relating to the status of the German minority and to rights demanded by the diaspora community, such as a right to residence. The German and Czech governments have only recently managed to find and express their consensus in a joint declaration, which might prove to be the beginning of reconciliation, not just at the bilateral level but also between two communities which have both incurred tremendous suffering. Without such reconciliation it will not be possible to secure a future for the German minority in the Czech Republic.

This, Cordell has stated, has been accomplished in relation to Poland and the German minority living there. Territorially concentrated in the Upper Silesian region, the minority's relationship with the majority population and state authorities in Poland is no longer threatened by either assimilation or repression or by irredentist or secessionist aspirations. Favourable political conditions, providing guaranteed parliamentary representation and opportunities for the minority to organise itself in political parties and cultural associations, have enabled ethnic Germans to maintain viable community structures and preserve, develop, and express their ethno-cultural identity despite the exodus of members of the minority that occurred in the late 1980s and early 1990s. Over the past years, the German minority has successfully striven to become a bridge between Poland and Germany. This success has been possible because the German federal government has placed great emphasis on its relationship with Poland, while the Polish government has recognised the 'value' of the German minority as a catalyst of reconciliation and eventually of accession to NATO and the European Union. From this perspective, ethnic Germans in Poland can confidently look towards the future.

Stricker's analysis has revealed that the most complex situation has evolved in relation to ethnic Germans living in the Russian Federation. Deportation and decades of repression and finally emigration have resulted in the steady decline of the minority and its increasing assimilation. This process continues despite increasing efforts by the German government to improve the living conditions of the minority in Russia. Aid programmes in the areas of German language education, economic recovery, and culture have been put in place to slow down the process of assimilation and emigration. The success of these programmes will depend on the will of the minority to consolidate itself and survive as a distinct ethno-cultural group. In addition, the situation in Russia as a whole will have a great bearing on whether ethnic Germans will see their future in Russia or in Germany.

The dichotomy of fear and hope, therefore, is to some extent a condensation of the past, present, and future of German minorities in Central and Eastern Europe. Deportation, expulsion, repression, persecution, and assimilation stand not only for the past. The resurgence of ethno-nationalism in most countries hosting German minorities, even if they themselves may not necessarily always be its target, can diminish the little bit of hope that developed after the collapse of the communist regimes and the opening up of the societies in the region. With respect to the future, fear and hope symbolise assimilation and minority protection just as much as they exemplify the choice many members of ethnic German communities, particularly on the territory of the former Soviet Union, have to make between remaining in their host-countries and emigrating to the Federal Republic. Thus, what is similar for all German-speaking minorities in Central and Eastern Europe is the fact that, although the conditions under which their members live have generally improved over the last decade, their survival as distinct ethno-cultural communities is by no means certain.

Assessing the Current Status and Future Prospects of German Minorities

Even though the situations in which the German-speaking minorities in Europe live are different, the factors that determine their status at present, and thus influence their future, are essentially the same. They can be grouped into three categories – intra-minority conditions, the situation in the host-country, and the state of bilateral relationships between the host-country and the Federal Republic of Germany, or Austria in the case of South Tyrol and, to a lesser degree, Hungary.

Among the intra-minority conditions, the most important aspects are demographic in their nature and relate to the degree of assimilation. The size of the minority, whether it lives territorially concentrated or dispersed, in its traditional settlement areas or in areas to which it had been deported at some point, and the age and social structure of the minority community influence its vitality as a distinct ethno-cultural group, and thus determine its future chances of survival or complete linguistic and cultural assimilation. The degree of political and social integration characterises to what extent the minority has been accepted as an equal part into its host-society.

Integration is thus linked closely to the general situation in the host-country. Three dimensions are essential in this respect – the degree to which minorities and their rights are explicitly protected in constitutional and simple legislation, the commitment with which ethno-cultural distinctiveness is recognised and supported, and the way in which popular and government sentiments influence the implementation of legal directives.

In terms of the bilateral dimension, historic and contemporary issues are important, as they both influence the considerations of the minority and its host and kin-states in relation to each other. The existence of a bilateral treaty including provisions related to the minority group, its right to engage in cross-border cooperation and to receive formal support from the German government as well as the emigrant community are the three most important factors in this context that will contribute to how the particular minority community locates itself both in relation to its host-state as well as to its kin-nation.

In view of the wide variety of geographic, social, political, and cultural contexts in which German-speaking minorities find themselves today, no generalisation is possible as to which of the above dimensions are the most significant and how each individual aspect must be shaped in order to facilitate the well-being of the different German communities in Western as well as Central and Eastern Europe. A detailed assessment, thus, can only be made on a case-by-case basis – a task that this book has sought to accomplish.

References

Alcock, A. E., *Geschichte der Südtirolfrage*, Vienna 1982.

Bundestagsdrucksache 12/6162.

Eisfeld, A., 'Zwischen Bleiben und Gehen: Die Deutschen in den Nachfolgestaaten der Sowjetunion', *Aus Politik und Zeitgeschichte*, no. 48, 1993, pp. 44–52.

Index